AUTHORS OF GREECE

LECTOR HOUSE PUBLIC DOMAIN WORKS

This book is a result of an effort made by Lector House towards making a contribution to the preservation and repair of original classic literature. The original text is in the public domain in the United States of America, and possibly other countries depending upon their specific copyright laws.

In an attempt to preserve, improve and recreate the original content, certain conventional norms with regard to typographical mistakes, hyphenations, punctuations and/or other related subject matters, have been corrected upon our consideration. However, few such imperfections might not have been rectified as they were inherited and preserved from the original content to maintain the authenticity and construct, relevant to the work. The work might contain a few prior copyright references as well as page references which have been retained, wherever considered relevant to the part of the construct. We believe that this work holds historical, cultural and/or intellectual importance in the literary works community, therefore despite the oddities, we accounted the work for print as a part of our continuing effort towards preservation of literary work and our contribution towards the development of the society as a whole, driven by our beliefs.

We are grateful to our readers for putting their faith in us and accepting our imperfections with regard to preservation of the historical content. We shall strive hard to meet up to the expectations to improve further to provide an enriching reading experience.

Though, we conduct extensive research in ascertaining the status of copyright before redeveloping a version of the content, in rare cases, a classic work might be incorrectly marked as not-in-copyright. In such cases, if you are the copyright holder, then kindly contact us or write to us, and we shall get back to you with an immediate course of action.

HAPPY READING!

AUTHORS OF GREECE

THOMAS WALLACE LUMB, CYRIL ALINGTON

ISBN: 978-93-90294-18-3

Published: -

© 2020
LECTOR HOUSE LLP

LECTOR HOUSE LLP
E-MAIL: lectorpublishing@gmail.com

AUTHORS OF GREECE

BY

THE REVEREND T. W. LUMB, M.A.

WITH AN INTRODUCTION BY
THE REVEREND CYRIL ALINGTON, D.D.

AUTHOR'S PREFACE

Greek literature is more modern in its tone than Latin or Medieval or Elizabethan. It is the expression of a society living in an environment singularly like our own, mainly democratic, filled with a spirit of free inquiry, troubled by obstinate feuds and still more obstinate problems. Militarism, nationalism, socialism and communism were well known, the preachers of some of these doctrines being loud, ignorant and popular. The defence of a maritime empire against a military oligarchy was twice attempted by the most quick-witted people in history, who failed to save themselves on both occasions. Antecedently then we might expect to find some lessons of value in the record of a people whose experiences were like our own.

Further, human thought as expressed in literature is not an unconnected series of phases; it is one and indivisible. Neglect of either ancient or modern culture cannot but be a maiming of that great body of knowledge to which every human being has free access. No man can be anything but ridiculous who claims to judge European literature while he knows nothing of the foundations on which it is built. Neither is it true to say that the ancient world was different from ours. Human nature at any rate was the same then as it is now, and human character ought to be the primary object of study. The strange belief that we have somehow changed for the better has been strong enough to survive the most devilish war in history, but few hold it who are familiar with the classics.

Yet in spite of its obvious value Greek literature has been damned and banned in our enlightened age by some whose sole qualification for the office of critic often turns out to be a mental darkness about it so deep that, like that of Egypt, it can be felt. Only those who know Greek literature have any right to talk about its powers of survival. The following pages try to show that it is not dead yet, for it has a distinct message to deliver. The skill with which these neglected liberators of the human mind united depth of thought with perfection of form entitles them at least to be heard with patience.

CONTENTS

Page

- AUTHOR'S PREFACE v
- INTRODUCTION 1
- HOMER 2
- AESCHYLUS 28
- SOPHOCLES 44
- EURIPIDES 62
- ARISTOPHANES 79
- HERODOTUS 92
- THUCYDIDES 102
- PLATO 113
- DEMOSTHENES 127

INTRODUCTION

I count it an honour to have been asked to write a short introduction to this book. My only claim to do so is a profound belief in the doctrine which it advocates, that Greek literature can never die and that it has a clear and obvious message for us to-day. Those who sat, as I did, on the recent Committee appointed by Mr. Lloyd George when Prime Minister to report on the position of the classics in this country, saw good reason to hope that the prejudice against Greek to which the author alludes in his preface was passing away: it is a strange piece of irony that it should ever have been encouraged in the name of Science which owes to the Greeks so incalculable a debt. We found that, though there are many parts of the country in which it is almost impossible for a boy, however great his literary promise, to be taught Greek, there is a growing readiness to recognise this state of affairs as a scandal, and wherever Greek was taught, whether to girls or boys, we found a growing recognition of its supreme literary value. There were some at least of us who saw with pleasure that where only one classical language can be studied there is an increasing readiness to regard Greek as a possible alternative to Latin.

On this last point, no doubt, classical scholars will continue to differ, but as to the supreme excellence of the Greek contribution to literature there can be no difference of opinion. Those to whom the names of this volume recall some of the happiest hours they have spent in literary study will be grateful to Mr. Lumb for helping others to share the pleasures which they have so richly enjoyed; he writes with an enthusiasm which is infectious, and those to whom his book comes as a first introduction to the great writers of Greece will be moved to try to learn more of men whose works after so many centuries inspire so genuine an affection and teach lessons so modern. They need have no fear that they will be disappointed, for Mr. Lumb's zeal is based on knowledge. I hope that this book will be the means of leading many to appreciate what has been done for the world by the most amazing of all its cities, and some at least to determine that they will investigate its treasures for themselves. They will find like the Queen of Sheba that, though much has been told them, the half remains untold.

C. A. ALINGTON.

HOMER

Greek literature opens with a problem of the first magnitude. Two splendid Epics have been preserved which are ascribed to "Homer", yet few would agree that Homer wrote them both. Many authorities have denied altogether that such a person ever existed; it seems certain that he could not have been the author of both the *Iliad* and the *Odyssey*, for the latter describes a far more advanced state of society; it is still an undecided question whether the *Iliad* was written in Europe or in Asia, but the probability is that the *Odyssey* is of European origin; the date of the poems it is very difficult to gauge, though the best authorities place it somewhere in the eighth century B.C. Fortunately these difficulties do not interfere with our enjoyment of the two poems; if there were two Homers, we may be grateful to Nature for bestowing her favours so liberally upon us; if Homer never existed at all, but is a mere nickname for a class of singer, the literary fraud that has been perpetrated is no more serious than that which has assigned Apocalyptic visions of different ages to Daniel. Perhaps the Homeric poems are the growth of many generations, like the English parish churches; they resemble them as being examples of the exquisite effects which may be produced when the loving care and the reverence of a whole people blend together in different ages pieces of artistic work whose authors have been content to remain unnamed.

It is of some importance to remember that the Iliad is not the story of the whole Trojan war, but only of a very small episode which was worked out in four days. The real theme is the Wrath of Achilles. In the tenth year of the siege the Greeks had captured a town called Chryse. Among the captives were two maidens, one Chryseis, the daughter of Chryses, a priest of Apollo, the other Briseis; the former had fallen to the lot of Agamemnon, the King of the Greek host, the latter to Achilles his bravest follower. Chryses, father of Chryseis, went to Agamemnon to ransom his daughter, but was treated with contumely; accordingly he prayed to the god to avenge him and was answered, for Apollo sent a pestilence upon the Greeks which raged for nine days, destroying man and beast. On the tenth day the chieftains held a counsel to discover the cause of the malady. At it Chalcas the seer before revealing the truth obtained the promise of Achilles' protection; when Agamemnon learned that he was to ransom his captive, his anger burst out against the seer and he demanded another prize in return. Achilles upbraided his greed, begging him to wait till Troy was taken, when he would be rewarded fourfold. Agamemnon in reply threatened to take Achilles' captive Briseis, at the same time describing his follower's character. "Thou art the most hateful to me of all Kings sprung of Zeus, for thou lovest alway strife and wars and battles. Mighty though thou art, thy might is the gift of some god. Briseis I will take, that thou mayest know how far stronger I am than thou, and that another may shrink from deeming himself my equal, rivalling me to my face." At this insult Achilles half drew his sword to slay the King, but was checked by Pallas Athena, who bade him confine his resentment to taunts, for the time would come when Agamemnon would offer him splendid gifts to atone for the wrong. Obeying the goddess Achilles reviled his foe, swearing a solemn oath that he would not help the Greeks when Hector swept them away. In vain did Nestor, the wise old counsellor who had seen two generations of heroes, try to make up the quarrel, beseeching Agamemnon not to outrage his best warrior and Achilles not to contend with his leader. The meeting broke up; Achilles departed to his huts, whence the heralds in obedience to Agamemnon speedily carried away Briseis.

Going down to the sea-shore Achilles called upon Thetis his mother to whom he told the story of his ill-treatment. In deep pity for his fate (for he was born to a life of a short span), she promised that she would appeal to Zeus to help him to his revenge; she had saved Zeus from destruction by summoning the hundred-armed Briareus to check a revolt among the gods against Zeus' authority. For the moment the king of the gods was absent in Aethiopia; when he returned to Olympus on the twelfth day she would win him over. Ascending to heaven, she obtained the promise of Zeus' assistance, not without raising the suspicions of Zeus' jealous consort Hera; a quarrel between them was averted by their son Hephaestus, whose ungainly performance of the duties of cupbearer to the Immortals made them forget all resentments in laughter unquenchable.

True to his promise Zeus sent a dream to Agamemnon to assure him that he would at last take Troy. The latter determined to summon an Assembly of the host. In it the changeable temper of the Greeks is vividly pictured. First Agamemnon told how he had the promise of immediate triumph; when the army eagerly called for battle, he spoke yet again describing their long years of toil and advising them to break up the siege and fly home, for Troy was not to be taken. This speech was welcomed with even greater enthusiasm than the other, the warriors rushing down to the shore to launch away. Aghast at the coming failure of the enterprise Athena stirred up Odysseus to check the mad impulse. Taking from Agamemnon his royal sceptre as the sign of authority, he pleaded with chieftains and their warriors, telling them that it was not for them to know the counsel in the hearts of Kings.

> "We are not all Kings to bear rule here. 'Tis not good to have many Lords; let there be one Lord, one King, to whom the crooked-counselling son of Cronos hath given the rule."

Thus did Odysseus stop the flight, bringing to reason all save Thersites, "whose heart was full of much unseemly wit, who talked rashly and unruly, striving with Kings, saying what he deemed would make the Achaeans smile".

He continued his chatter, bidding the Greeks persist in their homeward flight. Knowing that argument with such an one was vain, Odysseus laid his sceptre across his back with such heartiness that a fiery weal started up beneath the stroke. The host praised the act, the best of the many good deeds that Odysseus had done before Troy.

When the Assembly was stilled, Odysseus and Nestor and Agamemnon told the plan of action; the dream bade them arm for a mighty conflict, for the end could not be far off, the ten years' siege that had been prophesied being all but completed. The names of the various chieftains and the numbers of their ships are found in the famous catalogue, a document which the Greeks treasured as evidence of united action against a common foe. With equal eagerness the Trojans poured from their town commanded by Hector; their host too has received from Homer the glory of an everlasting memory in a detailed catalogue.

Literary skill of a high order has brought upon the scene as quickly as possible the chief figures of the poem. When the armies were about to meet, Paris, seeing Menelaus whom he had wronged, shrank from the combat. On being upbraided by Hector who called him "a joy to his foes and a disgrace to himself", Paris was stung to an act of courage. Hector's heart was as unwearied as an axe, his spirit knew not fear; yet beauty too was a gift of the gods, not to be cast away. Let him be set to fight Menelaus in single combat for Helen and her wealth; let an oath be made between the two armies to abide by the result of the fight, that both peoples might end the war and live in peace. Overjoyed, Hector called to the Greeks telling them of Paris' offer, which Menelaus accepted. The armies sat down to witness the fight, while Hector sent to Troy to fetch Priam to ratify the treaty.

In Troy the elders were seated on the wall to watch the conflict, Priam among them. Warned by Iris, Helen came forth to witness the single combat. As she moved among them the elders bore their testimony to her beauty; its nature is suggested but not described, for the poet felt he was unable to paint her as she was.

> "Little wonder," they exclaimed, "that the Trojans and Achaeans should suffer woe for many a year for such a woman. She is marvellous like the goddesses to behold; yet albeit she is so fair let her depart in the ships, leaving us and our little ones no trouble to come."

Seeing her, Priam bade her sit by him and tell the names of the Greek leaders as they passed before his eyes. Agamemnon she knew by his royal bearing, Odysseus who moved along the ranks like a ram she marked out as the master of craft and deep counsel. Hearing her words, Antenor bore his witness to their truth, for once Odysseus had come with Menelaus to Troy on an embassy.

> "When they stood up Menelaus was taller, when they sat down Odysseus was more stately. But when they spake, Menelaus' words were fluent, clear but few; Odysseus when he spoke, fixed his eyes on the ground, turning his sceptre neither backwards nor forward, standing still like a man devoid of wit; one would have deemed him a churl and a very fool; yet when he sent forth his mighty voice from his breast in words as many as the snowflakes, no other man could compare with him."

Helen pointed out Ajax and Idomeneus and others, yet could not see her two brothers, Castor and Pollux; either they had not come from her home in Sparta, or they had refused to fight, fearing the shame and reproach of her name. "So she spake, yet the life-giving earth covered them there, even in Sparta, their native land."

When the news came to Priam of the combat arranged between Paris and Menelaus, the old King shuddered for his son, yet he went out to confirm the compact. Feeling he could not look upon the fight, he returned to the city. Meanwhile Hector had cast lots to decide which of the two should first hurl his spear. Paris failed to wound his enemy, but Menelaus' dart pierced Paris' armour; he followed it up with a blow of his sword which shivered to pieces in his hand. He then caught Paris' helmet and dragged him off towards the Greek army; but Aphrodite saved her favourite, for she loosed the chin-strap and bore Paris back to Helen in Troy. Menelaus in vain looked for him among the Trojans who were fain to see an end of him, "and would not have hidden him if they had seen him". Agamemnon then declared his brother the victor and demanded the fulfilment of the treaty.

Such an end to the siege did not content Hera, whose anger against the Trojans was such that she could have "devoured raw Priam and his sons". With Zeus' consent she sent down Pallas Athena to confound the treaty. Descending like some brilliant and baleful star the goddess assumed the shape of Laodocus and sought out the archer Pandarus. Him she tempted to shoot privily at Menelaus to gain the favour of Paris. While his companions held their shields in front of him the archer launched a shaft at his victim, but Athena turned it aside so that it merely grazed his body, drawing blood. Seeing his brother wounded Agamemnon ran to him, to prophesy the certain doom of the treaty breakers.

> "Not in vain did we shed the blood of compact and offer the pledges of a treaty. Though Zeus hath not fulfilled it now, yet he will at last and they will pay dear with their lives, they, their wives and children. Well I know in my heart that the day will come when sacred Troy will perish and Priam and his folk; Zeus himself throned on high dwelling in the clear sky will shake against them all his dark aegis in anger for this deceit."

While the leeches drew out the arrow from the wound, Agamemnon went round the host with words of encouragement or chiding to stir them up to the righteous conflict. They rushed on to battle to be met by the Trojans whose host

> "knew not one voice or one speech; their language was mixed, for they were men called from many lands."

In the fight Diomedes, though at first wounded by Pandarus, speedily returned refreshed and strengthened by Athena. His great deeds drew upon him Pandarus and Aeneas, the son of Aphrodite and the future founder of Rome's greatness. Diomedes quickly slew Pandarus and when Aeneas bestrode his friend's body, hurled at him a mighty stone which laid him low. Afraid of her son Aphrodite cast her arms about him and shrouded him in her robe. Knowing that she was but a weak goddess Diomedes attacked her, wounding her in the hand. Dropping her son, she fled to Ares who was watching the battle and besought him to lend her his chariot, wherein she fled back to Olympus. There her mother Dione comforted her with the story of the woes which other gods had suffered from mortals.

> "But this man hath been set upon thee by Athena. Foolish one, he knoweth not in his heart that no man liveth long who fighteth with the gods; no children lisp 'father' at his knees when he returneth from war and dread conflict. Therefore, albeit he is so mighty, let him take heed lest a better than thou meet him, for one day his prudent wife shall wail in her sleep awaking all her house, bereft of her lord, the best man of the Achaeans."

But Athena in irony deemed that Aphrodite had been scratched by some Greek woman whom she caressed to tempt her to forsake her husband and follow one of the Trojans she loved.

Aeneas when dropped by his mother had been picked up by Apollo; when Diomedes attacked the god, he was warned that battle with an immortal was not like man's warfare. Stirred by Apollo, Ares himself came to the aid of the Trojans, inspiring Sarpedon the Lycian to hearten his comrades, who were shortly gladdened by the return of Aeneas whom Apollo had healed. At the sight of Ares and Apollo fighting for Troy Hera and Athena came down to battle for the Greeks; they found Diomedes on the skirts of the host, cooling the wound Pandarus had inflicted. Entering his chariot by his side, Athena fired him to meet Ares and drive him wounded back to Olympus, where he found but little compassion from Zeus. The two goddesses then left the mortals to fight it out.

At this moment Helenus, the prophetic brother of Hector, bade him go to Troy to try to appease the anger of Athena by an offering, in the hope that Diomedes' progress might be stayed. In his absence Diomedes met in the battle Glaucus, a Lycian prince.

> "Who art thou?" he asked. "I have never seen thee before in battle, yet now thou hast gone far beyond all others in hardihood, for thou hast awaited my onset, and they are hapless whose sons meet my strength. If thou art a god, I will not fight with thee; but if thou art one of those who eat the fruit of the earth, come near, that thou mayest the quicker get thee to the gates of death."

In answer, Glaucus said:

> "Why askest thou my lineage? As is the life of leaves, so is that of men. The leaves are scattered some of them to the earth by the wind, others the wood putteth forth when it is in bloom, and they come on in the season of spring. Even so of men one generation groweth, another ceaseth."

He then told how he was a family friend of Diomedes and made with him a compact that if they met in battle they should avoid each the other; this they sealed by the exchange of armour, wherein the Greek had the better, getting gold weapons for bronze, the worth of a hundred oxen for the value of nine.

Coming to Troy Hector bade his mother offer Athena the finest robe she had; yet all in vain, for the goddess rejected it. Passing to the house of Paris, he found him polishing his armour, Helen at his side. Again rebuking him, he had from him a promise that he would be ready to re-enter the fight when Hector had been to his own house to see his wife Andromache. Hector's heart foreboded that it was the last time he would speak with her. She had with her their little son Astyanax. Weeping she besought him to spare himself for her sake.

> "For me there will be no other comfort if thou meetest thy doom, but sorrow. Father and mother have I none, for Achilles hath slain them and my seven brothers. Hector, thou art my father and my lady mother and my brother and thou art my wedded husband. Nay, come, pity me and abide on the wall, lest thou make thy son an orphan and thy wife a widow."

He answered, his heart heavy with a sense of coming death:

> "The day will come when Troy shall fall, yet I grieve not for father or mother or brethren so much as for thee, when some Achaean leads thee captive, robbing thee of thy day of freedom. Thou shalt weave at the loom in Argos or perchance fetch water, for heavy necessity shall be laid upon thee. Then shall many a one say when he sees thee shedding tears: 'Lo, this is the wife of Hector who was the best warrior of the Trojans when they fought for their town.' Thus will they speak and thou shalt have new sorrow for lack of such a man to drive away the day of slavery."

He stretched out his arms to his little son who was affrighted at the sight of the helmet as it nodded its plumes dreadfully from its tall top. Hector and Andromache laughed when they saw the child's terror; then Hector took off his helmet and prayed that the boy might grow to a royal manhood and gladden his mother's heart. Smiling through her tears, Andromache took the child from Hector, while he comforted her with brave words.

> "Lady, grieve not overmuch, I beseech thee, for no man shall thrust me to death beyond my fate. Methinks none can avoid his destiny, be he brave or a coward, when once he hath been born. Nay, go to the house, ply thy tasks and bid the maids be busy, but war is the business of the men who are born in Troy and mine most of all."

Thus she parted from him, looking back many a time, shedding plenteous tears. So did they mourn for Hector even before his doom, for they said he would never escape his foes and come back in safety.

Finding Paris waiting for him, Hector passed out to the battlefield. Aided by Glaucus he wrought great havoc, so much that Athena and Apollo stirred him to challenge the bravest of the Greeks. The victor was to take the spoils of the vanquished but to return the body for burial. At first the Greeks were silent when they heard his challenge, ashamed to decline it and afraid to take it up. At last eight of their bravest cast lots, the choice falling upon Ajax. A great combat ended in the somewhat doubtful victory of Ajax, the two parting in friendship after an exchange of presents. The result of the fighting had discouraged both sides; the

Greeks accordingly decided to throw up a mound in front of their ships, protected by a deep trench. This tacit confession of weakness in the absence of Achilles leads up to the heavy defeat which was to follow. On the other side the Trojans held a council to deliver up Helen. When Paris refused to surrender her but offered to restore her treasures, a deputation was sent to inform the Greeks of his decision. The latter refused to accept either Helen or the treasure, feeling that the end was not far off. That night Zeus sent mighty thunderings to terrify the besiegers.

So far the main plot of the *Iliad* has been undeveloped; now that the chief characters on both sides have played a part in the war, the poem begins to show how the wrath of Achilles works itself out under Zeus' direction. First the king of the gods warned the deities that he would allow none to intervene on either side and would punish any offender with his thunders. Holding up the scales of doom, he placed in them the lot of Trojans and of Greeks; as the latter sank down, he hurled at their host his lightnings, driving all the warriors in flight to the great mound they had built. For a time Teucer the archer brother of Ajax held them back, but when he was smitten by a mighty stone hurled of Hector all resistance was broken. A vain attempt was made by Hera and Athena to help the Greeks, but the goddesses quailed before the punishment wherewith Zeus threatened them. When night came the Trojans encamped on the open plain, their camp-fires gleaming like the stars which appear on some night of stillness.

Disheartened at his defeat, Agamemnon freely acknowledged his fault and suggested flight homewards. Nestor advised him to call an Assembly and depute some of the leading men to make up the quarrel with Achilles. The King listened to him, offering to give Achilles his own daughter in wedlock, together with cities and much spoil of war. Three ambassadors were chosen, Phoenix, Ajax and Odysseus. Reaching Achilles' tent, they found him singing lays of heroes, Patroclus his friend by his side. When he saw the ambassadors, he gave them a courtly welcome. Odysseus laid the King's proposals before him, to which Achilles answered with dignity.

> "I hate as sore as the gates of Death a man who hideth one thing in his heart and sayeth its opposite. Do the sons of Atreus alone of men love their wives? Methinks all the wealth which Troy contained before the Greeks came upon it, yea all the wealth which Apollo holds in rocky Pytho, is not the worth of life itself. Cattle and horses and brazen ware can be got by plunder, but a man's life cannot be taken by spoil nor recovered when once it passeth the barrier of his teeth. Nay, go back to the elders and bid them find a better plan than this. Let Phoenix abide by me here that he may return with me to-morrow in my ships if he will, for I will not constrain him by force."

Phoenix had been Achilles' tutor. In terror for the safety of the Greek fleet, he appealed to his friend to relent.

> "How can I be left alone here without thee, dear child? Thy father sent me to teach thee to be a speaker of words and a doer

of deeds. In thy childhood I tended thee, for I knew that I should never have a son and I looked to thee to save me from ruin. Tame thy great spirit. Even the gods know how to change, whose honour is greater, and their power. Men in prayer turn them by sacrifice when any hath sinned and transgressed. For Prayers are the daughters of great Zeus; they are halt and wrinkled and their eyes look askance. Their task it is to go after Ruin; for Ruin is strong and sound of foot, wherefore she far outrunneth them all and getteth before them in harming men over all the world. But they come after; whosoever honoureth the daughters of Zeus when they come nigh, him they greatly benefit and hear his entreaties, but whoso denieth them and stubbornly refuseth, they go to Zeus and ask that Ruin may dog him, that he may be requited with mischief. Therefore, Achilles, bring it to pass that honour follow the daughters of Zeus, even that honour which bendeth the heart of others as noble as thou."

When this appeal also failed, Ajax, a man of deeds rather than words, deemed it best to return at once, begging Achilles to bear them no ill-will and to remember the rights of hospitality which protected them from his resentment. When Achilles assured them of his regard for them and maintained his quarrel with Agamemnon alone, they departed and brought the heavy news to their anxious friends. On hearing it Diomedes briefly bade them get ready for the battle and fight without Achilles' help.

When the Trojan host had taken up its quarters on the plain, Nestor suggested that the Greeks should send one of their number to find out what Hector intended to do on the morrow. Diomedes offered to undertake the office of a spy, selecting Odysseus as his comrade. After a prayer to Athena to aid them, they went silently towards the bivouac. It chanced that Hector too had thought of a similar plan and that Dolon had offered to reconnoitre the Greek position. He was a wealthy man, ill-favoured to look upon, but swift of foot, and had asked that his reward should be the horses and the chariot of Achilles.

Hearing the sound of Dolon's feet as he ran, Diomedes and Odysseus parted to let him pass between them; then cutting off his retreat they closed on him and captured him. They learned how the Trojan host was quartered; at the extremity of it was Rhesus, the newly arrived Thracian King, whose white horses were a marvel of beauty and swiftness. In return for his information Dolon begged them to spare his life, but Diomedes deemed it safer to slay him. The two Greeks penetrated the Thracian encampment, where they slew many warriors and escaped with the horses back to the Greek armament.

When the fighting opened on the next day, Agamemnon distinguished himself by deeds of great bravery, but retired at length wounded in the hand. Zeus had warned Hector to wait for that very moment before pushing home his attack. One after another the Greek leaders were wounded, Diomedes, Odysseus, Machaon; Ajax alone held up the Trojan onset, retiring slowly and stubbornly towards the sea. Achilles, seeing the return of the wounded warrior Machaon, sent his friend

Patroclus to find out who he was. Nestor meeting Patroclus, told him of the rout of the army, and advised him to beg Achilles at least to allow the Myrmidons to sally forth under Patroclus' leadership, if he would not fight in person. The importance of this episode is emphasised in the poem. The dispatch of Patroclus is called "the beginning of his undoing", it foreshadows the intervention which was later to bring Achilles himself back into the conflict.

The Trojan host after an attempt to drive their horses over the trench stormed it in five bodies. As they streamed towards the wall, an omen of a doubtful nature filled Polydamas with some misgivings about the wisdom of bursting through to the sea. It was possible that they might be routed and that they would accordingly be caught in a trap, leaving many of their dead behind them. His advice to remain content with the success they had won roused the anger of Hector, whose headstrong character is well portrayed in his speech.

> "Thou biddest me consider long-winged birds, whereof I reck not nor care for them whether they speed to right or left. Let us obey the counsel of Zeus. One omen is the best, to fight for our country. Why dost thou dread war and tumult? Even if all we others were slain at the ships, there is no fear that thou wilt perish, for thy heart cannot withstand the foe and is not warlike. But if thou holdest from the fight or turnest another from war, straightway shalt thou lose thy life under the blow of my spear."

Thus encouraged the army pressed forward, the walls being pierced by the Lycian King Sarpedon, a son of Zeus. Taking up a mighty stone, Hector broke open the gate and led his men forward to the final onslaught on the ships.

For a brief space Zeus turned his eyes away from the conflict and Poseidon used the opportunity to help the Greeks. Idomeneus the Cretan and his henchman Meriones greatly distinguished themselves, the former drawing a very vivid picture of the brave man.

> "I know what courage is. Would that all the bravest of us were being chosen for an ambush, wherein a man's bravery is most manifest. In it the coward and the courageous man chiefliest appear. The colour of the one changeth and his spirit cannot be schooled to remain stedfast, but he shifteth his body, settling now on this foot now on that; his heart beateth mightily, knocking against his breast as he bodeth death, and his teeth chatter. But the good man's colour changeth not, nor is he overmuch afraid when once he sitteth in his place of ambush; rather he prayeth to join speedily in the dolorous battle."

Yet soon Idomeneus' strength left him; Hector hurried to the centre of the attack, where he confronted Ajax.

At this point Hera determined to prolong the intervention of Poseidon in favour of the Greeks. She persuaded Aphrodite to lend her all her spells of beauty on the pretence that she wished to reconcile Ocean to his wife Tethys. Armed with the goddess' girdle, she lulled Zeus to sleep and then sent a message to Poseidon to give the Greeks his heartiest assistance. Inspired by him the fugitives turned on their pursuers; when Ajax smote down Hector with a stone the Trojans were hurled in flight back through the gate and across the ramparts.

When Zeus awakened out of slumber and saw the rout of the Trojans, his first impulse was to punish Hera for her deceit. He then restored the situation, bidding Poseidon retire and sending Apollo to recover Hector of his wound. The tide speedily turned again; the Trojans rushed through the rampart and down to the outer line of the Greek ships, where they found nobody to resist them except the giant Ajax and his brother Teucer. After a desperate fight in which Ajax single-handed saved the fleet, Hector succeeded in grasping the ship of Protesilaus and called loud for fire. This was the greatest measure of success vouchsafed him; from this point onwards the balance was redressed in favour of the Greeks.

Achilles had been watching the anguish of Patroclus' spirit when this disaster came upon their friends.

> "Why weepest thou, Patroclus, like some prattling little child who runneth to her mother and biddeth her take her up, catching at her garment and checking her movement and gazing at her tearfully till she lifteth her? Even so thou lettest fall the big tears."

Patroclus begged his friend to allow him to wear his armour and lead the Myrmidons out to battle, not knowing that he was entreating for his own ruin and death. After some reluctance Achilles gave him leave, yet with the strictest orders not to pursue too far. Fresh and eager for the battle the Myrmidons drove the Trojans back into the plain. Patroclus' course was challenged by the Lycians, whose King Sarpedon faced him in single combat. In great sorrow Zeus watched his son Sarpedon go to his doom; in his agony he shed tear-drops of blood and ordered Death and Sleep to carry the body back to Lycia for burial.

The great glory Patroclus had won tempted him to forget his promise to Achilles. He pursued the Trojans back to the walls of the town, slaying Cebriones the charioteer of Hector. In the fight which took place over the body Patroclus was assailed by Hector and Euphorbus under the guidance of Apollo. Hector administered the death-blow; before he died Patroclus foretold a speedy vengeance to come from Achilles.

A mighty struggle arose over his body. Menelaus slew Euphorbus, but retreated at the approach of Hector, who seized the armour of Achilles and put it on. A thick cloud settled over the combatants, heightening the dread of battle. The gods came down to encourage their respective warriors; the Greeks were thrust back over the plain, but the bravery of Ajax and Menelaus enabled the latter to save Patroclus' body and carry it from the dust of battle towards the ships.

When the news of his friend's death came to Achilles his grief was so mighty that it seemed likely that he would have slain himself. He burst into a lamentation so bitter that his mother heard him in her sea-cave and came forth to learn what new sorrow had taken him. Too late he learned the hard lesson that revenge may be sweet but is always bought at the cost of some far greater thing.

> "I could not bring salvation to Patroclus or my men, but sit at the ships a useless burden upon the land, albeit I am such a man as no other in war, though others excel me in speech. Perish strife from among men and gods, and anger which inciteth even a prudent man to take offence; far sweeter than dropping honey it groweth in a man's heart like smoke, even now as Agamemnon hath roused me to a fury."

Being robbed of his armour he could not sally out to convey his companion's body into the camp. Hera therefore sent Iris to him bidding him merely show himself at the trenches and cry aloud. At the sound of his thrice-repeated cry the Trojans shrank back in terror, leaving the Greeks to carry in Patroclus' body unmolested; then Hera bade the sun set at once into the ocean to end the great day of battle.

Polydamas knew well what the appearance of Achilles portended to the Trojans, for he was the one man among them who could look both before and after; his advice was that they should retire into the town and there shut themselves up. It was received with scorn by Hector. In the Greek camp Achilles burst into a wild lament over Patroclus, swearing that he would not bury him before he had brought in Hector dead and twelve living captives to sacrifice before the pyre. That night his mother went to Hephaestus and persuaded him to make divine armour for her son, which the poet describes in detail.

On receiving the armour from his mother Achilles made haste to reconcile himself with Agamemnon. His impatience for revenge and the oath he had taken made it impossible for him to take any food. His strength was maintained by Athena who supplied him with nectar. On issuing forth to the fight he addressed his two horses:

> "Xanthus and Balius, bethink you how ye may save your charioteer when he hath done with the battle, and desert him not in death as ye did Patroclus."

In reply they prophesied his coming end.

> "For this we are not to blame, but the mighty god—and violent Fate. We can run quick as the breath of the North wind, who men say is the swiftest of all, but thy fate it is to die by the might of a god and a man."

The Avenging Spirits forbade them to reveal more. The awe of the climax of the poem is heightened by supernatural interventions. At last the gods themselves received permission from Zeus to enter the fray. They took sides, the shock of their meeting causing the nether deity to start from his throne in fear that his realm should collapse about him. Achilles met Aeneas and would have slain him had not Poseidon saved him. Hector withdrew before him, warned by Apollo not to meet him face to face. Disregarding the god's advice he attacked Achilles, but for the moment was spirited away. Disappointed of his prey Achilles sowed havoc among the lesser Trojans.

Choked by the numerous corpses the River-God Scamander begged him cease his work of destruction. When the Hero disregarded him, he assembled all his waters and would have overwhelmed him but for Athena who gave him power to resist; the river was checked by the Fire-God who dried up his streams. The gods then plunged into strife, the sight whereof made Zeus laugh in joy. Athena quickly routed Aphrodite and Hera Artemis. Apollo deemed it worthless to fight Poseidon.

> "Thou wouldst not call me prudent were I to strive with thee for cowering mortals, who like leaves sometimes are full of fire, then again waste away spiritless. Let us make an end of our quarrel; let men fight it out themselves."

Deserted by their protectors the Trojans broke before Achilles, who nearly took the town.

Baulked a second time of his vengeance by Apollo, Achilles vowed he would have punished the god had he the power. Hector had at last decided to face his foe at the Scaean Gate. His father and his mother pleaded with him in a frenzy of grief to enter the town, but the dread of Polydamas' reproaches fixed his resolve. When Achilles came rushing towards him, his heart failed; he ran three times round the walls of the city. Meanwhile the gods held up the scales of doom; when his life sank down to death Apollo left him for ever.

Athena then took the shape of Deiphobus, encouraging him to face Achilles. Seeing unexpectedly a friend, he turned and stood his ground, for she had already warned Achilles of her plot. Hector launched his spear which sped true, but failed to penetrate the divine armour. When he found no Deiphobus at his side to give him another weapon, he knew his end had come. Drawing himself up for a final effort, he darted at Achilles; the latter spied a gap in the armour he had once worn, through which he smote Hector mortally. Lying in approaching death, the Trojan begged that his body might be honoured with a burial, but Achilles swore he should never have it, rather the dogs and carrion birds should devour his flesh. Seeing their great foe dead the Greeks flocked around him, not one passing by him without stabbing his body. Achilles bored through his ankles and attached him to his car; then whipping up his horses, he drove full speed to the camp, dragging Hector in disgrace over the plain. This scene of pure savagery is succeeded by the laments of Priam, Hecuba and Andromache over him whom Zeus allowed to be outraged in his own land.

That night the shade of Patroclus visited Achilles, bidding him bury him speedily that he might cross the gates of death; the dust of his ashes was to be stored up in an urn and mixed with Achilles' own when his turn came to die. After the funeral Achilles held games of great splendour in which the leading athletes contended for the prizes he offered.

Yet nothing could make up for the loss of his friend. Every day he dragged Hector's body round Patroclus' tomb, but Apollo in pity for the dead man kept away corruption, maintaining the body in all its beauty of manhood. At last on the twelfth day Apollo appealed to the gods to end the barbarous outrage.

"Hath not Hector offered to you many a sacrifice of bulls and goats? Yet ye countenance the deeds of Achilles, who hath forsaken all pity which doth harm to men and bringeth a blessing too. Many another is like to lose a friend, but he will weep and let his foe's body go, for the Fates have given men an heart to endure. Good man though he be, let Achilles take heed lest he move us to indignation by outraging in fury senseless clay."

Zeus sent to fetch Thetis whom he bade persuade her son to ransom the body; meanwhile Iris went to Troy to tell Priam to take a ransom and go to the ships without fear, for the convoy who should guide him would save him from harm.

On hearing of Priam's resolve Hecuba tried to dissuade him, but the old King would not be turned. That night he went forth alone; he was met in the plain by Hermes, disguised as a servant of Achilles, who conducted him to the hut where Hector lay. Slipping in unseen, Priam caught Achilles' knees and kissed the dread hands that had slain his son. In pity for the aged King Achilles remembered his own father, left as defenceless as Priam. Calling out his servants he bade them wash the corpse outside, lest Priam at the sight of it should upbraid him and thus provoke him to slay him and offend against the commands of Zeus. As they supped, Priam marvelled at the stature and beauty of Achilles and Achilles wondered at Priam's reverend form and his words. While Achilles slept, Hermes came to Priam to warn him of his danger if he were found in the Greek host. Hastily harnessing the chariot, he led him back safely to Troy, where the body was laid upon a bed in Hector's palace.

The laments which follow are of great beauty. Andromache bewailed her widowhood, Hecuba her dearest son; Helen's lament is a masterpiece.

"Hector, far the dearest to me of all my brethren, of a truth Paris is my lord, who brought me hither—would I had died first. This is the tenth year since I left my native land, yet have I never heard from thee a word cruel or despiteful; rather, if any other chode me, thy sister or a brother's wife or thy mother—though thy father is gentle to me always as he were my own sire—thou didst restrain such with words of persuasion and kindness and gentleness all thine own. Wherefore I grieve for thee and for myself in anguish, for there is no other friend in broad Troy kind and tender, but all shudder at me."

Then with many a tear they laid to his rest mighty Hector.

Such is the *Iliad*. To modern readers it very often seems a little dull. Horace long ago pointed out that it is inevitable that a long poem should flag; even Homer nods sometimes. Some of the episodes are distinctly wearisome, for they are invented to give a place in this national Epic to lesser heroes who could hardly be mentioned if Achilles were always in the foreground. Achilles himself is not a pleasing person; his character is wayward and violent; he is sometimes childish, always liable to be carried away by a fit of pettishness and unable to retain our real respect; further, a hero who is practically invulnerable and yet dons divine armour to attack those who are no match for him when he is without it falls below the ordinary "sportsman's" level. Nor can we feel much reverence for many of the gods; Hera is odious, Athena guilty of flat treachery, Zeus, liable to allow his good nature to overcome his judgment—Apollo alone seems consistently noble. More, we shall look in vain in the *Iliad* for any sign of the pure battle-joy which is so characteristic of northern Epic poetry; the Greek ideal of bravery had nothing of the Berserker in it. Perhaps these are the reasons why the sympathy of nearly all readers is with the Trojans, who are numerically inferior, are aided by fewer and weaker gods and have less mighty champions to defend them.

What then is left to admire in the *Iliad*? It is well to remember that the poem is not the first but the last of a long series; its very perfection of form and language makes it certain that it is the result of a long literary tradition. As such, it has one or two remarkable features. We shall not find in many other Epics that sense of wistful sorrow for man's brief and uncertain life which is the finest breath of all poetry that seeks to touch the human heart. The marks of rude or crude workmanship which disfigure much Epic have nearly all disappeared from the *Iliad*. The characterisation of many of the figures of the poem is masterly, their very natures being hit off in a few lines—and it is important to remember that it is not really the business of Epic to attempt analysis of character at all except very briefly; the story cannot be kept waiting. But the real Homeric power is displayed in the famous scenes of pure and worthy pathos such as the parting of Andromache from Hector and the laments over his body. Those who would learn how to touch great depths of sorrow and remain dignified must see how it has been treated in the *Iliad*.

A few vigorous lines hit off the plan of the *Odyssey*.

> "Sing, Muse, of the man of much wandering who travelled right far after sacking sacred Troy, and saw the cities of many men and knew their ways. Many a sorrow he suffered on the sea, trying to win a return home for himself and his comrades; yet he could not for all his longing, for they died like fools through their own blindness."

Odysseus, when the poem opens, was in Calypso's isle pitied of all the gods save Poseidon. In a council Zeus gave his consent that Hermes should go to Calypso, while Athena should descend to Ithaca to encourage Odysseus' son Telemachus to seek out news of his father.

Taking the form of Mentes, Athena met Telemachus and informed him that his father was not yet dead. Seeing the suitors who were wooing his mother Penelope and eating up the house in riot, she advised him to dismiss them and visit Nestor in Pylos. A lay sung by Phemius brought Penelope from her chamber, who was astonished at the immediate change which her son's speech showed had come upon him, transforming him to manhood.

Next day Telemachus called an Assembly of the Ithacans; his appeal to the suitors to leave him in peace provoked an insulting speech from their ringleader Antinous who held Penelope to blame for their presence; she had constantly eluded them, on one occasion promising to marry when she had woven a shroud for

Laertes her father-in-law; the work she did by day she undid at night, till she was betrayed by a serving-woman. Telemachus then asked the suitors for a ship to get news of his father. When the assembly broke up, Athena appeared in answer to Telemachus' prayer in the form of Mentor and pledged herself to go with him on his travels. She prepared a ship and got together a crew, while Telemachus bade his old nurse Eurycleia conceal from his mother his departure.

In Pylos Nestor told him all he knew of Odysseus, describing the sorrows which came upon the Greek leaders on their return and especially the evil end of Agamemnon. He added that Menelaus had just returned to Sparta and was far more likely to know the truth than any other, for he had wandered widely over the seas on his home-coming. Bidding Nestor look after Telemachus, Athena vanished from his sight, but not before she was recognised by the old hero. On the morrow Telemachus set out for Sparta, accompanied by Pisistratus, one of Nestor's sons.

Menelaus gave them a kindly welcome and a casual mention of his father's name stirred Telemachus to tears. At that moment Helen entered; her quicker perception at once traced the resemblance between the young stranger and Odysseus. When Telemachus admitted his identity, Helen told some of his father's deeds. Once he entered Troy disguised as a beggar, unrecognised of all save Helen herself. "After he made her swear an oath that she would not betray him, he revealed all the plans of the Greeks. Then, after slaying many Trojans, he departed with much knowledge, while Helen's heart rejoiced, for she was already bent on a return home, repenting of the blindness which Aphrodite had sent her in persuading her to abandon home and daughter and a husband who lacked naught, neither wit not manhood." Menelaus then recounted how Odysseus saved him when they were in the wooden horse, when one false sound would have betrayed them. On the next morning Telemachus told the story of the ruin of his home; Menelaus prophesied the end of the suitors, then preceded to recount how in Egypt he waylaid and captured Proteus, the changing god of the sea, whom he compelled to relate the fate of the Greek leaders and to prophesy his own return; from him he heard that Odysseus was with Calypso who kept him by force. On learning this important piece of news Telemachus was eager to return to Ithaca with all speed.

Meanwhile the suitors had learned of the departure of Telemachus and plotted to intercept him on his return. Their treachery was told to Penelope, who was utterly undone on hearing it; feeling herself left without a human protector she prayed to Athena, who appeared to her in a dream in the likeness of her own sister to assure her that Athena was watching over her, but refusing to say definitely whether Odysseus was alive.

The poem at this point takes up the story of Odysseus himself. Going to the isle where he was held captive, Hermes after admiring its great beauty delivered Zeus' message to Calypso to let the captive go. She reproached the gods for their jealousy and reluctantly promised to obey. She found Odysseus on the shore, eating out his heart in the desire for his home. When she informed him that she intended to let him go, he first with commendable prudence made her swear that she did not design some greater evil for him. Smiling at his cunning, she swore the most solemn of all oaths to help him, then supplied tools and materials for the building of his boat. When he was out on the deep, Poseidon wrecked his craft, but a sea goddess Leucothea, once a mortal, gave him a scarf to wrap round him, bidding him cast it from him with his back turned away when he got to land. After two nights and two days on the deep he at length saw land. Finding the mouth of a small stream, he swam up it, then utterly weary flung himself down on a heap of leaves under a bush, guarded by Athena.

The next episode introduces one of the most charming figures in ancient literature. Nausicaa was the daughter of Alcinous, King of Phaeacia, on whose island Odysseus had landed. To her Athena appeared in a dream, bidding her obtain from her father leave to go down to the sea to wash his soiled garments. The young girl obeyed, telling her father that it was but seemly that he, the first man in the kingdom, should appear at council in raiment white as snow. He gave her the leave she desired. After their work was done, she and her handmaids began a game of ball; their merry cries woke up Odysseus, who started up on hearing human voices. Coming forward, he frightened by his appearance the handmaids, but Nausicaa, emboldened by Athena, stood still and listened to his story. She supplied him with clean garments after she had given him food and drink. On the homeward journey Nausicaa bade Odysseus bethink him of the inconvenient talk which his presence would occasion if he were seen with her near the city. She therefore judged it best that she should enter first, at the same time she gave him full information of the road to the palace; when he entered it he was to proceed straight to the Queen Arete, whose favour was indispensable if he desired a return home.

Just outside the city Athena met him in the guise of a girl to tell him his way; she further cast about him a thick cloud to protect him from curious eyes. Passing through the King's gardens, which were a marvel of beauty and fruitfulness, Odysseus entered the palace and threw his arms in supplication about Arete's knees. She listened kindly to him and begged Alcinous give him welcome. When all the courtiers had retired to rest, Arete, noticing that the garments Odysseus wore had been woven by her own hands, asked him whence he had them and how he had come to the island. On hearing the story of his shipwreck Alcinous promised him a safe convoy to his home on the morrow.

At an assembly Alcinous consulted with his counsellors about Odysseus; all agreed to help in providing him with a ship and rowers. At a trial of skill Odysseus, after being taunted by some of the Phaeacians, hurled the quoit beyond them all. Later, a song of the wooden horse of Troy moved him to tears; though unnoticed by the others, he did not escape the eye of Alcinous who bade him tell them plainly who he was. Then he revealed himself and told the marvellous story of his wanderings.

First he and his companions reached the land of the Lotus-eaters. Finding out that the lotus made all who ate it lose their desire for home, Odysseus sailed away with all speed, forcing away some who had tasted the plant. Thence they reached the island of the Cyclopes, a wild race who knew no ordinances; each living in his cave was a law to himself, caring nothing for the others. Leaving his twelve ships, Odysseus proceeded with some of his men to the cave of one of the Cyclopes, a son of Poseidon, taking with him a skin of wine. When the one-eyed monster returned with his flock of sheep, he shut the mouth of the cave with a mighty stone which no mortal could move; then lighting a fire he caught sight of his visitors and asked who they were. Odysseus answered craftily, whereupon the monster devoured six of his company. Odysseus opened his wine-skin and offered some of the wine; when the Cyclops asked his name, Odysseus told him he was called Noman; in return for his kindness in offering him the strangely sweet drink the Cyclops promised to eat him last of all. But the wine soon plunged the monster into a slumber, from which he was awakened by the burning end of a great stake which Odysseus thrust into his eye. On hearing his cries of agony the other Cyclopes came to him, but went away when they heard that Noman was killing him. As it was impossible for anyone but the Cyclops to open the cave, Odysseus tied his men beneath the cattle, putting the beast which carried a man between two which were unburdened; he himself hung on to the ram. As the animals passed out, the Cyclops was a little surprised that the ram went last, but thought he did so out of grief for his master. When they were all safely outside, Odysseus freed his friends and made haste to get to the ship. Thrusting out, when he was at what seemed a safe distance he shouted to the Cyclops, who then remembered an old prophecy and hurled a huge rock which nearly washed them back; a second rock which he hurled on learning Odysseus' real name narrowly missed the ship. Then the Cyclops prayed to Poseidon to punish Odysseus; the god heard him, persecuting him from that time onward. Reassembling his ships, Odysseus proceeded on his voyage.

He next called at the isle of Aeolus, king of the winds, who gave him in a bag all the winds but one, a favouring breeze which was to waft him to his own island. For nine days Odysseus guarded his bag, but at last, when Ithaca was in sight, he sank into a sleep of exhaustion. Thinking that the bag concealed some treasure, his men opened it, only to be blown back to Aeolus who bid him begone as an evil man when he begged aid a second time.

After visiting the Laestrygones, a man-eating people, who devoured all the fleet except one ship's company, the remainder reached Aeaea, the island where lived the dread goddess Circe. Odysseus sent forward Eurylochus with some twenty companions who found Circe weaving at a loom. Seeing them she invited them within; then after giving them a charmed potion she smote them with her rod, turning them into swine. Eurylochus who had suspected some trickery hurried back to Odysseus with the news. The latter determined to go alone to save his friends. On the way he was met by Hermes, who showed him the herb moly, an antidote to Circe's draught. Finding that her magic failed, she at once knew that her visitor was Odysseus whose visit had been prophesied to her by Hermes. He bound her down by a solemn oath to refrain from further mischief and persuaded her to restore to his men their humanity. When Odysseus desired to depart home, she told him of the wanderings that awaited him. First he must go to the land of the dead to consult the shade of Teiresias, the blind old prophet, who would help him.

Following the goddess' instructions, they sailed to the land of the Cimmerians on the confines of the earth. There Odysseus dug a trench into which he poured the blood of slain victims which he did not allow the dead spirits to touch till Teiresias appeared. The seer told him of the sorrows that awaited him and vaguely indicated that his death should come upon him from the sea; he added that any spirit he allowed to touch the blood would tell him truly all whereof he was as yet ignorant, and that those ghosts he drove away would return to the darkness.

First arose the spirit of his dead mother Anticleia who told him that his wife and son were yet alive and his father was living away from the town in wretchedness.

> "For me, it was not the visitation of Apollo that took me, nor any sickness whose corruption drove the life from my frame; rather it was longing for thee and thy counsels and thy gentleness which spoiled me of my spirit."

Thrice he tried to embrace her, and thrice the ghost eluded him, for it was "as a dream that had fled away from the white frame of the body". A procession of famous women followed, then came the wraith of Agamemnon who told how he had been foully slain by his own wife, as faithless as Penelope was prudent. Achilles next approached; when Odysseus tried to console him for his early death by reminding him of the honour he had when he was alive, he answered:

> "Speak not comfortingly of death; I would rather be a clown and a thrall on earth to another man than rule among the departed."

On hearing that his son Neoptolemus had won great glory in the capture of Troy, the spirit left him, exulting with joy that his son was worthy of him. Ajax turned from Odysseus in anger at the loss of Achilles' armour for the possession of which they had striven. The last figure that came was the ghost of Heracles, though the hero himself was with the gods in Olympus.

> "Round him was the whirr of the dead as of birds fleeing in panic. Like to black night, with his bow ready and an arrow on the string, he glared about him terribly, as ever intending to shoot. Over his breast was flung a fearful belt, whereon were graven bears and lions and fights, battles, murders and man-slayings."

He recognised Odysseus before he passed back to death; when a crowd of terrifying apparitions came thronging to the trench, Odysseus fled to his ship lest the Gorgon might be sent from the awful Queen of the dead.

Returning to Circe, he learned from her of the remaining dangers. The first of these was the island of the Sirens, who by the marvellous sweetness of their song charmed to their ruin all who passed. Odysseus filled the ears of his crews with wax, bidding them to tie him to the mast of his ship and to row hard past the temptresses in spite of his strugglings. They then entered the dangerous strait, on one side of which was Scylla, a dreadful monster who lived in a cave near by, on the other was the deadly whirlpool of Charybdis. Scylla carried off six of his men who called in vain to Odysseus to save them, stretching out their hands to him in their last agony. From the strait they passed to the island of Trinacria, where they found grazing the cattle of the Sun. Odysseus had learned from both Teiresias and Circe that an evil doom would come upon them if they touched the animals; he therefore made his companions swear a great oath not to touch them if they landed. For a whole month they were wind-bound in the island and ate all the provisions which Circe had given them. At a time when Odysseus had gone to explore the island Eurylochus persuaded his men to kill and eat; as he returned Odysseus smelled the savour of their feast and knew that destruction was at hand. For nine days the feasting continued. When the ship put out to sea Zeus, in answer to the prayer of the offended Sun-God, sent a storm which drowned all the crew and drove Odysseus back to the dreaded strait. Escaping through it with difficulty, he drifted helplessly over the deep and on the tenth day landed on the island of "the dread goddess who used human speech", Calypso, who tended him and kept him in captivity.

On the next day the Phaeacians loaded Odysseus with presents and landed him on his own island while he slept. Poseidon in anger at the arrival of the hero changed the returning Phaeacian ship into stone when it was almost within the harbour of the city. When Odysseus awoke he failed to recognise his own land. Athena appeared to him disguised as a shepherd, telling him he was indeed in Ithaca:

> "Thou art witless or art come from afar, if thou enquirest about this land. It is not utterly unknown; many know it who dwell in the East and in the West. It is rough and unfitted for steeds, yet it is not a sorry isle, though narrow. It hath plenteous store of corn and the vine groweth herein. It hath alway rain and glistening dew. It nourisheth goats and cattle and all kinds of woods and its streams are everlasting."

Such is the description of the land for which Odysseus forsook Calypso's offer of immortality. After smiling at Odysseus' pretence that he was a Cretan Athena counselled him how to slay the suitors and hurried to fetch Telemachus from Sparta. The poet tells why Athena loved Odysseus more than all others.

> "Crafty would he be and a cunning trickster who surpassed thee in wiles, though it were a god who challenged thee. We know craft enough, both of us, for thou art by far the best of mortals in speech and counsel and I among the gods am famed for devices and cunning."

Transformed by her into an old beggar, Odysseus went to the hut of his faithful old swineherd Eumaeus; the dogs set upon him, but Eumaeus scared them away and welcomed him to his dwelling. In spite of Odysseus' assurance that the master would return Eumaeus, who had been often deceived by similar words, refused to believe. Feigning himself to be a Cretan, Odysseus saw for himself that the old servant's loyalty was steadfast; a deft touch brings out his care for his master's substance:

> "laying a bed for Odysseus before the fire, he went out and slept among the dogs in a cave beneath the breath of the winds."

By the intervention of Athena the two leading characters are brought together. She stood beside the sleeping Telemachus in Sparta, warning him of the ambush set for him in Ithaca and bidding him to land on a lonely part of the coast whence he was to proceed to the hut of Eumaeus. On his departure from Sparta an omen was interpreted by Helen to mean that Odysseus was not far from home. As he was on the point of leaving Pylos on the morrow a bard named Theoclymenus appealed to him for protection, for he had slain a man and was a fugitive from justice. Taking him on board Telemachus frustrated the ambush, landing in safety; he proceeded to Eumaeus' hut, where Odysseus had with some difficulty been persuaded to remain.

The dogs were the first to announce the arrival of a friend, gambolling about him. After speaking a word of cheer to Eumaeus Telemachus enquired who the stranger was; hearing that he was a Cretan he lamented his inability to give him a welcome in his home owing to the insolence of his enemies. Remembering the anxiety of his mother during his absence he sent Eumaeus to the town to acquaint her with his arrival. Athena seized the opportunity to reveal Odysseus to his son, transforming him to his own shape. After a moment of utter amazement at the marvel of the change, Telemachus ran to his father and fell upon his neck, his joy finding expression in tears. The two then laid their plans for the destruction of the suitors. By the time Eumaeus had returned Odysseus had resumed his sorry and tattered appearance.

Telemachus went to the town alone, bidding Eumaeus bring the stranger with him. They were met by one Melanthius a goatherd, who covered them with insults. "In truth one churl is leading another, for the god ever bringeth like to like. Whither art thou taking this glutton, this evil pauper, a kill-joy of the feast? He hath learned many a knavish trick and is like to refuse to labour; creeping among the people he would rather ask alms to fill his insatiate maw." Leaping on Odysseus, he kicked at him, yet failed to stir him from the pathway. Swallowing the insult Odysseus walked towards his house. A superb stroke of art has created the next incident. In the courtyard lay Argus, a hound whom Odysseus had once fed. Neglected in the absence of his master he had crept to a dung-heap, full of lice. When he marked Odysseus coming towards him he wagged his tail and dropped his ears, but could not come near his lord. Seeing him from a little distance Odysseus wiped away his tears unnoticed of Eumaeus and asked whose the hound was. Eumaeus told the story of his neglect: "but the doom of death took Argus straightway after seeing Odysseus in the twentieth year". In the palace Telemachus sent his father food, bidding him ask a charity of the wooers. Antinous answered by hurling a stool which struck his shoulder. The noise of the high words which followed brought down Penelope who protested against the godless behaviour of the suitors and asked to interview the stranger in hope of learning some tidings of her husband, but Odysseus put her off till nightfall when they would be less likely to suffer from the insolence of the suitors.

In Ithaca was a beggar named Irus, gluttonous and big-boned but a coward. Encouraged by the winkings and noddings of the suitors he bade Odysseus begone. A quiet answer made him imagine he had to deal with a poltroon and he challenged him to a fight. The proposal was welcomed with glee by the suitors, who promised on oath to see fair play for the old man in his quarrel with a younger. But when they saw the mighty limbs and stout frame of Odysseus, they deemed that Irus had brought trouble on his own head. Chattering with fear Irus had to be forced to the combat. One blow was enough to lay him low; the ease with which Odysseus had disposed of his foe made him for a time popular with the suitors.

Under an inspiration of Athena, Penelope came down once more to chide the wooers for their insolence; she also upbraided them for their stinginess.

> "Yours is not the custom of wooers in former days who were wont to sue for wedlock with the daughter of a rich man and contend among themselves. Such men offer oxen and stout cattle and glorious gifts; they will never consume another's substance without payment."

Stung by the taunt, they gave her the accustomed presents, while Odysseus rejoiced that she flattered their heart in soft words with a different intent in her spirit. The insolence of the suitors was matched by the pertness of the serving maids, of whom Melantho was the most impudent. A threat from Odysseus drew down upon him the wrath of the suitors who were with difficulty persuaded by Telemachus to depart home to their beds.

That night Odysseus and his son removed the arms from the walls, the latter being told to urge as a pretext for his action the necessity of cleaning from them the rust and of removing a temptation to violence when the suitors were heated with wine. At the promised interview with his wife Odysseus again pretended he was a Cretan; describing the very dress which Odysseus had worn, he assured her that he would soon return with the many treasures which he had collected. Half persuaded by the exact description of a garment she had herself made, she bade her maids look to him, but he would not suffer any of them to approach him save his old nurse Eurycleia. As she was washing him in the dim light of the fireside her fingers touched the old scar above his knee, the result of an accident in a boar-hunt during his youth.

> "Dropping the basin she fell backwards; joy and grief took her heart at once, her eyes filled with tears and her utterance was checked. Catching him by his beard, she said: 'In very sooth thou art Odysseus, my dear boy; and I knew thee not before I had touched the body of my lord.' So speaking she looked at Penelope, fain to tell her that her lord was within. But Odysseus laid his hand upon the nurse's mouth, with the other he drew her to him and whispered: 'Nurse, wouldst thou ruin me? Thou didst nourish me at thy breast, and now I am come back after mighty sufferings. Be silent, lest another learn the news, or I tell thee that when I have punished the suitors I will not even refrain from thee when I destroy the other women in my halls.'"

Concealing the scar carefully under his rags by the fireside he put a good interpretation on a strange dream which had visited his wife.

That night Odysseus with his own eyes witnessed the intrigues between his women and the suitors. He heard his wife weeping in her chamber for him and prayed to Zeus for aid in the coming trial. On the morrow he was again outraged; the suitors were moved to laughter by a prophecy of Theoclymenus:

> "Yet they were laughing with alien lips, the meat they ate was dabbled with blood, their eyes were filled with tears and their hearts boded lamentation. Among them spake Theoclymenus; 'Wretched men, what is this evil that is come upon you? Your heads and faces and the knees beneath you are shrouded in night, mourning is kindled among you, your cheeks are bedewed with tears, the walls and the fair pillars are sprinkled with blood, the forecourt and the yard is full of spectres hastening to the gloom of Erebus; the sun hath perished from the heaven and a mist of ruin hath swept upon you.'"

In answer Eurymachus bade him begone if all within was night; taking him at his word, the seer withdrew before the coming ruin.

Then Athena put it into the heart of Penelope to set the suitors a final test. She brought forth the bow of Odysseus together with twelve axes. It had been an exercise of her lord to set up the axes in a line, string the bow and shoot through the heads of the axes which had been hollowed for that purpose. She promised to follow at once the suitor who could string the bow and shoot through the axes. First Telemachus set up the axes and tried to string the weapon; failing three times he would have succeeded at the next effort but for a glance from his father. Leiodes vainly tried his strength, to be rebuked by Antinous who suggested that the bow should be made more pliant by being heated at the fire.

Noticing that Eumaeus and Philoetius had gone out together Odysseus went after them and revealed himself to them; the three then returned to the hall. After all the suitors had failed except Antinous, who did not deem that he should waste a feast-day in stringing bows, Odysseus begged that he might try, Penelope insisting on his right to attempt the feat. When she retired Eumaeus brought the bow to Odysseus, then told Eurycleia to keep the woman in their chambers while Philoetius bolted the hall door.

> "But already Odysseus was turning the bow this way and that testing it lest the worms had devoured it in his absence. Then when he had balanced it and looked it all over, even as when a man skilled in the lyre and song easily putteth a new string about a peg, even so without an effort Odysseus strung his mighty bow. Taking it in his right hand he tried the string which sang sweetly beneath his touch like to the voice of a swallow. Then he took an arrow and shot it with a straight aim through the axes, missing not one. Then he spake to Telemachus: 'Thy guest bringeth thee no shame as he sitteth in thy halls, for I missed not the mark nor spent much time in the stringing. My strength is yet whole within me. But now it is time to make a banquet for the Achaeans in the

light of day and then season it with song and dance, which are the crown of revelry.' So speaking he nodded, and his son took a sword and a spear and stood by him clad in gleaming bronze."

The first victim was Antinous, whom Odysseus shot through the neck as he was in the act of drinking, never dreaming that one man would attack a multitude of suitors. Eurymachus fell after vainly attempting a compromise. Melanthius was caught in the act of supplying arms to the rest and was left bound to be dealt with when the main work was done. Athena herself encouraged Odysseus in his labour of vengeance, deflecting from him any weapons that were hurled at him. At length all was over, the serving women were made to cleanse the hall of all traces of bloodshed; the guiltiest of them were hanged, while Melanthius died a horrible death by mutilation. Odysseus then summoned his wife to his presence.

Eurycleia carried the message to her, laughing with joy so much that Penelope deemed her mad. The story of the vengeance which Odysseus had exacted was so incredible that it must have been the act of a god, not a man. When she entered the hall Telemachus upbraided her for her unbelief, but Odysseus smiled on hearing that she intended to test him by certain proofs which they two alone were aware of. He withdrew for a time to cleanse him of his stains and to put on his royal garments, after ordering the servants to maintain a revelry to blind the people to the death of their chief men.

When he reappeared, endued with grace which Athena gave him, he marvelled at the untoward heart which the gods had given his wife and bade his nurse lay him his bed. Penelope caught up his words quickly; the bed was to be laid outside the chamber which he himself had made. The words filled Odysseus with dismay:

"Who hath put my bed elsewhere? It would be a hard task for any man however cunning, except a god set it in some other place. Of men none could easily shift it, for there is a wonder in that cunningly made bed whereat I laboured and none else. Within the courtyard was growing the trunk of an olive; round it I built my bed-chamber with thick stones and roofed it well, placing in it doors that shut tight. Then I cut away the olive branches, smoothed the trunk, made a bedpost, and bored all with a gimlet. From that foundation I smoothed my bed, tricking it out with gold and silver and ivory and stretching from its frame thongs of cow-hide dyed red. Such is the wonder I tell of, yet I know not, Lady, whether the bed is yet fixed there, or whether another hath moved it, cutting the foundation of olive from underneath."

On hearing the details of their secret Penelope ran to him casting her arms about him and begging him to forgive her unbelief, for many a pretender had come, making her ever more and more suspicious. Thus reunited the two spent the night in recounting the agonies of their separation; Odysseus mentioned the strange prophecy of Teiresias, deciding to seek out his father on the morrow.

A vivid description tells how the souls of the suitors were conducted to the realm of the dead, the old comrades of Odysseus before Troy recognising in the vengeance all the marks of his handiwork. Odysseus found his father in a wretched old age hoeing his garden, clad in soiled garments with a goat-skin hat on his head which but increased his sorrow. At the sight Odysseus was moved to tears of compassion. Yet even then he could not refrain from his wiles, for he told how he had indeed seen Odysseus though five years before. In despair the old man took the dust in his hands and cast it about his head in mighty grief.

> "Then Odysseus' spirit was moved and the stinging throb smote his nostrils. Clinging to his father he kissed him and told him he was indeed his son, returned after twenty years."

For a moment the old man doubted, but believed when Odysseus showed the scar and told him the number and names of the trees they had planted together in their orchard.

Meanwhile news of the death of the wooers had run through the city. The father of Antinous raised a tumult and led a body of armed men to demand satisfaction. The threatening uproar was stopped by the intervention of Athena who thus completed the restoration of her favourite as she had begun it.

It is strange that this poem, which is such a favourite with modern readers, should have made a less deep impression on the Greeks. To them, Homer is nearly always the *Iliad*, possibly because Achilles was semi-divine, whereas Odysseus was a mere mortal. But the latter is for that very reason of more importance to us, we feel him to be more akin to our own life. Further, the type of character which Odysseus stands for is really far nobler than the fervid and somewhat incalculable nature of the son of Thetis. Odysseus is patient endurance, common sense, self-restraint, coolness, resource and strength; he is indeed a manifold personality, far more complex than anything attempted previously in Greek literature and therefore far more modern in his appeal. It is only after reading the *Odyssey* that we begin to understand why Diomedes chose Odysseus as his companion in the famous Dolon adventure in Noman's land. Achilles would have been the wrong man for this or any other situation which demanded first and last a cool head.

The romantic elements which are so necessary a part of all Epic are much more convincing in the *Odyssey*; the actions and adventures are indeed beyond experience, but they are treated in such a masterly style that they are made inevitable; it would be difficult to improve on any of the little details which force us to believe the whole story. Added to them is another genuine romantic feature, the sense of wandering in strange new lands untrodden before of man's foot; the beings who move in these lands are gracious, barbarous, magical, monstrous, superhuman, dreamy, or prophetic by turns; they are all different and all fascinating. The reader is further introduced to the life of the dead as well as of the living and the memory of his visit is one which he will retain for ever. Not many stories of adventure can impress themselves indelibly as does the *Odyssey*.

To English readers the poem has a special value, for it deals with the sea and its wonders. The native land of its hero is not very unlike our own, "full of mist and rain", yet able to make us love it far more than a Calypso's isle with an offer of immortality to any who will exchange his real love of home for an unnatural haven of peace. A splendid hero, a good love-story, admirable narrative, romance and excitement, together with a breath of the sea which gives plenty of space and pure air have made the *Odyssey* the companion of many a veteran reader in whom the Greek spirit cannot die.

Of the impression which Homer has made upon the mind of Europe it would be difficult to give an estimate. The Greeks themselves early came to regard his text with a sort of veneration; it was learned by heart and quoted to spellbound audiences in the cities and at the great national meetings at Olympia. Every Greek boy was expected to know some portion at least by heart; Plato evidently loved Homer and when he was obliged to point out that the system of morality which he stood for was antiquated and needed revision, apologised for the criticism he could not avoid. It is sometimes said that Homer was the Bible of the Greeks; while this statement is probably inaccurate—for no theological system was built on him nor did he claim any divine revelation—yet it is certain that authors of all ages searched the text for all kinds of purposes, antiquarian, ethical, social, as well as religious. This careful study of Homer culminated in the learned and accurate work of the great Alexandrian school of Zenodotus and Aristarchus.

In Roman times Homer never failed to inspire lesser writers; Ennius is said to have translated the *Odyssey*, while Virgil's *Aeneid* is clearly a child of the Greek Homeric tradition. In the Middle Ages the Trojan legend was one of the four great cycles which were treated over and over again in the Chansons. Even drama was glad to borrow the great characters of the *Iliad*, as Shakespeare did in *Troilus and Cressida*. In England a number of famous translations has witnessed to the undying appeal of the first of the Greek masters. Chapman published his *Iliad* in 1611, his *Odyssey* in 1616; Pope's version appeared between 1715 and 1726; Cowper issued his translation in 1791. In the next century the Earl Derby retranslated the *Iliad*, while an excellent prose version of the *Odyssey* by Butcher and Lang was followed by a prose version of the *Iliad* by Lang Myers and Leaf. At a time when Europe had succeeded in persuading itself that the whole story of a siege of Troy was an obvious myth, a series of startling discoveries on the site of Troy and on the mainland of Greece proved how lamentably shallow is some of the cleverest and most destructive Higher Criticism.

The marvellous rapidity and vigour of these two poems will save them from death; the splendid qualities of direct narration, constructive skill, dignity and poetical power will always make Homer a name to love. Those who know no Greek and therefore fear that they may lose some of the directness of the Homeric appeal might recall the famous sonnet written by Keats who had had no opportunity to learn the great language. His words are no doubt familiar enough; that they have become inseparable from Homer must be our apology for inserting them here.

> Much have I travelled in the realms of gold,
> And many goodly states and Kingdoms seen;
> Round many western islands have I been
> Which bards in fealty to Apollo hold.

Oft of one wide expanse had I been told
That deep-browed Homer ruled as his demesne:
Yet never did I breathe its pure serene
Till I heard Chapman speak out loud and bold.

Then felt I like some watcher of the skies
When a new planet swims into his ken,
Or like stout Cortes, when with eagle eyes
He stared at the Pacific—and all his men
Look'd at each other with a wild surmise—
Silent, upon a peak in Darien.

TRANSLATIONS. AS INDICATED IN THE TEXT OF THE ESSAY.

The whole of the Homeric tradition is affected by the recent discoveries made in Crete. The civilisation there unearthed raises questions of great interest; the problems it suggests are certain to modify current ideas of Homeric study.

See *Discoveries in Crete*, by R. Burrows (Murray, 1907).

A very good account of the early age of European literature is in *The Heroic Age*, by Chadwick (Cambridge, 1912).

The best interpretation of Greek poetry is Symonds' *Greek Poets*, 2 vols. (Smith Elder).

Jebb's *Homer* is the best introduction to the many difficulties presented by the poems.

Flaxman's engravings for the *Iliad* and *Odyssey* are of the highest order.

AESCHYLUS

Towards the end of the sixth century before Christ, one of the most momentous advances in literature was made by the genius of Aeschylus. European drama was created and a means of utterance was given to the rapidly growing democratic spirit of Greece. Before Aeschylus wrote, rude public exhibitions had been given of the life and adventures of Dionysus, the god of wine. Choruses had sung odes to the deity and variety was obtained by a series of short dialogues between one of the Chorus and the remainder. Aeschylus added a second actor to converse with the first; he thus started a movement which eventually ousted the Chorus from its place of importance, for the interest now began to concentrate on the two actors; it was their performance which gave drama its name. In time more characters were added; the Chorus became less necessary and in the long run was felt to be a hindrance to the movement of the story. This process is plainly visible in the extant works of the Attic tragedians.

Aeschylus was born at Eleusis in 525; before the end of the century he was writing tragedies. In 490 he fought in the great battle of Marathon and took part in the victory of Salamis in 480. This experience of the struggle for freedom against Persian despotism added a vigour and a self-reliance to his writing which is characteristic of a growing national spirit. He is said to have visited Sicily in 468 and again in 458, various motives being given for his leaving Athens. His death at Gela in 456 is said to have been due to an eagle, which dropped a tortoise upon his head which he mistook for a stone. He has left to the world seven plays in which the rapid development of drama is conspicuous.

One of the earliest of his plays is the *Suppliants*, little read owing to the uncertainty of the text and the meagreness of the dramatic interest. The plot is simple enough. Danaus, sprung from Io of Argos, flees from Egypt with his fifty daughters who avoid wedlock with the fifty sons of Aegyptus. He sails to Argos and lays suppliant boughs on the altars of the gods, imploring protection. The King of Argos after consultation with his people decides to admit the fugitives and to secure them from Aegyptus' violence. A herald from the latter threatens to take the Danaids back with him, but the King intervenes and saves them. There is little in this play but long choral odes; yet one or two Aeschylean features are evident. The King dreads offending the god of suppliants

> "lest he should make him to haunt his house, a dread visitor
> who quits not sinners even in the world to come."

The Egyptian herald reverences no gods of Greece "who reared him not nor brought him to old age". The Chorus declare that "what is fated will come to pass, for Zeus' mighty boundless will cannot be thwarted". Here we have the three leading ideas in the system of Aeschylus—the doctrine of the inherited curse, of human pride and impiety, and the might of Destiny.

The *Persians* is unique as being the only surviving historical play in Greek literature. It is a poem rather than a drama, as there is little truly dramatic action. The piece is a succession of very vivid sketches of the incidents in the great struggle which freed Europe from the threat of Eastern despotism. A Chorus of Persian elders is waiting for news of the advance of the great array which Xerxes led against Greece in 480. They tell how Persia extended her sway over Asia. Yet they are uneasy, for

> "what mortal can avoid the crafty deception of Heaven? In seeming kindness it entices men into a trap whence they cannot escape."

The Queen-mother Atossa enters, resplendent with jewels; she too is anxious, for in a dream she had seen Xerxes yoke two women together who were at feud, one clad in Persian garb, the other in Greek. The former was obedient to the yoke, but the latter tore the car to pieces and broke the curb. The Chorus advises her to propitiate the gods with sacrifice, and to pray to Darius her dead husband to send his son prosperity. At that moment a herald enters with the news of the Greek victory at Salamis. Xerxes, beguiled by some fiend or evil spirit, drew up his fleet at night to intercept the Greeks, supposed to be preparing for flight. But at early dawn they sailed out to attack, singing mightily

> "Ye sons of Greece, onward! Free your country, your children and wives, the shrines of your fathers' gods, and your ancestral tombs. Now must ye fight for all."

Winning a glorious victory, they landed on the little island (Psyttaleia) where the choicest Persian troops had been placed to cut off the retreat of the Greek navy, and slew them all. Later, they drove back the Persians by land; through Boeotia, Thessaly and Macedonia the broken host retreated, finally recrossing to Asia over the Hellespont.

On hearing the news Atossa disappears and the Persian Chorus sing a dirge. The Queen returns without her finery, attired as a suppliant; she bids the Chorus call up Darius, while she offers libations to the dead. The ghost of the great Empire-builder rises before the astonished spectators, enquiring what trouble has overtaken his land. His release from Death is not easy, "for the gods of the lower world are readier to take men's spirits than to let them go". On learning that his son has been totally defeated, he delivers his judgment. The oracles had long ago prophesied this disaster; it was hurried on by Xerxes' rashness, for when a man is himself hurrying on to ruin Heaven abets him. He had listened to evil counsellors, who bade him rival his father's glory by making wider conquests. The ruin of Persia is not yet complete, for when insolence is fully ripe it bears a crop of ruin and reaps a harvest of tears. This evil came upon Xerxes through the sacrilegious demolition of altars and temples. Zeus punishes overweening pride, and his correcting hand is heavy. Darius counsels Atossa to comfort their son and to prevent him from attacking Greece again; he further advises the Chorus to take life's pleasures while they can, for after death there is no profit in wealth. A distinctly grotesque touch is added by the appearance of Xerxes himself, broken and defeated, filling the scene with lamentations for lost friends and departed glory, unable to answer the Chorus when they demand the whereabouts of some of the most famous Persian warriors.

The play is valuable as the result of a personal experience of the poet. As a piece of literature it is important, for it is a poetic description of the first armed conflict between East and West. It directly inspired Shelley when he wrote his *Hellas* at a time when Greece was rousing herself from many centuries of Eastern oppression. As a historical drama it is of great value, for it is substantially accurate in its main facts, though Aeschylus has been compelled to take some liberties with time and human motives in order to satisfy dramatic needs. From Herodotus it seems probable that Darius himself hankered after the subjugation of Greece, while Xerxes at the outset was inclined to leave her in peace.

One or two characteristic features are worth note. The genius of Aeschylus was very bold; it was a daring thing to bring up a ghost from the dead, for the supernatural appeal does not succeed except when it is treated with proper insight; yet even Aeschylus' genius has not quite succeeded in filling his canvas, the last scenes being distinctly poor in comparison with the splendour of the main theme. On the other hand a notable advance in dramatic power has been made. The main actors are becoming human; their wills are beginning to operate. Tragedy is based on a conflict of some sort; here the wilful spirit of youth is portrayed as defying the forces of justice and righteousness; it is insolence which brings Xerxes to ruin. The substantial creed of Aeschylus is contained in Darius' speech; as the poet progresses in dramatic cunning we shall find that he constantly finds his sources of tragic inspiration in the acts of the sinners who defy the will of the gods.

The Seven against Thebes was performed in 472. It was one of a trilogy, a series of three plays dealing with the misfortunes of Oedipus' race. After the death of Oedipus his sons Polyneices and Eteocles quarrelled for the sovereignty of Thebes. Polyneices, expelled and banished by his younger brother, assembled an army of chosen warriors to attack his native land. Eteocles opens the play with a speech which encourages the citizens to defend their town. A messenger hurries in telling how he left the besiegers casting lots to decide which of the seven gates of Thebes each should attack. Eteocles prays that the curse of his father may not destroy the town and leaves to arrange the defences. In his absence the Chorus of virgins sing a wild prayer to the gods to save them. Hearing this, the King returns to administer a vigorous reproof; he declares that their frenzied supplications fill the city with terrors, discouraging the fighting men. He demands from them obedience, the mother of salvation; if at last they are to perish, they cannot escape the inevitable. His masterful spirit at last cows them into a better frame of mind; this scene presents to us one of the most manly characters in Aeschylus' work.

After a choral ode a piece of intense tragic horror follows. The messenger tells the names of the champions who are to assault the gates. As he names them and the boastful or impious mottoes on their shields, the King names the Theban champions who are to quell their pride in the fear of the gods. Five of the insolent attackers are mentioned, then the only righteous one of the invading force, Amphiaraus the seer; he it was who rebuked the violence of Tydeus, the evil genius among the besiegers, and openly reviled Polyneices for attacking his own native land. He had prophesied his own death before the city, yet resolved to meet his fate nobly; on his shield alone was no device, for he wished to be, not to seem, a good man. The pathos of the impending ruin of a great character through evil associations is heightened by the terror of what follows. Only one gate remains without an assailant, the gate Eteocles is to defend; it is to be attacked by the King's own brother, Polyneices. Filled with horror, the Chorus begs him send another to that gate, for "there can be no old age to the pollution of kindred bloodshed". Recognising that his father's curse is working itself out, he departs to kill and be killed by his own brother, for "when the gods send evil none can avoid it".

In an interval the Chorus reflect on their King's impending doom. His father's curse strikes them with dread; Oedipus himself was born of a father Laius who, though warned thrice by Apollo that if he died without issue he would save his land, listened to the counsels of friends and in imprudence begat his own destroyer. Their song is interrupted by a messenger who announces that they have prospered at six gates, but at the seventh the two brothers have slain each other. This news inspires another song in which the joy of deliverance gradually yields to pity for an unhappy house, cursed and blighted, the glory of Oedipus serving but to make more acute the shame of his latter end and the triumph of the ruin he invoked on his sons. The agony of this scene is intensified by the entry of Ismene and Antigone, Oedipus' daughters, the latter mourning for Polyneices, the former for Eteocles. The climax is reached when a herald announces a decree made by the senate and people. Eteocles, their King who defended the land, was to be buried with all honours, but Polyneices was to lie unburied. Calmly and with great dignity Antigone informs the herald that if nobody else buries her brother, she will. A warning threat fails to move her. The play closes with a double note of terror at the doom of Polyneices and pity for the death of a brave King.

Further progress in dramatic art has been made in this play. One of the main sources of the pathos of human life is the operation of what seems to us to be mere blind chance. Just as the casual dropping of Desdemona's handkerchief gave Iago his opportunity, so the casual allotting of the seven gates brings the two brothers into conflict. But behind it was the working of an inherited curse; yet Aeschylus is careful to point out that the curse need never have existed at all but for the wilfulness of Laius; he was the origin of all the mischief, obstinately refusing to listen to a warning thrice given him by Apollo. Another secret of dramatic excellence has been discovered by the poet, that of contrast. Two brothers and two sisters are balanced in pairs against one another. The weaker sister Ismene laments the stronger brother, while the more unfortunate Polyneices is championed by the more firmly drawn sister. Equally admirable is the contrast between the righteous Amphiaraus and his godless companions. The character of each of these is a masterpiece. War, horror, kindred bloodshed, with a promise of further agonies to arise from Antigone's resolve are the elements which Aeschylus has fused together in this vivid play.

"There was war in Heaven" between the new gods and the old. The *Prometheus Bound* contains the story of the proud tyranny of Zeus, the latest ruler of the gods. Hephaestus, the god of fire, opens a conversation with Force and Violence who are pinning Prometheus with chains of adamant to the rocks of Caucasus. Hephaestus performs his task with reluctance and in pity for the victim, the deep-counselling son of right-minded Law. Yet the command of Zeus his master is urgent, overriding the claims of kindred blood. Force and Violence, full of hatred, hold down the god who has stolen fire, Hephaestus' right, and given it to men. They bid the Fire-God make the chains fast and drive the wedge through Prometheus' body. When the work is done they leave him with the taunt:

> "Now steal the rights of the gods and give them to the creatures of the day; what can mortals do to relieve thy agonies? The gods wrongly call thee a far-seeing counsellor, who thyself lackest a counsellor to save thee from thy present lot."

Abandoned of all, Prometheus breaks out into a wild appeal to earth, air, the myriad laughter of the sea, the founts and streams to witness his humiliation; but soon he reflects that he had foreseen his agony and must bear it as best he can, for the might of Necessity is not to be fought against. A sound of lightly moving pinions strikes his ears; sympathisers have come to visit him; they are the Chorus, the daughters of Ocean, who have heard the sound of the riveted chains and hurried forth in their winged car Awestruck, they come to see how Zeus is smiting down the mighty gods of old. It would be difficult to imagine a more natural and touching motive for the entry of a Chorus.

In the dialogue that follows the tragic appeal to pity is quickly blended with a different interest. By a superb stroke of art Aeschylus excites the audience to an intense curiosity. Though apparently subdued, Prometheus has the certainty of ultimate triumph over his foe; he alone has secret knowledge of something which will one day hurl Zeus from his throne; the time will come when the new president of Heaven will hurry to him in anxious desire for reconciliation; when ruin threatens him he will forsake his pride and beg Prometheus to save him. But no words will prevail on the sufferer till he is released from his bonds and receives ample satisfaction for his maltreatment. The Chorus bids him tell the whole history of the quarrel. To them he unfolds the story of Zeus' ingratitude. There was a discord among the older gods, some wishing to depose Cronos and make Zeus their King. Warned by his mother, Prometheus knew that only counsel could avail in the struggle, not violence. When he failed to persuade the Titans to use cunning, he joined Zeus who with his aid hurled his foes down to Tartarus. Securing the sovereignty, Zeus distributed honours to his supporters, but was anxious to wipe out the human race and create a new stock. Prometheus resisted him, giving mortals fire the creator of many arts and ridding them of the dread of death. This act brought him into conflict with Zeus. He invites the Chorus to step down from their car and hear the rest of his story. At this point Ocean enters, one of the older gods. He offers to act as a mediator with Zeus, but Prometheus warns him to keep out of the conflict; he has witnessed the sorrows of Atlas, his own brother, and of

Typhos, pinned down under Etna, and desires to bring trouble upon no other god; he must bear his agonies alone till the time of deliverance is ripe. Ocean departing, Prometheus continues his story. He gave men writing and knowledge of astronomy, taught them to tame the wild beasts, invented the ship, created medicine, divination and metallurgy. Yet for all this, his art is weaker far than Necessity, whereof the controllers are Fate and the unforgetting Furies. Terror-struck at his sufferings, the Chorus point out how utterly his goodness has been wasted in helping the race of mortals who cannot save him. He warns them that a time would come when Zeus should be no longer King; when they ask for more knowledge, he turns them to other thoughts, bidding them hide the secret as much as possible. Their interest is drawn away to another of Zeus' victims, who at this moment rushes on the scene; it is Io, cajoled and abandoned by Zeus, plagued and tormented by the dread unsleeping gadfly sent by Zeus' consort Hera. She relates her story to the wondering Chorus, and then Prometheus tells her the long tale of misery and wandering that await her as she passes from the Caucasus to Egypt, where she is promised deliverance from her tormentor.

The play now moves to its awful climax. The sight of Io stirs Prometheus to prophesy more clearly the end in store for Zeus. There would be born one to discover a terror far greater than the thunderbolt, and smite Zeus and his brother Poseidon into utter slavery. On hearing this Zeus sends from heaven his messenger Hermes to demand fuller knowledge of this new monarch. Disdaining his threats, Prometheus mocks the new gods and defies their ruler to do his worst. Hermes then delivers his warning. Prometheus would be overwhelmed with the terrors of thunder and lightning, while the red eagle would tear out his heart unceasingly till one should arise to inherit his agonies, descending to the depths of Tartarus. He advises the Chorus to depart from the rebel, lest they too should share in the vengeance. They remain faithful to Prometheus, ready to suffer with him; then descend the thunderings and lightnings, the mountains rock, the winds roar, and the sky is confounded with sea; the dread agony has begun.

Once more the bold originality of Aeschylus displays itself. Here is a theme unique in Greek literature. The strife between the two races of gods opens out a vista of the world ages before man was created. It will provide a solution to a very difficult problem which will confront us in a later play. The conflict between two stubborn wills is the source of a sublime tragedy in which our sympathies are with the sufferer; Zeus, who punishes Prometheus for "unjustly" helping mortals, himself falls below the level of human morality; he is tyrannous, ungrateful and revengeful—in short, he displays all the wrong-headedness of a new ruler. No doubt in the sequel these defects would have disappeared; experience would have induced a kindlier temper and the sense of an impending doom would have made it essential for him to relent in order to learn the great secret about his successor.

Pathos is repeatedly appealed to in the play. Hephaestus is one of the kindliest figures in Greek tragedy; the noble-hearted young goddesses cannot fail to hold our affection. They are the most human Chorus in all drama; their entry is admirable; in the sequel we should have found them still near Prometheus after his cycle of tortures. But the subject-matter is calculated to win the admiration of all humanity; it is the persecution of him to whom on Greek principles mankind owes all that it is of value in its civilisation. We cannot help thinking of another God, racked and tormented and nailed to a cross of shame to save the race He loved. The very power and majesty of Aeschylus' work has made it difficult for successors to imitate him; few can hope to equal his sublime grandeur; Shelley attempted it in his *Prometheus Unbound*, but his Prometheus becomes abstract Humanity, ceasing to be a character, while his play is really a mere poem celebrating the inevitable victory of man over the evils of his environment and picturing the return of an age of happiness.

Nearly all the characters in Greek tragedy were the heroes of well-known popular legends. In abandoning the well-trodden circle Aeschylus has here ensured an undying freshness for his work—it is novel, free and unconventional; more than that, it is dignified.

The slightest error of taste would have degraded if to the level of a comedy; throughout it maintains a uniform tone of loftiness and sincerity. The language is easy but powerful, the art with which the story is told is consummate. Finally, it is one of the few pieces in the literature of the world which are truly sublime; it ranks with Job and Dante. The great purpose of creation, the struggles of beings of terrific power, the majesty of gods, the whole universe sighing and lamenting for the agonies of a deity of wondrous foresight, saving others but not himself—such is the theme of this mighty and affecting play.

In 458 Aeschylus wrote the one trilogy which is extant. It describes the murder of Agamemnon, the revenge of Orestes and his purification from blood-guiltiness. It will be necessary to trace the history of Agamemnon's family before we can understand these plays. His great-grandfather was Tantalus, who betrayed the secrets of the gods and was subjected to unending torture in Hades. Pelops, his son, begat two sons, Atreus and Thyestes. The former killed Thyestes' son, invited the father to a banquet and served up his own son's body for him to eat. The sons of Atreus were Agamemnon and Menelaus, who married respectively Clytemnestra and Helen, daughters of Zeus and Leda, both evil women; the son of Thyestes was Aegisthus, a deadly foe of his cousins who had banished him. The "inherited curse" then had developed itself in this unhappy stock and it did not fail to ruin it.

When Helen abandoned Menelaus and went to Troy with Paris, Agamemnon led a great armament to recover the adulteress. The fleet was wind-bound at Aulis, because the Greeks had offended Artemis. Chalcas the seer informed Agamemnon that it would be impossible for him to reach Troy unless he offered his eldest daughter Iphigeneia to Artemis. Torn by patriotism and fatherly affection, Agamemnon resorted to a strategem to bring his daughter to the sacrifice. He sent a messenger to Clytemnestra saying he wished to marry their child to Achilles. When the mother and daughter arrived at Aulis they learned the bitter truth. Iphigeneia was indeed sacrificed, but Artemis spirited her away to the country now called Crimea, there to serve as her priestess. Believing that her daughter was dead, Clytemnestra returned to Argos to plot destruction for her husband, forming an illicit union with his foe Aegisthus, nursing her revenge during the ten years of the siege.

AESCHYLUS

The *Agamemnon*, the first play of the trilogy, opens in a romantic setting. It is night. A watchman is on the wall of Argos, stationed there by the Queen. For ten years he had waited for the signal of the beacon-fire to be lit at Nauplia, the port of Argos, to announce the fall of Troy. At last the expected signal is given. He hurries to tell the news to the Queen, a woman with the resolution of a man; in his absence the Chorus of Argive Elders enter the stage, singing one of the finest odes to be found in any language. It likens Agamemnon and his brother to two avenging spirits sent to punish the sinner. The Chorus are past military age, and are come to learn from Clytemnestra why there is sacrifice throughout all Argos. They remember the woes at the beginning of the campaign, how Chalcas prophesied that in time Troy would be taken, yet hinted darkly of some blinding curse of Heaven hanging over the Greeks, his burden being

"Sing woe, sing woe, but let the good prevail."

"Yea, the law of Zeus is, wisdom by suffering, for thus soberness of thought comes to those who wish not for it. First men are emboldened by ill-counselling foolish frenzy which begins their troubles; even as Agamemnon, through sin against Artemis, was compelled to slay his daughter to save his armament. Her cries for a father's mercy, her unuttered appeals to her slayers—these he disregarded. What is to come of it, no man knows; yet it is useless to lament the issue before it comes, as come it will, clear as the light of day."

Clytemnestra enters, the sternest woman figure in all literature. She reminds the Chorus that she is no child and is not known to have a slumbering wit. When they enquire how she has learned so quickly of the capture of Troy, she describes with great brilliance the long chain of beacon fires she has caused to be made, stretching from Ida in Troyland to Argos. She imagines the wretched fate of the conquered and the joy of the victors, rid for ever of their watchings beneath the open sky. Striking the same ominous note as Chalcas did, she continues:

"If they reverence the Gods of Troy and their shrines, they shall not be caught even as they have taken the city. May no lust of plundering fall upon the army, for it needs a safe return home. Yet even if the army sins not against the gods, the anger of the slain may awake, though no new ills arise. But let the right prevail, for all to see it clearly."

This speech inspires the Chorus to sing another solemn ode. Too much prosperity leads to godlessness; Paris carried away Helen in pride and infatuation, stealing the light of Menelaus' eyes, leaving him only the torturing memories of her beauty which visited him in his dreams. But there is a spirit of discontent in every city of Greece; all had sent their young men to Troy in the glory of life, and in return they had a handful of ashes, asking why their sons should fall in murderous strife for another man's wife. At night the dark dread haunts Argos that the gods care not for men who shed much blood, who succeed by injustice, who are well spoken of overmuch. Often these are smitten full in the face by the thunderbolt;

and perhaps this beacon message is mere imagining or a lie sent from heaven.

Hearing this the Queen comes forth to prove the truth of her story. A herald at that moment advances to confirm it, for Troy has been sacked.

> "Altars and shrines have been demolished and all the seed of land destroyed. Thus is Agamemnon the happiest man of mortals, most worthy of honour, for Paris and his city cannot say that their crime was greater than its punishment."

Immediately after learning this story, Clytemnestra makes the first of a number of speeches charged with a dreadful double meaning.

> "When the first news came, I shouted for joy, but now I shall hear the story from the King himself. And I will use all diligence to give my lord the best of all possible welcomes. Bid him come with speed. May he find in the house a wife as faithful as he left her! I know of no wanton pleasure with another man more than I know how to dye a sword."

The Chorus understand well the hidden force of this sinister speech and bid the messenger speak of Menelaus, the other beloved King of the land. In reply he tells how a dreadful storm sent by the angry gods descended upon the Greek fleet. In it fire and water, those ancient foes, forsook their feud, conspiring to destroy the unhappy armament. Whether Menelaus was alive or not was uncertain; if he lived, it was only by the will of Zeus who desired to save the royal house. The Chorus who look at things with a deeper glance than the herald, hear his story with a growing uneasiness.

> "Helen, the cause of the war, at first was a spirit of calm to Troy, but at the latter end she was their bane, the evil angel of ruin. For one act of violence begets many others like it, until righteousness can no longer dwell within the sinner."

They touch a more joyous chord of welcome and loyalty when at last they see the actual arrival of Agamemnon himself.

The King enters the stage accompanied by Cassandra, the prophetic daughter of Priam, thus giving visible proof of his contempt for Apollo, the Trojan protector and inspirer of the prophetess. He has heard the Chorus' welcome and promises to search out the false friends and administer healing medicine to the city. Clytemnestra replies in a second speech of double significance.

> "The Argive Elders well know how dearly she loves her lord and the impatience of her life while he was at Troy. Often stories came of his wounds; were they all true, he would have more scars than a net has holes. Orestes their son has been sent away, lest he should be the victim of some popular uprising in the King's absence. Her fount of tears is dried up, not a drop being left."

After some words of extravagant flattery, she bids her waiting women lay down purple carpets on which Justice may bring him to a home which he never hoped to see. Agamemnon coldly deprecates her long speech; the honour she suggests is one for the gods alone; his fame will speak loud enough without gaudy trappings, for a wise heart is Heaven's greatest gift. But the Queen, not to be denied, overcomes his scruples. Giving orders that Cassandra is to be well treated, he passes over the purple carpets, led by Clytemnestra who avows that she would have given many purple carpets to get him home alive. Thus arrogating to himself the honours of a god, he proceeds within the palace, while she lingers behind for one brief moment to pray openly to Zeus to fulfil her prayers and to bring his will to its appointed end. Thoroughly alarmed, the Chorus give free utterance to the vague forebodings which shake them, the song of the avenging Furies which cries within their hearts.

> "Human prosperity often strikes a sunken rock; bloodshed calls to Heaven for vengeance; yet there is comfort, for one destiny may override another, and good may yet come to pass."

These pious hopes are broken by the entry of the Queen who summons Cassandra within: when the captive prophetess answers her not a word, Clytemnestra declares she has no time to waste outside the palace: already there stands at the altar the ox ready for sacrifice, a joy she never looked to have; if Cassandra will not obey, she must be taught to foam out her spirit in blood.

In the marvellous scene which follows Aeschylus reaches the pinnacle of tragic power. Cassandra advances to the palace, but starts back in horror as a series of visions of growing vividness comes before her eyes. These find utterance in language of blended sanity and madness, creating a terror whose very vagueness increases its intensity. First she sees Atreus' cruel murder of his brother's children; then follows the sight of Clytemnestra's treacherous smile and of Agamemnon in the bath, hand after hand reaching at him; quickly she sees the net cast about him, the murderess' blow. In a flash she foresees her own end and breaks out into a wild lament over the ruin of her native city. Her words work up the Chorus into a state of confused dread and foreboding; they can neither understand nor yet disbelieve. When their mental confusion is at its height, relief comes in a prophecy of the greatest clearness, no longer couched in riddling terms. The palace is peopled by a band of kindred Furies, who have drunk their fill of human blood and cannot be cast out; they sit there singing the story of the origin of its ruin, loathing the murder of the innocent children. Agamemnon himself would soon pay the penalty, but his son would come to avenge him. Foretelling her own death, she hurls away the badges of her office, the sceptre and oracular chaplets, things which have brought her nothing but ridicule. She prays for a peaceful end without a struggle; comparing human life to a shadow when it is fortunate and to a picture wiped out by a sponge when it is hapless, she moves in calmly to her fate.

There is a momentary interval of reflection, then Agamemnon's dying voice is heard as he is stricken twice. Frantic with horror, the Chorus prepare to rush within but are checked by the Queen, who throws open the door and stands glorying in the triumph of self-confessed murder. Her real character is revealed in her speech.

> "This feud was not unpremeditated; rather, it proceeds from an ancient quarrel, matured by time. Here I stand where I smote

him, over my handiwork. So I contrived it, I freely confess, that he could neither escape his fate nor defend himself. I cast over him the endless net, and I smote him twice—in two groans he gave up the ghost—adding a third in grateful thanksgiving to the King of the dead in the nether world. As he fell he gasped out his spirit, and breathing a swift stream of gore he smote me with a drop of murderous dew, while I rejoiced even as does the cornfield under the Heavensent shimmering moisture when it brings the ears to the birth. Ye Argive Elders, rejoice if ye can, but I exult. If it were fitting to pour thank-offerings for any death, 'twere just, nay, more than just, to offer such for him, so mighty was the bowl of curses he filled up in his home, then came and drank them up himself to the dregs."

To their solemn warning that she would herself be cut off, banished and hated, she replies:

"He slew my child, my dearest birth-pang, to charm the Thracian winds. In the name of the perfect justice I have exacted for my daughter, in the name of Ruin and Vengeance, to whom I have sacrificed him, my hopes cannot tread the halls of fear so long as Aegisthus is true to me. There he lies, seducer of this woman, darling of many a Chryseis in Troyland. As for this captive prophetess, this babbler of oracles, she sat on the ship's bench by his side and both have fared as they deserved. He died as ye see; but she sang her swan-song of death and lies beside him she loved, bringing me a sweet relish for the luxury of my own love."

A little later she denies her very humanity.

"Call me not his spouse; rather the ancient dread haunting evil genius of this house has taken a woman's shape and punished him, a full-grown man in vengeance for little children."

Burial he should have, but without any dirges from his people.

"Let Iphigeneia, his daughter, as is most fitting, meet her father at the swift-conveying passage of woe, throw her arms about him and kiss him welcome."

The last scene of this splendid drama brings forward the poltroon Aegisthus who had skulked behind in the background till the deed was done. He enters to air his ancient grievance, reminding the Chorus how his father was outraged by Atreus, how he himself was a banished man, yet found his arm long enough to smite the King from far away. In contempt for the coward the Elders prepare to offer him battle; they appeal to Orestes to avenge the murder. The quarrel was stopped by Clytemnestra, who had had enough of bloodshed and was content to leave things as they were, if the gods consented thereto.

Before the sustained power of this masterpiece criticism is nearly dumb. The conception of the inherited curse is by now familiar to us; familiar too is the teaching that sacrilege brings its own punishment, that human pride may be flattered into assuming the privilege of a deity. These were enough to cause Agamemnon's undoing. But it is the part played by Clytemnestra which fixes the dramatic interest. She is inspired by a lust for vengeance, yet, had she known the truth that her daughter was not dead but a priestess, she would have had no pretext for the murder. This ignorance of essentials which originates some human action is called Irony; it was put to dramatic uses for the first time in European literature by Aeschylus. The horrible tragedy it may cause is clear enough in the *Agamemnon*; its power is terrible and its value as a dramatic source is inestimable. There is another and a far more subtle form of Irony, in which a character uses riddling speech interpreted by another actor in a sense different from the truth as it is known to the spectators; this too can be used in such a manner as to charge human speech with a sinister double meaning which bodes ruin under the mask of words of innocence. Few dramatic personages have used this device so effectively as Clytemnestra, certainly none with a more fiendish intent. Again, in this play the Chorus is employed with amazing skill; their vague uneasiness takes more and more definitely the shape of actual terror in every ode; this terror is raised to its height in the masterly Cassandra scene—it is then abated a little, perhaps it is just beginning to disappear, for nobody believed Cassandra, when the blow falls. This integral connection between the Chorus and the main action is difficult to maintain; that it exists in the *Agamemnon* is evidence of a constructive genius of the highest order.

The *Choephori* (Libation-bearers), the second play of the trilogy, opens with the entry of Orestes. He has just laid a lock of hair on his father's tomb and sees a band of maidens approaching, among them Electra, his sister. He retires with Pylades his faithful friend to listen to their conversation. The Chorus tell how in consequence of a dream of Clytemnestra they have been sent to offer libations to the dead, to appease their anger and resentment against the murderers. They give utterance to a wild hopeless song, full of a presentiment of disaster coming on successful wickedness enthroned in power. They are captives from Troy, obliged to look on the deeds of Aegisthus, whether just or unjust, yet they weep for the purposeless agonies of Agamemnon's house. When asked by Electra what prayers she should offer to her dead father, they bid her pray for some avenging god or mortal to requite the murderers. Returning to them from the tomb, she tells them of a strange occurrence; a lock of hair has been laid on the grave, and there are two sets of footprints on the ground, one of which corresponds with her own. Orestes then comes forward to reveal himself; as a proof of his identity, he bids her consider the garments which she wove with her own hands; urging her to restrain her joy lest she betray his arrival, he tells how Apollo has commanded him to avenge his father's death, threatening him with sickness, frenzy, nightly terrors, excommunication and a dishonoured death if he refuses.

In a long choral dialogue the actors tell of Clytemnestra's insolent treatment of the dead King; she had buried him without funeral rites or mourning, with no subjects to follow the corpse; she even mangled his body and thrust Electra out of the palace; thus she filled the cup of her iniquity. The Chorus remind Orestes of his duty to act, but first he inquires why oblations have been offered; on learning that they are the result of Clytemnestra's dreaming that she suckled a serpent that stung her, and that she hopes to appease the angry dead, he interprets the dream of himself. He then unfolds his plot. He and Pylades will imitate a Phocian dialect and will seek out and slay Aegisthus. An ode which succeeds recounts the legends of evil women, closing with the declaration that Justice is firmly seated in the world, that Fate prepares a sword for a murderer and a Fury punishes him with it.

Approaching the palace Orestes summons the Queen and tells her that a stranger called Strophius bade him bring to Argos the news that Orestes is dead. Clytemnestra commands her servants within the house to welcome him and sends out her son's old nurse Cilissa to take the news to Aegisthus. The nurse stops to speak to the Chorus in the very language of grief for the boy she had reared, like Constance in *King John*. The Chorus advise her to summon Aegisthus alone without his bodyguard, for Orestes is not yet dead; when she departs they pray that the end may be speedily accomplished and the royal house cleansed of its curse. Aegisthus crosses the stage into the palace to meet a hasty end; seeing the deed, a servant rushes out to call Clytemnestra, while Orestes bursts out from the house and faces his mother. For a moment his resolution wavers; Pylades reminds him of Apollo's anger if he fails. To his mother's plea that Destiny abetted her deed he replies that Destiny intends her death likewise; before he thrusts her into the palace she warns him of the avenging Furies she will send to persecute him. She then passes to her doom.

After the Chorus have sung an ode of triumph Orestes shows the bodies of the two who loved in sin while alive and were not separated in death. He then displays the net which Clytemnestra threw around her husband's body and the robe in which she caught his feet; he holds up the garment through which Aegisthus' dagger ran. But in that very moment the cloud of more agonies to come descends upon the hapless family. In obedience to Apollo's command he takes the suppliant's branch and chaplet, and prepares to hasten to Delphi, a wanderer cut off from his native land. The dreadful shapes of the avenging Furies close in upon him: the fancies of incipient madness thicken on his mind: he is hounded out, his only hope of rest being Apollo's sacred shrine. The play ends with a note of hopelessness, of calamity without end.

After the *Agamemnon* this play reads weak indeed. Yet it displays two marked characteristics. It is full of vigorous action; the plot is quickly conceived and quickly consummated; the business is soon over. Further, Aeschylus has discovered yet another source of tragic power, the conflict of duties. Orestes has to choose between obedience to Apollo and reverence for his mother. That these duties are incompatible is clear; whichever he performed, punishment was bound to follow. It is in this enforced choice between two evils that the pathos of life is often to be found; that Aeschylus should have so faithfully depicted it is a great contribution to the growth of drama.

The concluding play, the *Eumenides*, calls for a briefer description. It opens with one of the most awe-inspiring scenes which the imagination of man has conceived. The priestess of Delphi finds a man sitting as a suppliant at the central point of the earth, his hands dripping with blood, a sword and an olive branch in his hand. Round him is slumbering a troop of dreadful forms, beings from darkness, the avengers. When the scene is disclosed, Apollo himself is seen standing at Orestes' side. He urges Hermes to convey the youth with all speed to Athens where he is to clasp the ancient image of Athena. Immediately the ghost of Clytemnestra arises; waking the sleeping forms, she bids them fly after their victim. They arise and confront Apollo, a younger deity, whom they reproach for protecting one who should be abandoned to them. Apollo replies with a charge that they are prejudiced in favour of Clytemnestra, whom, though a murderess, they had never tormented.

The scene rapidly changes to Athens, where Orestes calls upon Athena; confident in the privilege of their ancient office the Chorus awaits the issue. The goddess appears and consents to try the case, the Council of the Areopagus acting as a jury. Apollo first defends his action in saving Orestes, asserting that he obeys the will of Zeus. The main question is, which of the two parents is more to be had in honour?

Athena herself had no mother; the female is merely the nurse of the child, the father being the true generative source. The Chorus points out that the sin of slaying a husband is not the same as that of murdering a mother, for the one implies kinship, while the other does not. Athena advises the Court to judge without fear or favour. When the votes are counted, it is found that they are exactly even. The goddess casts her vote for Orestes, who is thus saved and restored.

The Chorus threaten that ruin and sterility shall visit Athena's city; they are elder gods, daughters of night, and are overridden by younger deities. But Athena by the power of her persuasion offers them a full share in all the honours and wealth of Attica if they will consent to take up their abode in it. They shall be revered by countless generations and will gain new dignities such as they could not have otherwise obtained. Little by little their resentment is overcome; they are conducted to their new home to change their name and become the kindly goddesses of the land.

The boldness of Aeschylus is most evident in this play. Not content with raising a ghost as he had done in the *Persae*, he actually shows upon a public stage the two gods whom the Athenians regarded as the special objects of their worship. More than this, he has brought to the light the dark powers of the underworld in all their terrors; it is said that at the sight of them some of the women in the audience were taken with the pangs of premature birth. The introduction of these supernatural figures was the most vivid means at Aeschylus' disposal for bringing home to the minds of his contemporaries the seriousness of the dramatic issue. It will be remembered that the *Prometheus* was the last echo of the contest between two races of gods. The same strain of thought has made the poet represent the struggle in the mind of Orestes as a trial between the primeval gods and the newer stock; the result was the same, the older and perhaps more terrifying deities are beaten, being compelled to change their names and their character to suit the gentler spirit which a religion takes to itself as it develops. At any rate, such is Aeschylus' solution of the eternal question, "What atonement can be made for bloodshed and how can it be secured?" The problem is of the greatest interest; it may be that there is no real answer for it, but it is at least worth while to examine the attempts which have been made to solve it.

Before we begin to attempt an estimate of Aeschylus it is well to face the reasons which make Greek drama seem a thing foreign to us. We are at times aware that it is great, but we cannot help asking, "Is it real?" Modern it certainly is not. In the first place, the Chorus was all-important to the Greeks, but is non-existent with us. To them drama was something more than action, it was music and dancing as well. Yet as time went on, the Greeks themselves found the Chorus more and more difficult to manage and it was discarded as a feature of the main plot. Only in a very few instances could a play be constructed in such a manner as to allow the Chorus any real influence on the story. Aeschylus' skill in this branch of his art is really extraordinary; the Chorus does take a part, and a vital part too, in the play. Again, the number of Greek actors was limited, whereas in a modern play their number is just as great as suits playwright's convenience or his capacity. The impression then of a Greek play is that it is a somewhat thin performance compared with the vivacity and complexity of the great Elizabethans. The plot, where it exists, seems very narrow in Attic drama; it could hardly be otherwise in a society which was content with a repeated discussion of a rather close cycle of heroic legends. Yet here, too, we might note how Aeschylus trod out of the narrow circumscribed round, notably in the *Prometheus* and the *Persoe*. Lastly, the Greek play is short when compared with a full-bodied five-act tragedy. It must be remembered, however, that very often these plays are only a third part of the real subject dealt with by the playwright.

All Greek tragedy is liable to these criticisms; it is not fair to judge a process just beginning by the standards of an art which thinks itself full-blown after many centuries of history. Considering the meagre resources available for Aeschylus—the masks used by Greek actors made it impossible for any of them to win a reputation or to add to the fame of a play—we ought to admire the marvellous success he achieved. His defects are clear enough; his teaching is a little archaic, his plots are sometimes weak or not fully worked out, his tendency is to description instead of vigorous action, he has a superabundance of choric matter. Sometimes it is said that the doctrine of an inherited curse on which much of his work is written is false; let it be remembered that week by week a commandment is read in our churches which speaks of visiting the sins of the fathers upon the third and fourth generation of them that hate God; all that is needed to make Aeschylus' doctrine "real" in the sense of "modern" is to substitute the nineteenth-century equivalent Heredity. That he has touched on a genuine source of drama will be evident to readers of Ibsen's *Ghosts*. More serious is the objection that his work is not dramatic at all; the actors are not really human beings acting as such, for their wills and their deeds are under the control of Destiny. What then shall we say of this from Hamlet:—

> "There's a divinity that shapes our ends,
> Rough-hew them as we will?"

In this matter we are on the threshold of one of our insoluble problems—the freedom of the will. An answer to this real fault in Aeschylus will be found in the subsequent history of the Attic drama attempted in the next two chapters. Suffice it to say that, whether the will is free or not, we act as if it were, and that is enough to represent (as Aeschylus has done) human beings acting on a stage as we ourselves would do in similar circumstances, for the discussions about Destiny are very often to be found in the mouths not of the characters, but of the Chorus, who are onlookers.

The positive excellences of Aeschylus are numerous enough to make us thankful that he has survived. His style is that of the great sublime creators in art, Dante, Michaelangelo, Marlowe; it has many a "mighty line". His subjects are the Earth, the Heavens, the things under the Earth; more, he reveals a period of unsuspected antiquity, the present order of gods being young and somewhat inexperienced. He carries us back to Creation and shows us the primeval deities, Earth, Night, Necessity, Fate, powers simply beyond the knowledge of ordinary thoughtless men. His characters are cast in a mighty mould; he taps the deepest tragic springs; he teaches that all is not well when we prosper. The thoughtless, light-hearted, somewhat shallow mind which thinks it can speak, think, and act without having to render an account needs the somewhat stern tonic of these seven dramas; it may be chastened into some sobriety and learn to be a little less flippant and irreverent.

Aeschylus' influence is rather of the unseen kind. His genius is of a lofty type which is not often imitated. Demanding righteousness, justice, piety, and humility, he belongs to the class of Hebrew prophets who saw God and did not die.

TRANSLATIONS:—

Miss Swanwick; E. D. A. Morshead; Campbell (all in verse). Paley (prose).

Versions also appear in Verrall's editions of separate plays (Macmillan).

An admirable volume called *Greek Tragedy* by G. Norwood (Methuen) contains a summary of the latest views on the art of the Athenian dramatists.

See Symonds' *Greek Poets* as above.

SOPHOCLES

In Aeschylus' dramas the will of the gods tended to override human responsibility. An improvement could be effected by making the personages real captains of their souls; drama needed bringing down from heaven to earth. This process was effected by Sophocles. He was born at Colonus, near Athens, in 495, mixed with the best society in Periclean times, was a member of the important board of administrators who controlled the Delian League, the nucleus of the Athenian Empire, and composed over one hundred tragedies. In 468 he defeated Aeschylus, won the first prize twenty-two times and later had to face the more formidable opposition of the new and restless spirit whose chief spokesman was Euripides. For nearly forty years he was taken to be the typical dramatist of Athens, being nicknamed "the Bee"; his dramatic powers showed no abatement of vigour in old age, of which the *Oedipus Coloneus* was the triumphant issue. He died in 405, full of years and honours.

Providence has ordained it that his art, like his country's tutelary goddess Athena, should step perfect and fully armed from the brain of its creator. The *Antigone*, produced in 440, discusses one of the deepest problems of civilised life. On the morning after the defeat of the Seven who assaulted Thebes Polyneices' body lay dishonoured and unburied, a prey to carrion birds before the gates of the city which had been his home. His two sisters, Antigone and Ismene, discuss the edict which forbids his burial. Ismene, the more timid of the two, intends to obey it, but Antigone's stronger character rises in rebellion.

Loss of burial was the most awful fate which could overtake a Greek—before he died Sophocles was to see his country condemn ten generals to death for neglect of burial rites, though they had been brilliantly successful in a naval engagement. Rather than obey Antigone would die.

> "Bury him I will; I will lie in death with the brother I love, sinning in a righteous cause. Far longer is the time in which I must please the dead than men on earth, for among the former I shall dwell for ever. Do thou, if it please thee, hold in dishonour what is honoured by Heaven."

Here is the source of the tragedy, the will of the individual in conflict with established authority.

A chorus of Theban elders enters, singing an ode of deliverance and joy; they have been summoned by Creon, the new King, uncle of Oedipus' children. Full of the sense of his own importance Creon states the official view. Polyneices is to remain unburied.

> "Any man who considers private friendship to be more important than the State is a man of naught. In the name of all-seeing Zeus I would not hold my tongue if I saw ruin coming to the citizens instead of safety, nor would I make a friend of my country's enemy. Sure am I that it is the State that saves us; she is the ship that carries us; we make our friendships without overturning her."

The elders promise obedience, but grave news is reported by a guard who has been set to watch the corpse. Someone had scattered dust lightly over the dead and departed without leaving any trace; neither he nor his companions had done the deed.

When the Chorus suggest that it is the work of some deity, Creon answers in great impatience:

> "Cease, lest thou be proved a fool as well as old. Thy words are intolerable when thou sayest that the gods can have a care of this corpse. What, have they buried him in honour for his services to them? Did he not come to burn their pillared temples and offerings and precincts and shatter our laws?"

He angrily thrusts the watchman forth, threatening to hang him and his companions alive unless they find the culprit.

> "There are many marvels, but none greater than Man. He crosses the wintry sea, he wears away the hard earth with his plough, ensnareth the light-hearted race of birds, catcheth the wild beasts, trappeth the things of the deep, yoketh the horse and the unwearying ox. He hath taught himself speech and thought swift as the wind, hath learnt the moods of a city life and can avoid the shafts of the frost; he hath a device for every problem save Death—though disease he can escape. Sometimes he moveth to ill, again to good; his cities rear their heads when they reverence the laws and the gods; he wrecketh his city when he boldly forsakes the good. May an evil-doer never share my hearth or heart."

Such is the ordinary man's view of the action of Polyneices, for in Sophocles the Chorus certainly represents average public opinion. It is quickly challenged by the entry of Antigone with the Watchman, whose story Creon hastens out to hear. With no little self-satisfaction the Watchman tells how they caught the girl in the very act of replacing the dust they had removed and pouring libations over the dead. Antigone admits the deed. When asked how she dare defy the official ordinance, she replies—

> "It came neither from Zeus nor from Justice, nor did I deem that thy decrees had such power that a mortal could override the unwritten and unshaken laws of Heaven. These have not their life from now or yesterday, but from everlasting, and no man knows whence they have appeared. It was not likely that, through fear of

any man's will, I would pay Heaven's penalty for their infringement. Die I must, even hadst thou made no proclamation; if I die before my time, I count it all gain. If my act seem folly to thee, maybe it is a foolish judge who counts me mad."

Creon replies that this is sheer insolence; it is an insult that he, a man, should give way to a woman. He threatens to destroy both girls, but Antigone is sure that public opinion is with her, though for the moment it is muzzled through fear. Ismene is brought in and offers to die with her sister; Antigone refuses her offer, insisting that she alone has deserved chastisement.

In a second ode the gradual extinction of Oedipus' race is described, owing to foolish word and insensate thought, for "when Heaven leads a man to ruin it makes him believe that evil is good". A new interest is added by Creon's son Haemon, the affianced lover of Antigone, who comes to interview his father. This is the first instance in European drama of that without which much modern literature would have little reason for existing at all—the love element, wisely kept in check by the Greeks. A further conflict of wills adds to the dramatic effect of the play; Creon insists on filial obedience, for he cannot claim to rule a city if he fails to control his own family. Haemon answers with courtesy and deference; he points out that the force of public opinion is behind Antigone and suggests that the official view may perhaps be wrong because it is the expression of an individual's judgment. When he is himself charged thus directly with the very fault for which he claimed to punish Antigone, Creon lets his temper get the mastery; after a violent quarrel Haemon parts from him with a dark threat that the girl's death will remove more than one person, and vows never to cross his father's doorstep again.

Antigone is soon carried away to her doom; she is to be shut up in a cavern without food. In a dialogue of great beauty she confesses her human weakness—death is near, and with it banishment from the joys of life. Creon bids her make an end; her last speech concludes with a clear statement of the problem. Who knows if she is right? She herself will know after death. If she has erred, she will confess it; if the King is wrong, she prays he may not suffer greater woes than her own.

A reaction now occurs. Teiresias, the blind seer, seeks out Creon because of the failure of his sacrificial rites; the birds of the air are gorged with human blood, and fail to give the signs of augury. He bids Creon return to his right senses and quit his stubbornness. When the latter mockingly accuses the seer of being bribed, he learns the dread punishment his obstinacy has brought him.

> "Know that thou shalt not see out many hurrying rounds of the sun before thou shalt give one sprung from thine own loins in exchange for the dead, one in return for two, for thou hast thrust below one of the children of the light, penning up her spirit in a tomb with dishonour, and thou keepest above ground a body that belongs to the gods below, without its share of funerals, unrighteously; wherefore the late-punishing ruinous gods of death and the Furies lie in wait for thee, to catch thee in like agonies."

Cowed by the terror, the King hurries to undo his work, calling for pickaxes to open the tomb and himself going with all speed to set free its victim.

The sequel is told by a messenger who at the outset strikes a note of woe.

> "Creon I once envied, for he was the saviour of his land, and was the father of noble children. Now all is lost. When men lose pleasure, I deem that they are not alive but moving corpses. Heap up wealth and live in kingly state, but if there is no pleasure withal, I would not pay the worth of a shadow for all the rest. Haemon is dead."

Hearing the news, Eurydice the Queen comes out, and bids him tell his story in full. Creon found Haemon clasping the body of Antigone who had hung herself. Seeing his father, he made a murderous attack on him; when it failed, he drew his sword and fell on it—thus in death the two lovers were not separated. In an ominous silence the Queen departs. Creon enters with his son's body, to be utterly shattered by a second and an unexpected blow, for his wife has slain herself. Broken and helpless he admits his fault, while the Chorus sing in conclusion:—

> "By far the greatest part of happiness is wisdom; men should reverence the gods; mighty plagues repay the mighty words of the over-proud, teaching wisdom to the aged."

To Aeschylus the power that largely controlled men's acts was Destiny. A notable contrast is visible in the system of Sophocles. Destiny does not disappear, rather it retires into the background of his thought. To him the leading cause of ruin is evil counsel. Over and over again this teaching is driven home. All the leading characters mention it, Antigone, Haemon, Teiresias, and when it is disregarded, it is remorselessly brought home by disaster. The dramatic gain is enormous; man's sorrows are ascribed primarily to his own lack of judgment, the tragic character takes on a more human shape, for he is more nearly related to the ordinary persons we meet in our own experience. Another great advance is visible in the construction of the plot. It is more varied, more flexible; it never ceases developing, the action continuing to the end instead of stopping short at a climax. Further, the Chorus begins to fall into a more humble position, it exercises but little influence on the great figures of the plot, being content to mirror the opinions of the interested outside spectator. Truly drama is beginning to be master of itself—"the play's the thing".

But far more important is the subject of this play. It raises one of the most difficult problems which demand a solution, the harmonisation of private judgment with state authority. The individual in a growing civilisation sooner or later asks how far he ought to obey, who is the lord over his convictions, whether disobedience is ever justifiable. If a law is wrong how are we to make its immorality evident? In an age when a central authority is questioned or loses its hold on men's allegiance, this problem will imperiously demand an answer. When Europe was aroused from the slumber of the Middle Ages and the spiritual authority which had governed it for centuries was shattered, the same right of resistance as that which Antigone claimed was insisted upon by various reformers. It did not fail to bring with it tragic consequences, for the "power beareth not the sword in vain".

Its sequel was the Thirty Years' War which barbarised central Germany, leaving in many places a race of savage beings who had once been human. In our own days resistance is preached almost as a sacred duty. We have passive resisters, conscientious objectors, strikers and a host of young and imperfectly educated persons, some armed with the very serious power of voting, who claim to set their wills in flat opposition to recognised authority. One or two contributions to the solution of this problem may be found in the *Antigone*. The central authority must be prepared to prove that its edicts are not below the moral standard of the age; on the other hand, non-compliance must be backed by the force of public opinion; it must show that the action it takes will ultimately bring good to the whole community. It is of little use to appeal to the so-called conscience unless we can produce some credentials of the proper training and enlightenment of that rather vague and uncertain faculty, whose normal province is to condemn wrong acts, not to justify law-breaking. Most resisters talk the very language of Antigone, appealing to the will of Heaven; would that they could prove as satisfactorily as she did that the power behind them is that which governs the world in righteousness.

A somewhat similar problem reappears in the *Ajax*. This play opens at early dawn with a dialogue between Athena, who is unseen, and Odysseus; the latter has traced Ajax to his tent after a night of madness in which he has slain much cattle and many shepherds, imagining them to be his foes, especially Odysseus himself who had worsted him in the contest for the arms of Achilles. Athena calls out the beaten hero for a moment and the sight of him moves Odysseus to say:—

> "I pity him, though my foe; for I think of mine own self as much as of him. We men are but shadows, all of us, or fleeting shades."

To this Athena replies:—

> "When thou seest such sights, utter no haughty word against the gods and be not roused to pride, if thou art mightier than another in strength or store of wealth. One day can bring down or exalt all human state, but the gods love the prudent and hate the sinners."

A band of mariners from Salamis enter as the chorus; they are Ajax' followers who have come to learn the truth. They are confronted by Tecmessa, Ajax' captive, who confirms the grievous rumour, describing his mad acts. When the fit was over, she had left him in his tent prostrate with grief and shame among the beasts he had slain, longing for vengeance on his enemies before he died.

The business of the play now begins. Coming forth, Ajax in a long despairing speech laments his lot—persecuted by Athena, hated of Greeks and Trojans alike, the secret laughter of his enemies.

Where shall he go? Home to the father he has disgraced? Against Troy, leading a forlorn hope? He had already reminded Tecmessa with some sternness that silence is a woman's best grace; now she appeals to his pity. Bereft of him, she would speedily be enslaved and mocked; their son would be left defenceless; the many kindnesses she had done him cry for some return from a man of chivalrous nature, Ajax bade her be of good cheer; she must obey him in all things and first must bring his son Eurysaces. Taking him in his arms, he says:—

> "If he is my true son, he will not quail at the sight of blood. But he must speedily be broken into his father's warrior habit and imitate his ways. My son, I pray thou mayest be happier than thy sire, but like him otherwise, then thou shalt be no churl. Yet herein I envy thee that thou canst not feel my agonies. Life is sweetest in its careless years before it learns joy and pain; but when thou art come to that, show thy father's enemies thy nature and birth. Till then feed on the spirit of gladness, gambol in the life of boyhood and gladden thy mother's heart."

He reflects that his son will be safe as long as Teucer lives, whom he charges on his return to take the boy to his own father and mother to be their joy. His arms shall not be a prize to be striven for; they should be buried with him except his shield, which his son should take and keep. This ominous speech dashes the hopes which he had raised in Tecmessa's heart, even the Chorus sadly admitting that death is the best for a brainsick man, born of the highest blood, no longer true to his character.

Ajax re-enters, a sword in his hands. He feels his heart touched by Tecmessa's words and pities her helplessness. He resolves to go to the shore and there bury the accursed sword he had of Hector, which had robbed him of his peace. He will soon learn obedience to the gods and his leaders; all the powers of Nature are subject to authority, the seasons, the sea, night and sleep. He has but now learned that an enemy is to be hated as one who will love us later, while friendship will not always abide. Yet all will be well; he will go the journey he cannot avoid; soon all will hear that his evil destiny has brought him salvation. This splendid piece of tragic irony is interpreted at its surface value by the Chorus, who burst into a song of jubilation. But the words have a darker meaning; this transient joy is but the last flicker of hope before it is quenched in everlasting night.

A messenger brings the news that Teucer, Ajax' brother, on his return to the camp from a raid was nearly stoned to death as the kinsman of the army's foe. He inquires where Ajax is; hearing that he had gone out to make atonement, he knows the terror that is to come. Chalcas the seer adjured Teucer to use all means in his power to keep Ajax in his tent that day, for in it alone Athena's wrath would persecute him. She had punished him with madness for two proud utterances. On leaving his father he had boasted he would win glory in spite of Heaven, and later had bidden Athena assist the other Greeks, for the line would never break where he stood. Such was his pride, and such its punishment. Tecmessa hurries in and sends some to fetch Teucer, others to go east and west to seek out her lord. The scene rapidly changes to the shore, where Ajax cries to the gods, imprecates his foes, prays to Death, and after a remembrance of his native land falls on his sword.

The Chorus enter in two bands, but find nothing. Tecmessa discovers the body in a brake, and hides it under her robe. Distracted and haunted by the dread of slavery and ridicule, she gives way to grief. Teucer enters to learn of the tragedy;

after dispatching Tecmessa to save the child while there is yet time, he reflects on his own state. Telamon his father will cast him off for being absent in his brother's hour of weakness whom he loved as his own life. Sadly he bears out the truth of Ajax utterance, that a foe's gifts are fraught with ruin; the belt that Ajax gave Hector served to tie his feet to Achilles' car—and Hector's sword was in his brother's heart.

The plot now appeals to fiercer passions. Menelaus entering commands Teucer to leave the corpse where it is, for an enemy shall receive no burial. He strikes the same note as Creon:—

> "It is the mark of an ill-conditioned man that he, a commoner, should see fit to disobey the powers that be. Law cannot prosper in a city where there is no settled fear; where a man trembles and is loyal, there is salvation; when he is insolent and does as he will, his city soon or late will sink to ruin."

Teucer answers that Ajax never was a subject, but was always an equal. He fought, not for Helen, but for his oath's sake. The dispute waxes hot; the calm dignity of Teucer easily discomfits the Spartan braggart, who departs to bring aid. Meanwhile Tecmessa returns with the child whom Teucer in a scene of consummate pathos bids kneel at his father's side, holding in his hand a triple lock of hair—Teucer's, his mother's, his own; this sacred symbol, if violated, would bring a curse on any who dared outrage him. While the Chorus sing a song full of longings for home, Agamemnon advances to the place, followed by Teucer. The King is deliberately insolent, reviling Teucer for the stain on his birth. In reply the latter in a great speech reminds him that there was a time when the flames licked the Greek ships and there was none to save them but Ajax, who had faced Hector single-handed. With kindling passion he hurls the taunt of a stained birth back on Agamemnon and plainly tells him that Ajax shall be buried and that the King will rue any attempt at violence. Odysseus comes in to hear the quarrel. He admits that he had once been the foe of the dead man, who yet had no equal in bravery except Achilles. For all that, enmity in men should end where death begins. Astonished at this defence of a foe, Agamemnon argues a little with Odysseus, who gently reminds him that one day he too will need burial. This human appeal obtains the necessary permission; Odysseus, left alone with Teucer, offers him friendship. Too much overcome by surprise and joy to say many words, Teucer accepts his friendship and the play ends with a ray of sunlight after storm and gloom.

Once more Sophocles has filled every inch of his canvas. The plot never flags and has no diminuendo after the death of Ajax. The cause of the tragedy is not plainly indicated at the outset; with a skill which is masterly, Sophocles represents in the opening scene Athena and Odysseus as beings purely odious, mocking a great man's fall. With the progress of the action these two characters recover their dignity; Athena has just cause for her anger, while Odysseus obtains for the dead his right of burial. We should notice further how the pathos of this fine play is heightened by the conception of the "one day" which brought ruin to a noble warrior. Had he been kept within his tent that one day—had this fatal day been known, the ruin need not have happened. "The pity of it", the needless waste of human life, what a theme is there for a tragedy!

The *Ajax* has never exercised an acknowledged influence on literature. It was a favourite with the Greeks, but modern writers have strangely overlooked it. For us it has a good lesson. Here was a hero, born in an island, who unaided saved a fleet when his allies were forced back on their trenches and beyond them to the sea. His reward was such as Wordsworth tells of:—

> Alas! the gratitude of men
> Has oftener left me mourning.

We remember many a long month of agony during which another island kept destruction from a fleet and saved her allies withal. In some quarters this island has received the gratitude which Ajax had; her friends asked, "What has England done in the war, anyhow?" If it befits anybody to answer, it must be England's Teucer, who has built another Salamis overseas, just as he did. Our kindred across the oceans will give us the reward of praise; for us the chastisement of Ajax may serve to reinforce the warning which is to be found on the lips of not the least of our own poets:—

> "For frantic boast and foolish word
> Thy mercy on Thy people, Lord."

The *Electra* is Sophocles' version of the revenge of Orestes which Aeschylus described in the *Choephori* and is useful as affording a comparison between the methods of the two masters. An aged tutor at early dawn enters the scene with Orestes to whom he shows his father's palace and then departs with him to offer libations at the dead king's tomb. Electra with a Chorus of Argive girls comes forward, the former describing the insolent conduct of Clytemnestra who holds high revelry on the anniversary of her husband's death and curses Electra for saving Orestes. Chrysothemis, another daughter, comes out to talk with Electra; she is of a different mould, gentle and timid like Ismene, and warns Electra that in consequence of her obstinacy in revering her father's memory Aegisthus intends to shut her up in a rocky cavern as soon as he returns. She advises her to use good counsel, then departs to pour on Agamemnon's tomb some libations which Clytemnestra offers in consequence of a dream.

The Queen finds Electra ranging abroad as usual in the absence of Aegisthus. She defends the murder of her husband, but is easily refuted by Electra who points out that, if it is right to exact a life for a life, she ought to suffer death herself. Clytemnestra prays to Apollo to avert the omen of her dream, her prayer seemingly being answered immediately by the entry of the old tutor who comes to inform her of the death of Orestes, killed at Delphi in a chariot race which he brilliantly describes. Torn by her emotions, Clytemnestra can be neither glad nor sorry.

> "Shall I call this happy news, or dreadful but profitable? Hapless am I, if I save my life at the cost of my own miseries. Strong is the tie of motherhood; no parent hates a child even if outraged by him. Yet, now that he is gone, I shall have rest and peace from his threats."

Hearing so circumstantial a proof of her brother's death, Electra is plunged into the depths of misery.

But soon Chrysothemis returns in a state of high excitement. She has found a lock of Orestes' hair and some offerings at the tomb. Electra quickly informs her that her elation is groundless, for their brother is dead; she suggests that they two should strike the murderers, but Chrysothemis recoils in horror from the plot. Then Orestes enters with a casket in his hand; this he gives to Electra, saying it contains the mortal remains of the dead prince. In utter hopelessness Electra takes it and soliloquises over it. Seeing her misery, Orestes cannot refrain; gently taking the casket from her he gradually reveals himself. The tutor enters and recalls him to their immediate business. Electra asks who the stranger is and learns that it is the very man to whom she gave the infant boy her brother. The three advance to the palace which Orestes enters to dispatch his mother, Electra bidding him smite with double force, wishing only that Aegisthus were with her mother.

The end of Aegisthus himself is contrived with Sophoclean art. He comes in hurriedly to find the two strangers who have proof of Orestes' death.

Electra tells him they are in the palace; they have not only told her of the dead Orestes, but have shown him to her; Aegisthus himself can see the unenviable sight; he can rejoice at it, if there is any joy in it. Exulting, he sings a note of triumph at the removal of his fears and threatens to chastise all who try henceforth to thwart his will. He dashes open the door, and there sees the Queen lying dead. Orestes bids him enter the palace, to be slain on the very spot where his father was murdered.

Fortune has been kind in preserving us this play. The great difference between the art of Sophocles and that of Aeschylus is here apparent. Only one man has ventured to paint for us Aeschylus' Clytemnestra; Leighton has revealed her, stern as Nature herself, remorseless, armed with a sword to smite first, then argue if she can find time to do so. Sophocles' Clytemnestra is a woman, lost as soon as she begins to reason out her misdeeds. She prays to Apollo in secret, for fear lest Electra may overhear her prayer and make it void. But the crudity of Aeschylus' resources did not satisfy Sophocles, whose taste demanded a contrast to heighten the character of his heroine and found one in the Homeric story that Agamemnon had a second daughter. Aeschylus' stern nature did not shrink from the sight of a meeting between mother and son; Sophocles closed the doors upon the act of vengeance, though he represents Electra as encouraging her brother from outside the palace. The Aegisthus incident maintains the interest to the end in the masterly Sophoclean style of refined and searching irony. The tone of the play is singular; from misery it at first sinks to hopelessness, then to despair, and finally it soars to triumphant joy. Such a dangerous venture was unattempted before.

The most lovable woman in Greek literature is the heroine of the next play, the *Trachiniae*, produced at an uncertain date. Deianeira had been won and wed by Heracles; after a brief spell of happiness she found herself left more and more alone as her husband's labours called him away from her. For fifteen months she had heard no news of him. Her nurse suggests that she should send her eldest son to Euboea to seek him out, a rumour being abroad that he has reached that island. The mother in her loneliness is comforted by a band of girls of Trachis, the scene of the action. But her uneasiness is too great to be cheered; she describes the strange curse of womanhood:—

> "When it is young it groweth in a clime of its own, plagued by no heat of the sun nor rain nor wind; in careless gaiety it builds up its days till it is no longer maid, but wife; then in the night it hath its meed of cares, terrified for lord or children. Only such a one can know from the sight of her own sorrows what is my burden of grief."

But there is a deeper cause for anxiety; Heracles had said that if he did not return in fifteen months he would either die or be rid for ever of his labours; that very hour had come.

News reached her that Heracles is alive and triumphant; Lichas was coming to give fuller details. Very soon he enters with a band of captive maidens, telling how his master had been kept in slavery in Lydia; shaking off the yoke, he had sacked and destroyed the city of Eurytus who had caused his captivity, the girls were Heracles' offering of the spoils to Deianeira. Filled with pity at their lot, she looked closely at them and was attracted by one of them, a silent girl of noble countenance. Lichas when questioned denied all knowledge of her identity and departed. When he had gone, the messenger desired private speech with Deianeira. Lichas had lied; the girl was Iole, daughter of Eurytus; it was for her sake that his master destroyed the city, for he loved the maid and intended to keep her in his home to be a rival to his wife. Lichas on coming out was confronted by the messenger, and attempted to dissemble, but Deianeira appealed to him thus:—

> "Nay, deceive me not. Thou shalt not speak to a woman of evil heart, who knoweth not the ways of men, how that they by a law of their own being delight not always in the same thing. 'Tis a fool who standeth up to battle against Love who ruleth even gods as he will, and me too; then why not another such as I? Therefore if I revile my lord when taken with this plague, I am crazed indeed—or this woman is, who hath brought me no shame or sorrow. If my lord teacheth thee to lie, thy lesson is no good one; if thou art schooling thyself to falsehood in a desire to be kind to me, thou shalt prove unkind. Speak all the truth; it is an ignoble lot for a man of honour to be called false."

Completely won by this appeal, Lichas confesses the truth.

During the singing of a choral ode Deianeira has had time to reflect. The reward of her loyalty is to take a second place. The girl is young and her beauty is fast ripening; she herself is losing her charm. But no prudent woman should fly into a passion; happily she has a remedy, for in the first days of her wedded life Heracles had shot Nessus, a half-human monster, for insulting her. Before he died Nessus bade her steep her robe in his blood and treasure it as a certain charm for recovering his waning affection. Summoning Lichas, she gives him strict orders to take the robe to Heracles who was to allow no light of the sun or fire to fall upon it before wearing it. After a short interval, she returns in the greatest agitation; a little tuft of wool which she had anointed with the monster's blood had caught the sunlight and shrivelled up to dust. If the robe proved a means of death, she determined to slay herself rather than live in disgrace. At that moment Hyllus bursts in to describe the horrible tortures which seized Heracles when he put on the poisoned mantle; the hero commanded his son to ferry him across from Euboea to witness the curse which his mother's evil deed would bring with it. Hearing these tidings Deianeira leaves the scene without uttering a word.

The old nurse quickly rushes in from the palace to tell how Deianeira had killed herself—while Hyllus was kissing her dead mother's lips in vain self-reproach, bereft of both his parents. Heracles himself is borne in on a litter, tormented with the slow consuming poison. In agony, he prays for death; when he learns of the decease of his wife and her beguilement by Nessus into an unintentional crime, his resentment softens. In a flash of inspiration the double meaning of the oracle comes over him, his labour is indeed over. Commanding Hyllus to wed Iole he passes on his last journey to the lonely top of Oeta, to be consumed on the funeral pyre.

The Sophoclean marks are clear enough in this play—the tragic moment, the life and movement, the splendid pathos, breadth of outlook and fascination of language. Yet there is a serious fault as well, for Sophocles, like the youngest of dramatists, can strangely enough make mistakes. The entry of Heracles practically makes the play double, marring its continuity. The necessary and remorseless sequence of events which is looked for in dramatic writing is absent. This tendency to disrupt a whole into parts brilliant but unrelated is a feature of Euripides' work; it may perhaps find a readier pardon exactly because Sophocles himself is not able to avoid it always. But the greatest triumph is the character of Deianeira. It is such as one would rarely find in warm-blooded Southern peoples. She dreads that loss of her power over her husband which her waning beauty brings; she is grossly insulted in being forced to countenance a rival living in the same house after she has given her husband the best years of her life; yet she hopes on, and perhaps she would have won him back by her very gentleness. This creation of a type of almost perfect human nature is the justification of a poet's existence; it was a saying of Sophocles that he painted men as they ought to be, Euripides painted them as they are.

The rivalry of the younger poet produced its effect on another play with which Sophocles gained the first prize in 409. *Philoctetes*, the hero after whom it is named, had lit the funeral pyre of Heracles on Oeta and had received from him his unconquerable bow and arrows. When he went to Troy he was bitten in the foot by a serpent in Tenedos. As the wound festered and made him loathsome to the army he was left in Lemnos in the first year of the war. An oracle declared that Troy could not be taken without him and his arrows; at the end of the siege, as Achilles and Ajax were dead, Philoctetes, outraged and abandoned, became necessary to the Greeks. How could they win him over to rejoin them?

Odysseus his bitterest foe takes with him Neoptolemus, the young son of

Achilles. Landing at Lemnos, they find the cave in which Philoctetes lives, see his rude bed, rough-hewn cup and rags of clothing, and lay their plot. Neoptolemus is to say that he is Achilles' son, homeward bound in anger with the Greeks for the loss of his father's arms. As he was not one of the original confederacy, Philoctetes will trust him. He is then to obtain the bow and arrows by treachery, for violence will be useless. The young man's soul rises against the idea of foul play but Odysseus bids him surrender to shamelessness for one day, to reap eternal glory. Left alone with the Chorus, composed of sailors from his ship, Neoptolemus pities the hero's deserted existence, wretched, famished and half-brutalised. He comes along towards them, creeping and crying in agony. Seeing them he inquires who they are; Neoptolemus answers as he had been bidden and wins the heart of Philoctetes who describes the misery of his life, his desertion and the unquenchable malady that feeds on him. In return Neoptolemus tells how he was beguiled to Troy by the prophecy that he should capture it after his father's death; arriving there he obtained possession of all Achilles' property except the arms, which Odysseus had won. He pretends to return to his ship, but Philoctetes implores him to set him once more in Greece. The great pathos of his appeal wins the youth's consent; they prepare to depart when a merchant enters with a sailor; from him they learn that Odysseus with Diomedes are on the way to bring Philoctetes by force or persuasion to Troy which cannot fall without his aid. The mere mention of Odysseus' name fills Philoctetes with anger and he retires to the cave, taking Neoptolemus with him.

When they reappear, a violent attack of the malady prostrates Philoctetes who gives his bow to Neoptolemus, praying him to burn him and put an end to his agony. Noticing a strange silence in the youth, suspicions seem to be aroused in him, but when he falls into a slumber the Chorus takes a decided part in the action, advising the youth to fly with the bow and to talk in a whisper for fear of waking the sleeper. The latter unexpectedly starts out of slumber, again begging to be taken on board. Again Neoptolemus' heart smites him at the villainy he is about to commit; he reveals that his real objective is Troy. Betrayed and defenceless, Philoctetes appeals to Heaven, to the wild things, to Neoptolemus' better self to restore the bow which is his one means of procuring him food. A profound pity overcomes Neoptolemus, who is in the act of returning the weapon when Odysseus appears. Seeing him Philoctetes knows he is undone. Odysseus invites him to come to Troy of his own freewill, but is met with a curse; as he refuses to rejoin the Greeks, Odysseus and Neoptolemus depart bearing with them the bow for Teucer to use.

Left without that which brought him his daily food Philoctetes bursts out into a wild lyric dialogue with the Chorus. They advise him to make terms with Odysseus, but he bids them begone. When they obey, he recalls them to ask one little boon, a sword. At this moment Neoptolemus runs in, Odysseus close behind him. He has come to restore the bow he got by treachery. A violent quarrel ends in the temporary retirement of Odysseus. Advancing to Philoctetes, Neoptolemus gives him his property; Philoctetes takes it and is barely restrained from shooting at Odysseus who appears for a moment, only to take refuge in flight. Neoptolemus then tells him the whole truth about the prophecy, promising him great glory if he will go back to Troy which can fall only through him. In vain Neoptolemus assures him of a perfect cure; nothing will satisfy the broken man but a full redemption of the promise he had to be landed once more in Greece. When Neoptolemus tells him that such action will earn him the hatred of the Greeks, Philoctetes promises him the succour of his unerring shafts in a conflict.

The action has thus reached a deadlock. The problem is solved by the sudden appearance of the deified Heracles. He commands his old friend to go to Troy which he is to sack, and return home in peace. His lot is inseparably connected with that of Neoptolemus and a cure is promised him at the hands of Asclepius. This assurance overcomes his obstinacy; he leaves Lemnos in obedience to the will of Heaven.

Such is the work of an old dramatist well over eighty years old. It is exciting, vigorous, pathetic and everywhere dignified. The characters of the old hero and the young warrior are masterly. The Chorus takes an integral part in the action — its whisperings to Neoptolemus remind the reader of the evil suggestions of which Satan breathed into Eve's equally guileless ears in *Paradise Lost*. But the most remarkable feature of the piece is its close resemblance to the new type of drama which Euripides had popularised. The miserable life of Philoctetes, his rags, destitution and sickness are a parallel to the Euripidean Telephus; most of all, the appearance of a god at the end to untie the knot is genuine Euripides. But there is a great difference; of the disjointed actions which disfigure later tragedy and are not absent from Sophocles' own earlier work there is not a trace. The odes are relevant, the Chorus is indispensable; in short, Sophocles has shown Euripides that he can beat him even on his own terms. Melodramatic the play may be, but it wins for its author our affection by the sheer beauty of a boyish nature as noble as Deianeira's; the return of Neoptolemus upon his own baseness is one of the many compliments Sophocles has paid to our human kind.

Many years previously Sophocles had written his masterpiece, the *Oedipus Tyrannus*. It cannot easily be treated separately from its sequel. A mysterious plague had broken out in Thebes; Creon had been sent to Delphi by Oedipus to learn the cause of the disaster. Apollo bade the Thebans cast out the murderer of the last King Laius, who was still lurking in Theban territory. Oedipus on inquiry learns that there are several murderers, but only one of Laius' attendants escaped alive. In discovering the culprit Oedipus promises the sternest vengeance on his nearest friends, nay, on his own kin, if necessary. After a prayer from the Chorus of elders he repeats his determination even more emphatically, invoking a curse on the assassin in language of a terrible double meaning, for in every word he utters he unconsciously pronounces his own doom. With commendable foresight he had summoned the old seer Teiresias, but the seer for some reason is unwilling to appear. When at last he confronts the King, he craves permission to depart with his secret unsaid. Oedipus at once flies into a towering passion, finally accusing him without any justification of accepting bribes from Creon. With equal heat Teiresias more and more clearly indicates in every speech the real murderer, though his words are dark to him who could read the Sphinx's riddle.

The Chorus break out into an ode full of uneasy surmises as to the identity of the culprit. When Creon enters, Oedipus flies at him in headlong passion accusing him of bribery, disloyalty and eventually of murder. With great dignity he clears himself, warning the King of the pains which hasty temper brings upon itself. Their quarrel brings out Jocasta, the Queen and sister of Creon, who succeeds in settling the unseemly strife. She bids Oedipus take no notice of oracles; one such had declared that Laius would be slain by his own son, who would marry her, his mother. The oracle was false, for Laius had died at the hands of robbers in a place where three roads met. Aghast at hearing this, Oedipus inquires the exact scene of the murder, the time when it was committed, the actual appearance of Laius. Jocasta supplies the details, adding that the one survivor had implored her after Oedipus became King to live as far away as possible from the city. Oedipus commands him to be sent for and tells his life story. He was the reputed son of Polybus and Merope, rulers of Corinth. One day at a wine-party a man insinuated that he was not really the son of the royal pair. Stung by the taunt he went to Delphi, where he was warned that he should kill his father and marry his mother. He therefore fled away from Corinth towards Thebes. On the road he was insulted by an old man in a chariot who thrust him rudely from his path; in anger he smote the man at the place where three ways met. If then this man was Laius, he had imprecated a curse on himself; his one hope is the solitary survivor whom he had sent for; perhaps more than one man had killed Laius after all.

An ominous ode about destiny and its workings is followed by the entry of the Queen who describes the mad terrors of Oedipus. She is come to pray to Apollo to solve their troubles. At that moment a messenger enters from Corinth with the tidings that Polybus is dead. In eager joy Jocasta summons Oedipus, sneering at the truth of oracles. The King on his appearance echoes her words after hearing the tidings-only to sink back again into gloomy despondency. What of Merope, is she also dead? The messenger assures him that his anxiety about her is groundless, for there is no relationship between them. Little by little he tells Oedipus his true history. The messenger himself found him on Cithaeron in his infancy, his feet pierced through. He had him from a shepherd, a servant of Laius, the very man whom Oedipus had summoned. Suddenly turning to Jocasta, the King asks her if she knows the man. Appalled at the horror of the truth which she knows cannot be concealed much longer she affects indifference and beseeches him search no further. When he obstinately refuses, bidding the man be brought at once, she leaves the stage with the cry:

> "Alack, thou unhappy one; that is all I may call thee and never address thee again."

Oedipus by a masterstroke of art is made to imagine that she has departed in shame, fearing he may be proved the son of a slave.

> "But I account myself the son of Fortune, who will never bring me to dishonour; my brethren are the months, who marked me out for lowliness and for power. Such being my birth, I shall never prove false to it and faint in finding out who I am."

The awful power of this astonishing scene is manifest.

The bright joyousness of the King's impulsive speech prepares the way for the coming horror. When the shepherd appears, the messenger faces him claiming his acquaintance. The shepherd doggedly attempts to deny all knowledge of him, cursing him for his mad talkativeness. Oedipus threatens torture to open his lips. Line by line the truth is dragged from him; the abandoned child came from another—from a creature of Laius—was said to be his son—was given him by Jocasta—to be destroyed because of an oracle—why then passed over to the Corinthian messenger?—"through pity, and he saved the child alive, for a mighty misery. If thou art that child, know that thou art born a hapless man".

When the King rushes madly into the palace, the Chorus sings of his departed glory. The horrors increase with the appearance of a messenger from within, who tells how Oedipus dashed into Jocasta's apartment to find her hanging in suicide; then he blinded himself on that day of mourning, ruin, death and shame. He comes out a little later, an object of utter compassion. How can he have rest on earth? How face his murdered father in death? The memories of Polybus and Merope come upon him, then the years of unnatural wedlock. Creon, whom he has wantonly insulted, comes not to mock at him, but to take him into the palace where neither land nor rain nor light may know him. Oedipus begs him to let him live on Cithaeron, beseeching him to look after his two daughters whose birth is so stained that no man can ever wed them. Creon gently takes him within, to be kept there till the will of the gods is known. The end is a sob of pity for the tragic downfall of the famous man who solved the Sphinx' enigma.

No man can ever do justice to this masterpiece. It is so constructed that every detail leads up inevitably to the climax. Slowly, and playing upon all the deepest human emotions, anxiety, hope, gloom, terror and horror, Sophocles works on us as no man had ever done before. It is a sin against him to be content with a mere outline of the play; the words he has chosen are significant beyond description. Again and again they fascinate the reader and always leave him with the feeling that there are still depths of thought left unsounded. The casual mention of the shepherd at the beginning of the play is the first stroke of perfect art; Jocasta's disbelief in oracles is the next; then follows the contrast between the Queen's real motive for leaving and the reason assigned to it by her son; finally, the shepherd in torture is forced to tell the secret which plunges the torturer to his ruin. Where is the like of this in literature? To us it is heart-searching enough. What was it to the Greeks who were familiar with the plot before they entered the theatre? When they who knew the inevitable end watched the King trace out his own ruin in utter ignorance, their feelings cannot have remained silent; they must have found relief in sobbing or crying aloud.

The fault in Oedipus is his ungovernable temper. It is firmly drawn in the play; he is equally unrestrained in anger, despair and hope. He is the typical instance of the lack of good counsel which we have seen was to Sophocles the prime source of a tragedy. Indeed, only a headlong man would hastily marry a widowed queen after he had committed a murder which fulfilled one half of a terrible oracle. He should have first inquired into the history of the Theban royal house. Imagining that the further he was fleeing from Corinth the more certain he was to make his doom impossible of fulfilment, he inevitably drew nearer to it. This is our human lot; we cannot see and we misinterpret warnings; how shall not weaker men tremble for themselves when Oedipus' wisdom could not save him from evil counsel?

In 405 Sophocles showed in his last play how Oedipus passed from earth in the poet's own birthplace, Colonus. Oedipus enters with Antigone, and on inquiry from a stranger finds that he is on the demesne of the Eumenides. At once he sends to Theseus, King of Athens, and refuses to move from the spot, for there he is fated to find his rest. A Chorus from Colonus comes to find out who the suppliant is. When they hear the name of Oedipus they are horror-struck and wish to thrust him out. After much persuasion they consent to wait till Theseus arrives. Presently Ismene comes with the news that Eteocles has dispossessed his elder brother Polyneices; further, an oracle from Delphi declares that Oedipus is all-important to Thebes in life and after death. His sons know this oracle and Creon is coming to force him back. Declaring he will do nothing for the sons who abandoned him, Oedipus obstinately refuses his city any blessing. He sends Ismene to offer a sacrifice to the Eumenides; in her absence Theseus enters, offers him protection and asks why he has come. Oedipus replies that he has a secret to reveal which is of great importance to Athens; at present there is peace between her and Thebes:

> "but in the gods alone is no age or death; all else Time confounds, mastering everything. Strength of the Earth and of the body wastes, trust dies, disloyalty grows, the same spirit never stands firm among friends or allies. To some men early, to others late, pleasures become bitter and then again sweet."

The secret Oedipus will impart at the proper time. The need for protection soon comes. Creon attempts to persuade Oedipus to return to Thebes but is met by a curse, whereupon the Theban guards lay hold of Antigone—they had already seized Ismene—and menace Oedipus himself. Theseus hearing the alarm rushes back, reproaches Creon for his insolence and quickly returns with the two girls. He has strange news to tell; another Theban is a suppliant at the altar of Poseidon close by, craving speech with Oedipus. It is Polyneices, whom Antigone persuades her father to interview. The youth enters, ashamed of his neglect of his father, and begs a blessing on the army he has mustered against Thebes. He is met by a terrible curse which Oedipus invokes on both his sons. In despair Polyneices goes away to his doom.

> "For me, my path shall be one of care, disaster and sorrows sent me by my sire and his guardian angels; but, my sisters, be yours a happy road, and when I am dead fulfil my heart's desire, for while I live you may never perform it."

A thunderstorm is heard approaching; the Chorus are terrified at its intensity, but Oedipus eagerly dispatches a messenger for Theseus. When the King arrives he hears the secret; Oedipus' grave would be the eternal protection of Attica, but no man must know its site save Theseus who has to tell it to his heir alone, and he to his son, and so onwards for ever. The proof of Oedipus' word would be a miracle which soon would transform him back to his full strength. Presently he arises, endued with a mysterious sight, beckoning the others to follow him. The play concludes with a magnificent description of his translation. A voice from Heaven called him, chiding him for tarrying; commending his daughters to the care of Theseus, he greeted the earth and heaven in prayer and then without pain or sorrow passed away. On reappearing Theseus promised to convey the sisters back to Thebes and to stop the threatened fratricidal strife.

The *Oedipus Coloneus*, like the *Philoctetes*, the other play of Sophocles' old age, closes in peace. The old fiery passions still burn fiercely in Oedipus, as they did in Lear; yet both were "every inch a king" and "more sinned against than sinning". Oedipus' miraculous return to strength before he departs is curiously like the famous end of Colonel Newcome. There are subtle but unmistakable marks of the Euripidean influence on this drama; such are the belief that Theban worthies would protect Athens, the Theseus tradition, and the recovery of worn-out strength. These features will meet us in the next chapter. But it is again noteworthy that Sophocles has added those touches which distinguish his own firm and delicate handiwork. There is nothing of melodrama, nothing inconsequent, nothing exaggerated. It is the dramatist's preparation for his own end. Shakespeare put his valediction into the mouth of Prospero; Sophocles entrusted his to his greatest creation Oedipus. Like him, he was fain to depart, for the gods called. Our last sight of him is of one beckoning us to follow him to the place where calm is to be found; to find it we must use not the eyes of the body, but the inward illumination vouchsafed by Heaven.

To the Athenians of the Periclean age Sophocles was the incarnation of their dramatic ideal. His language is a delight and a despair. It tantalises; it suggests other meanings besides its plain and surface significance. This riddling quality is the daemonic element which he possessed in common with Plato; because of it these two are the masters of a refined and subtle irony, a source of the keenest pleasure. His plots reveal a vivid sense of the exact moment which will yield the intensest tragic effects—only on one particular day could Ajax die or Electra be saved. Accordingly, Sophocles very often begins his play with early dawn, in order to fill the few all-important hours with the greatest possible amount of action. He has put the maximum of movement into his work, only the presence of the Chorus and the conventional messengers (two features imposed on him by the law of the Attic theatre) making the action halt.

But it is in the sum-total of his art that his greatness lies; the sense of a whole is its controlling factor; details are important, indeed, he took the utmost pains to see that they were necessary and convincing—yet they were details, subordinate, closely related, not irrelevant nor disproportionate. This instinct for a definite plan first is the essence of the classical spirit; exuberance is rigorously repressed, symmetry and balance are the first, last and only aim. To some judges Sophocles is like a Greek temple, splendid but a little chilly; they miss the soaring ambition of Aeschylus or the more direct emotional appeal of Euripides. Yet it is a cardinal error to imagine that Sophocles is passionless; his life was not, neither are his characters. Like the lava of a recent eruption, they may seem ashen on the surface, but there is fire underneath; it betrays itself through the cracks which appear when their substance is violently disturbed.

> They, much enforced, show a hasty spark
> And straight are cold again.

Repression, avoidance of extremes, dignity under provocation are the marks of the gentle Sophoclean type and it is a very high type indeed.

For we have in him the very fountain of the whole classical tradition in drama. Sophocles is something far more important than a mere influence; he is an ideal, and as such is indestructible. To ask the names of writers who came most under his "influence" is as sensible as to ask the names of the sculptors who most faithfully followed the Greek tradition of statuary. He is Classical tragedy. The main body of Spanish and English drama is romantic, the Sophoclean ideal is that of the small but powerful body of University men in Elizabeth's time headed by Ben Jonson, of the typically French school of dramatists, of Moratin, Lessing, Goethe, of the exponents of the Greek creed in nineteenth-century England, notably Matthew Arnold and Walter Pater, and of Robert Bridges. To this school the cultivation of emotional expression is suspicious, if not dangerous; it leads to eccentricity, to the revelation of feelings which frequently are not worth experiencing, to sentimental flabbiness, to riot and extravagance. Perhaps in dread of the ridiculous the Classical school represses itself too far, creating characters of marble instead of flesh. These creations are at least worth looking at and bring no shame; they are better than the spectral psychological studies which many dramatists, now dead or dying, have bidden us believe are real men and women.

TRANSLATIONS:

Jebb (Cambridge). This is by far the best; it renders with success the delicacy of the original.

Storr (Loeb Series).

Verse translations by Whitelaw and Campbell.

See Symonds' *Greek Poets*, and Norwood *Greek Tragedy*, as above.

EURIPIDES

No-Man's Land was the scene of many tragedies during the Great War. There has come down to us a remarkable tragedy, called the *Rhesus*, about a similar region. It treats first of the Dolon incident of the Iliad. Hector sent out Dolon to reconnoitre, and soon afterwards some Phrygian shepherds bring news that Rhesus has arrived that very night with a Thracian army. Reviled by Hector for postponing his arrival till the tenth year of the war, Rhesus answers that continual wars with Scythia have occupied him, but now that he is come he will end the strife in a day. He is assigned his quarters and departs to take up his position.

Having learned the password from Dolon, Diomedes and Odysseus enter and reach the tents of Hector who has just left with Rhesus. Diomedes is eager to kill Aeneas or Paris or some other leader, but Odysseus warns him to be content with the spoils they have won. Athena appears, counselling them to slay Rhesus; if he survives that night, neither Achilles nor Ajax can save the Greeks. Paris approaches, having heard that spies are abroad in the night; he is beguiled by Athena who pretends to be Aphrodite. When he is safely got away, the two slay Rhesus.

The King's charioteer bursts on to the stage with news of his death. He accuses Hector of murder out of desire for the matchless steeds. Hector recognises in the story all the marks of Odysseus' handiwork. The Thracian Muse descends to mourn her son's death, declaring that she had saved him for many years, but Hector prevailed upon him and Athena caused his end.

This play is not only about No-man's land; it is a No-man's land, for its author is unknown; it is sometimes ascribed to Euripides, though it contains many words he did not use, on the ground that it reflects his art. For it shows in brief the change which came over Tragedy under Euripides' guidance. It is exciting, it seizes the tragic moment, the one important night, it has some lovely lyrics, the characters are realistic, the gods descend to untie the knot of the play or to explain the mysterious, some detail is unrelated to the main plot—Paris exercises no influence on the real action—it is pathetic.

Sophocles said that he painted men as they ought to be, Euripides as they are. This realistic tendency, added to the romanticism whence realism always springs, is the last stage of tragedy before it declines. A Euripides is inevitable in literary history.

Born at Salamis on the very day of the great victory of 480, Euripides entered into the spirit of revolution in all human activities which was stirring in contemporary Athens. He won the first prize on five occasions, was pilloried by the Conservatives though he was a favourite with the masses. Towards the end of his life

EURIPIDES

he migrated to Macedonia, where he wrote not the least splendid of his plays, the *Bacchae*. On the news of his death in 406 Sophocles clothed his Chorus in mourning as a mark of his esteem.

The famous *Alcestis* won the second prize in 438. Apollo had been the guest of Admetus and had persuaded Death to spare him if a substitute could be found. Admetus' parents and friends failed him, but his wife Alcestis for his sake was content to leave the light. After a series of speeches of great beauty and pathos she dies, leaving her husband desolate. Heracles arrives at the palace on the day of her death; he notices that some sorrow is come upon his host, but being assured that only a relation has died he remains. Meanwhile Admetus' parents arrive to console him; he reviles them for their selfishness in refusing to die for him, but is sharply reminded by them that parents rejoice to see the sun as well as their children; in reality, he is his wife's murderer.

Heracles' reckless hilarity shocked the servants who were unwilling to look after an unfeeling guest. He enters the worse for liquor and advises a young menial to enjoy life while he can. After a few questions he learns the truth. Sobered, he hurries forth unknown to Admetus to wrestle with Death for Alcestis. Admetus, distracted by loss of his wife, becomes aware that evil tongues will soon begin to talk of his cowardice. Heracles returns with a veiled woman, whom he says he won in a contest, and begs Admetus keep her till he returns. After much persuasion Admetus takes her by the hand, and on being bidden to look more closely, sees that it is Alcestis. The great deliverer then bids farewell with a gentle hint to him to treat guests more frankly in future.

This play must be familiar to English readers of Browning's *Balaustion's Adventure*. It has been set to music and produced at Covent Garden this very year. The specific Euripidean marks are everywhere upon it. The selfish male, the glorious self-denial of the woman, the deep but helpless sympathy of the gods, the tendency to laughter to relieve our tears, the wonderful lyrics indicate a new arrival in poetry. The originality of Euripides is evident in the choice of a subject not otherwise treated; he was constantly striving to pass out of the narrow cycle prescribed for Attic tragedians. A new and very formidable influence has arisen to challenge Sophocles who may have felt as Thackeray did when he read one of Dickens' early emotional triumphs.

In 431 he obtained the third prize with the *Medea*, the heroine of the world-famous story of the Argonauts related for English readers in Morris' *Life and Death of Jason*. A nurse tells the story of Jason's cooling love for Medea and of his intended wedlock with the daughter of Creon, King of Corinth, the scene of the play. Appalled at the effect the news will produce on her mistress' fiery nature, she begs the Tutor to save the two children. Medea's frantic cries are heard within the house; appearing before a Chorus of Corinthian women she plunges into a description of the curse that haunts their sex.

> "Of all things that live and have sense women are the most hapless. First we must buy a husband to lord it over our bodies; our next anxiety is whether he will be good or bad, for divorce is

not easy or creditable. Entering upon a strange new life we must divine how best to treat our spouse. If after this agony we find one to live with us without chafing at the yoke, a happy life is ours—if not, better to die. But when a man is surfeited with his mate he can find comfort outside with friend or compeer; but we perforce look to one alone. They say of us that we live a life free from danger, but they fight in wars. It is false. I would rather face battle thrice than childbirth once."

Desolate, far away from her father's home, she begs the Chorus to be silent if she can devise punishment for Jason.

Creon comes forth, uneasy at some vague threats which Medea has uttered and afraid of her skill as a sorceress. He intends to cast her out of Corinth before returning to his palace, but is prevailed upon to grant one day's grace. Medea is aghast at this blow, but decides to use the brief respite. After a splendid little ode which prophesies that women shall not always be without a Muse, Jason emerges. Pointing out that her violent temper has brought banishment he professes to sympathise, offering money to help her in exile. She bursts into a fury of indignation, recounting how she abandoned home to save and fly with him to Greece. He argues that his gratitude is due not to her, but to Love who compelled her to save him; he repeats his offer and is ready to come if she sends for him. Salvation comes unexpectedly. Aegeus, the childless King of Athens, accidentally visits Corinth. Medea wins his sympathy and promises him children if he will offer her protection. He willingly assents and she outlines her plan. Sending for Jason, she first pretends repentance for hasty speech, then begs him to get her pardon from the new bride and release from exile for the two children. She offers as a wedding gift a wondrous robe and crown which once belonged to her ancestor the Sun. In the scene which follows is depicted one of the greatest mental conflicts in literature. To punish Jason she must slay her sons; torn by love for them and thirsting for revenge she wavers. The mother triumphs for a moment, then the fiend, then the mother again—at last she decides on murder. This scene captured the imagination of the ancient world, inspiring many epigrams in the Anthology and forming one of the mural paintings of Pompeii.

A messenger rushes in. The robe and crown have burnt to death Glauce the bride and her father who vainly tried to save her: Jason is coming with all speed to punish the murderess. She listens with unholy joy, retires and slays the children. Jason runs in and madly batters at the door to save them. He is checked by the apparition of Medea seated in her car drawn by dragons. Reviled by him as a murderess, she replies that the death of the children was agony to her as well and prophesies a miserable death for him.

This marvellous character is Euripides' Clytemnestra. Yet unlike her, she remains absolutely human throughout; her weak spot was her maternal affection which made her hesitate, while Clytemnestra was past feeling, "not a drop being left". Medea is the natural Southern woman who takes the law into her own hands. In the *Trachiniae* is another, outraged as Medea was, yet forgiving. Truly Sophocles said he painted men as they ought to be, Euripides as they were.

The *Hippolytus* in 429 won the first prize. It is important as introducing a revolutionary practice into drama. Aphrodite in a prologue declares she will punish Hippolytus for slighting her and preferring to worship Artemis, the goddess of hunting. The young prince passes out to the chase; as he goes, his attention is drawn to a statue of Aphrodite by his servants who warn him that men hate unfriendly austerity, but he treats their words with contempt. His stepmother Phaedra enters with the Nurse, the Chorus consisting of women of Troezen, the scene of the play. A secret malady under which Phaedra pines has so far baffled the Nurse who now learns that she loves her stepson. She had striven in vain against this passion, only to find like Olivia that

> Such a potent fault it is
> That it but mocks reproof.

She decided to die rather than disgrace herself and her city Athens. The Nurse advises her not to sacrifice herself for such a common passion; a remedy there must be: "Men would find it, if women had not found it already". "She needs not words, but the man." Scandalised by this cynicism the Queen bids her be silent; the woman tells her she has potent charms within the house which will rid her of the malady without danger to her good name or her life. Phaedra suspects her plan and absolutely forbids her to speak with Hippolytus. The answer is ambiguous:

> "Be of good cheer; I will order the matter well. Only Queen
> Aphrodite be my aid. For the rest, it will suffice to tell my plan to
> my friends within."

A violent commotion arises in the palace; Hippolytus is heard indistinctly uttering angry words. He and the Nurse come forth; in spite of her appeal for silence, he denounces her for tempting him. When she reminds him of his oath of secrecy, he answers "My tongue has sworn, but not my will"—a line pounced upon as immoral by the poet's many foes. Hippolytus' long denunciation of women has been similarly considered to prove that the poet was an enemy of their sex. Left alone with the Nurse Phaedra is terror-stricken lest her husband Theseus should hear of her disgrace. She casts the Nurse off, adding that she has a remedy of her own. Her last speech is ominous.

> "This day will I be ruined by a bitter love. Yet in death I will
> be a bane to another, that he may know not to be proud in my
> woes; sharing with me in this weakness he will learn wisdom."

Her suicide plunges Theseus into grief. Hanging to her wrist he sees a letter which he opens and reads. There he finds evidence of her passion for his son. In mad haste he calls on Poseidon his father to fulfil one of the three boons he promised to grant him; he requires the death of his son. Hearing the tumult the latter returns. His father furiously attacks him, calling him hypocrite for veiling his lusts under a pretence of chastity. The youth answers with dignity; when confronted with the damning letter, he is unable to answer for his oath's sake. He sadly obeys the decree of banishment pronounced on him, bidding his friends farewell.

A messenger tells the sequel. He took the road from Argos along the coast in his chariot. A mighty wave washed up a monster from the deep. Plunging in terror the horses became unruly; they broke the car and dashed their master's body against the rocks. Theseus rejoices at the fate which has overtaken a villain, yet pities him as his son. He bids the servants bring him that he may refute his false claim to innocence. Artemis appears to clear her devotee. The letter was forged by the Nurse, Aphrodite causing the tragedy. "This is the law among us gods; none of us thwarts the will of another but always stands aside." Hippolytus is brought in at death's door. He is reconciled to his father and dies blessing the goddess he has served so long.

The play contains the first indication of a sceptical spirit which was soon to alter the whole character of the Drama. The running sore of polytheism is clear. In worshipping one deity a man may easily offend another, Aeschylus made this conflict of duties the cause of Agamemnon's death, but accepted it as a dogma not to be questioned. Such an attitude did not commend itself to Euripides; he clearly states the problem in a prologue, solving it in an appearance of Artemis by the device known as the *Deus ex machina*. It is sometimes said this trick is a confession of the dramatist's inability to untie the knot he has twisted. Rather it is an indication that the legend he was compelled to follow was at variance with the inevitable end of human action. The tragedies of Euripides which contain the *Deus ex machina* gain enormously if the last scene is left out; it was added to satisfy the craving for some kind of a settlement and is more in the nature of comedy perhaps than we imagine. Hippolytus is a somewhat chilly man of honour, the Nurse a brilliant study of unscrupulous intrigue. Racine's *Phèdre* is as disagreeable as Euripides' is noble. Like *Hamlet*, the play is full of familiar quotations.

Two Euripidean features appear in the *Heracleidae*, of uncertain date. Iolaus the comrade of Heracles flees with the hero's children to Athens. They sit as suppliants at an altar from which Copreus, herald of their persecutor Eurystheus, tries to drive them.

Unable to fight in his old age Iolaus begs aid. A Chorus of Athenians rush in, followed by the King Demophon, to hear the facts. First Copreus puts his case, then Iolaus refutes him. The King decides to respect the suppliants, bidding Copreus defy Eurystheus in his name. As a struggle is inevitable Iolaus refuses to leave the altars till it is over.

Demophon returns to say that the Argive host is upon them and that Athens will prevail if a girl of noble family freely gives her life; he cannot compel his subjects to sacrifice their children for strangers, for he rules a free city. Hearing his words, Macaria comes from the shrine where she had been sheltering with her sisters and Alcmena, her father's mother. When she hears the truth, she willingly offers to save her family and Athens.

> "Shall I, daughter of a noble sire, suffer the worst indignity? Must I not die in any wise? We may leave Attica and wander again; shall I not hang my head if I hear men say, 'Why come ye here with suppliant boughs, cleaving to life? Depart; we will not help cowards.' Who will marry such a one? Better death than such disgrace."

A messenger announces that Hyllus, Heracles' son, has returned with succours and is with the Athenian army. Iolaus summons Alcmena and orders his arms; old though he is, he will fight his foe in spite of Alcmena's entreaties. In the battle he saw Hyllus and begged him to take him into his chariot. He prayed to Zeus and Hebe to restore his strength for one brief moment. Miraculously he was answered. Two stars lit upon the car, covering the yoke with a halo of light. Catching sight of Eurystheus Iolaus the aged took him prisoner and brought him to Alcmena. At sight of him she gloats over the coming vengeance. The Athenian herald warns her that their laws do not permit the slaughter of captives, but she declares she will kill him herself. Eurystheus answers with great dignity; his enmity to Heracles came not from envy but from the desire to save his own throne. He does not deprecate death, rather, if he dies, his body buried in Athenian land will bring to it a blessing and to the Argive descendants of the Heracleidae a curse when they in time invade the land of their preservers.

Though slight and weakly constructed, this play is important. Its two features are first, the love of argument, a weakness of all the Athenians who frequented the Law Courts and the Assembly; this mania for discussing pros and cons spoils one or two later plays. Next, the self-sacrificing girl appears for the first time. To Euripides the worthier sex was not the male, possessed of political power and therefore tyrannous, but the female. He first drew attention to its splendid heroism. He is the champion of the scorned or neglected elements of civilisation.

The *Andromache* is a picture of the hard lot of one who is not merely a woman, but a slave. Hector's wife fell to Neoptolemus on the capture of Troy and bore him a son called Molossus. Later he married Hermione, daughter of Menelaus and Helen; the marriage was childless and Hermione, who loved her husband, persecuted Andromache. She took advantage of her husband's absence to bring matters to a head. Andromache exposed her child, herself flying to a temple of Thetis when Menelaus arrived to visit his daughter. Hermione enters richly attired, covered with jewels "not given by her husband's kin, but by her father that she may speak her mind." She reviles Andromache as a slave with no Hector near and commands her to quit sanctuary. Menelaus brings the child; after a long discussion he threatens to kill him if Andromache does not abandon the altar, but promises to save him if she obeys. In this dilemma she prefers to die if she can thus save her son; but when Menelaus secures her he passes the child to his daughter to deal with him as she will. Betrayed and helpless, Andromache breaks out into a long denunciation of Spartan perfidy.

Peleus, grandfather of Neoptolemus, hearing the tumult intervenes. After more rhetoric he takes Andromache and Molossus under his protection and cows Menelaus, who leaves for Sparta on urgent business. When her father departs, Hermione fears her husband's vengeance on her maltreatment of the slave and child whom he loves. Resolving on suicide, she is checked by the entry of Orestes who is passing through Phthia to Dodona. She begs him to take her away from the land or back to her father. Orestes reminds her of the old compact which their parents made to unite them; he has a grievance against Neoptolemus apart from his frustrated wedlock, for he had called him a murderer of his mother. He had therefore taken measures to assassinate him at Delphi, whither he had gone to make his peace with Apollo.

Hearing of Hermione's flight Peleus returns, only to hear more serious news. Orestes' plot had succeeded and Neoptolemus had been overwhelmed. In consternation he fears the loss of his own life in old age. His goddess-wife Thetis appears and bids him marry Andromachus to Hector's brother Helenus; Molossus would found a mighty kingdom, while Peleus would become immortal after the burial of Neoptolemus.

A very old criticism calls this play "second rate". Dramatically it is worthless, for it consists of three episodes loosely connected. The motives for Menelaus' return and Hermione's flight with an assassin from a husband she loved are not clear, while the *Deus ex machina* adds nothing to the story. It is redeemed by some splendid passages, but is interesting as revealing a further development of Euripides' thought. He here makes the slave, another downtrodden class, free of the privileges of literature, for to him none is vile or reprobate. The famous painting *Captive Andromache* indicates to us the loneliness of slavery.

The same subject was treated more successfully in the *Hecuba*: she has received her immortality in the famous players' scene in *Hamlet*. The shade of Polydorus, Hecuba's son, outlines the course of the action. Hecuba enters terrified by dreams about him and her daughter Polyxena. Her forebodings are realised when she hears from a Chorus of fellow-captives that the shade of Achilles has demanded her daughter's sacrifice. Odysseus bids her face the ordeal with courage. She replies in a splendid pathetic appeal. Reminding him how she saved him from discovery when he entered Troy in disguise, she demands a requital.

> "Kill her not, we have had enough of death. She is my comfort, my nurse, the staff of my life and guide of my way. She is my joy in whom I forget my woes. Victors should not triumph in lawlessness nor think to prosper always. I was once but now am no more, for one day has taken away my all."

He sympathises but dare not dishonour the mighty dead. Polyxena intervenes to point out the blessings death will bring her.

> "First, its very unfamiliar name makes me love it. Perhaps I might have found a cruel-hearted lord to sell me for money, the sister of Hector; I might have had the burden of making bread, sweeping the house and weaving at the loom in a life of sorrow. A slave marriage would degrade me, once thought a fit mate for kings."

Bidding Odysseus lead her to death, she takes a touching and beautiful farewell. Her latter end is splendidly described by Talthybius.

A serving woman enters with the body of Polydorus; she is followed by Agamemnon who has come to see why Hecuba has not sent for Polyxena's corpse. In hopeless grief she shows her murdered son, begging his aid to a revenge and promising to exact it without compromising him. A message brings on the scene

Polymestor, her son's Thracian host with his sons. In a dialogue full of terrible irony Hecuba inquires about Polydorus, saying she has the secret of a treasure to reveal. He enters her tent where is nobody but some Trojan women weaving. Dismissing his guards, he lets the elder women dandle his children, while the younger admire his robes. At a signal they arose, slew the children and blinded him. On hearing the tumult, Agamemnon hurries in; turning to him, the Thracian demands justice, pretending he had slain Polydorus to win his favour. Hecuba refutes him, pointing out that it was the lust for her son's gold which caused his death. Agamemnon decides for Hecuba, whereupon Polymestor turns fay, prophesying the latter end of Agamemnon, Hecuba and Cassandra.

The strongest and weakest points of Euripides' appeal are here apparent. The play is not one but two, the connection between the deaths of both brother and sister being a mere dream of their mother. The poet tends to rely rather upon single scenes than upon the whole and is so far romantic rather than classical. His power is revealed in the very stirring call he makes upon the emotions of pity and revenge; because of this Aristotle calls him the most tragic of the poets.

The *Supplices*, written about 421, carries a little further the history of the Seven against Thebes. A band of Argive women, mothers of the defeated Seven, apply to Aethra, mother of Theseus, to prevail on her son to recover the dead bodies. Adrastus, king of Argos, pleads with Theseus who at first refuses aid but finally consents at the entreaties of his mother. His ultimatum to Thebes is delayed by the arrival of a herald from that city. A strange discussion of the comparative merits of democracy and tyranny leads to a violent scene in which Theseus promises a speedy attack in defence of the rights of the dead.

In the battle the Athenians after a severe struggle won the victory; in the moment of triumph Theseus did not enter the city, for he had come not to sack it but to save the dead. Reverently collecting them he washed away the gore and laid them on their biers, sending them to Athens. In an affecting scene Adrastus recognises and names the bodies. At this moment Evadne enters, wife of the godless Capaneus who was smitten by the thunderbolt; she is demented and wishes to find the body to die upon it. Her father Iphis comes in search of her and at first does not see her, as she is seated on a rock above him. His pleadings with her are vain; she throws herself to her death. At the sight Iphis plunges into a wild lament.

> "She is no more, who once kissed my face and fondled my head. To a father the sweetest joy is his daughter; son's soul is greater, but less winsome in its blandishments."

Theseus returns with the children of the dead champions to whom he presents the bodies. He is about to allow Adrastus to convey them home when Athena appears. She advises him to exact an oath from Adrastus that Argos will never invade Attica. To the Argives she prophecies a vengeance on Thebes by the Epigoni, sons of the Seven.

This play is very like the *Heraclidae* but adds a new feature; drama begins to be used for political purposes. The play was written at the end of the first portion of the Peloponnesian war, when Argos began to enter the world of Greek diplomacy. This illegitimate use of Art cannot fail to ruin it; Art has the best chance of making itself permanent when it is divorced from passing events. But there are other weaknesses in this piece; it has some fine and perhaps some melodramatic situations; here and there are distinct touches of comedy.

The *Ion* is a return to Euripides' best manner. Hermes in a prologue explains what must have been a strange theme to the audience. Ion is a young and nameless boy who serves the temple of Apollo in Delphi. There is a mystery in his birth which does not trouble his sunny intelligence. Creusa, daughter of Erectheus King of Athens, is married to Xuthus but has no issue. Unaware that Ion is her son by Apollo, she meets him and is attracted by his noble bearing. A splendid dialogue of tragic irony represents both as wishing to find the one a mother, the other a son. Creusa tells how she has come to consult the oracle about a friend who bore a son to the god and exposed him. Ion is shocked at the immorality of the god he serves; he refuses to believe that an evil god can claim to deliver righteous oracles. Addressing the gods as a body, he states the problem of the play.

> "Ye are unjust in pursuing pleasure rather than wisdom; no longer must we call men evil, if we imitate your evil deeds; rather the gods are evil, who instruct men in such things."

Xuthus embraces Ion as his son in obedience to a command he has just received to greet as his child the first person he meets on leaving the shrine. Ion accepts the god's will but longs to know who is his mother. Seeing an unwonted dejection in him Xuthus learns the reason. Ion is afraid of the bar on his birth which will disqualify him from residence at Athens, where absolute legitimacy was essential; his life at Delphi was in sharp contrast, it was one of perfect content and eternal novelty. Xuthus tells him he will take him to Athens merely as a sightseer; he is afraid to anger his wife with his good fortune; in time he will win her consent to Ion's succession to the throne.

Creusa enters with an old man who had been her father's Tutor. She learns from the Chorus that she can never have a son, unlike her more lucky husband who has just found one. The Tutor counsels revenge; though a slave, he will work for her to the end.

> "Only one thing brings shame to a slave, his name. In all else he is every whit the equal of a free man, if he is honest."

The two decide to poison Ion when he offers libations. But the plot failed owing to a singular chance. The birds in the temple tasted the wine and one that touched Ion's cup died immediately. Creusa flees to the altar, pursued by Ion who reviles her for her deed. At that moment the old Prophetess appears with the vessel in which she first found Ion. Creusa recognises it and accurately describes the child's clothing which she wove with her own hands; mother and son are thus united. The play closes with an appearance of Athena, who prophesies that Ion shall be the founder of the great Ionian race, for Apollo's hand had protected him and Creusa throughout.

The central problem of this piece is whether the gods govern the world righteously or not. No more vital issue could be raised; if gods are wicked they must fall below the standard of morality which men insist on in their dealings with one another. Ion is the Greek Samuel; his naturally reverent mind is disturbed at any suggestion of evil in a deity. His boyish faith in Apollo is justified and Euripides seems to teach in another form the lesson that "except we become as children, we cannot enter the kingdom of Heaven."

The *Hercules Furens* belongs to Euripides' middle period. Amphitryon, father of Heracles, and Megara, the hero's wife, are in Theban territory waiting for news. They are in grave danger, for Lycus, a new king, threatens to kill them with Heracles' children, as he had already slain Megara's father. He has easy victims in Amphitryon, "naught but an empty noise", and Megara, who is resigned to the inevitable. Faced with this terror, Amphitryon exclaims:—

> "O Zeus, thou art a worse friend than I deemed. Though a mortal, I exceed thee in worth, god though thou art, for I have never abandoned my son's children. Thou canst not save thy friends; either thou art ignorant or unjust in thy nature."

As they are led out to slaughter, Amphitryon makes what he is sure is a vain appeal to Heaven to send succour. At that moment the hero himself appears. Seeing his family clad in mourning, he inquires the reason. At first his intention is to attack Lycus openly, but Amphitryon bids him wait within; he will tell Lycus that his victims are sitting as suppliants on the hearth; when the King enters Heracles may slay him without trouble.

When vengeance has been taken Iris descends from heaven, sent by Hera to stain Heracles with kindred bloodshed. She summons Madness who is unwilling to afflict any man, much less a famous hero. Reluctantly consenting she sets to work. A messenger rushes out telling the sequel. Heracles slew two of his children and was barely prevented from destroying his father by the intervention of Athena. He reappears in his right mind, followed by Amphitryon who vainly tries to console him. Theseus who accompanied Heracles to the lower world hurries in on hearing a vague rumour. To him Heracles relates his life of never-ending sorrow. Conscious of guilt and afraid of contaminating any who touch him, he at length consents to go to Athens with Theseus for purification. He departs in sorrow, bidding his father bury the slain children.

Like the *Hecuba*, this play consists of two very loosely connected parts. The second is decidedly unconvincing. Madness has never been treated in literature with more power than in Hamlet and Lear. Besides Shakespeare's work, the description in the mouth of a messenger, though vivid enough, is less effective, for "what is set before the eyes excites us more than what is dropped into our ears" as Horace remarks. But the point of the play is the seemingly undeserved suffering which is the lot of a good character. This is the theme of many a Psalm in the Bible; its answer is just this—"Whom the Lord loveth He chasteneth."

In 415 Euripides told how Hecuba lost her last remaining child Cassandra. The plot of the *Trojan Women* is outlined by Poseidon and Athena who threaten the Greeks with their hatred for burning the temples of Troy. After a long and powerful lament the captive women are told their fate by the herald Talthybius.

Cassandra is to be married to Agamemnon. She rushes in prophesying wildly. On recovering calm speech she bids her mother crown her with garlands of victory, for her bridal will bring Agamemnon to his death, avenging her city and its folk. Triumphantly she passes to her appointed work of ruin.

Andromache follows her, assigned to Neoptolemus. She sadly points out how her faithfulness to Hector has brought her into slavery with a proud master.

> "Is not Polyxena's fate agony less than mine? I have not that thing which is left to all mortals, hope, nor may I flatter my mind heart with any good to come, though it is sweet to even to dream of it."

This despair is rendered more hopeless when she learns that the Greeks have decided to throw her little son Astyanax from the walls.

Menelaus comes forward, gloating at the revenge he hopes to wreak on Helen. On seeing him Hecuba first prays:—

> "Thou who art earth's support and hast thy seat on earth, whoever thou art, past finding out, Zeus, whether thou art a natural Necessity or man's Intelligence, to thee I pray. Moving in a noiseless path thou orderest all things human in righteousness."

She continues:—

> "I praise thee, Menelaus, if thou wilt indeed slay thy wife, but fly her sight, lest she snare thee with desire. She catcheth men's eyes, sacketh cities, burneth homes, so potent are her charms. I know her as thou dost and all who have suffered from her."

Hecuba and Helen then argue about the responsibility for the war. The latter in shameless impudence pleads that she has saved Greece from invasion and that Love who came with Paris to Sparta was the cause of her fault. Hecuba ridicules the idea that Hera and Artemis could desire any prize of beauty. It was lust of Trojan gold that tempted Helen; never once was she known to bewail her sin in Troy, rather she always tried to attract men's eyes. Such a woman's death would be a crown of glory to Greece. Menelaus says her fate will be decided in Argos. Talthybius brings in the body of Astyanax, over which Hecuba bursts into a lament of exceptional beauty and then passes out to slavery.

In this drama Euripides draws upon all his resources of pathos. It is a succession of brilliantly conceived sorrows. Cassandra's exulting prophecy of the revenge she is to bring is one of the great things in Euripides. In this play we have a most vivid picture of the destructive effects of evil, an inevitable consequence of which it is that the woman, however innocent she may be, always pays. Hecuba drank the cup of bereavement to the very last drop.

The *Electra*, acted about 418, is characteristic. Electra has been compelled to marry a Mycenean labourer, a man of noble instincts who respects the princess and treats her as such. Both enter the scene; the man goes to labour for Electra, "for no lazy man by merely having God's name on his lips can make a livelihood without toil". Orestes and Pylades at first imagine Electra to be a servant; learning the truth they come forward and question her. She tells the story of her mother's shame and Aegisthus' insolence which Orestes promises to recount to her brother, "for in ignorant men there is no spark of pity anywhere, only in the learned." The labourer returns and by his speech moves Orestes to declare that birth is no test of nobility. Electra sends him to fetch an old Tutor of her father to make ready for her two guests; he departs remarking that there is just enough food in the house for one day.

The old Tutor arrives in tears; he has found a lock of hair on Agamemnon's tomb. Gazing intently on the two strangers, he recognises Orestes by a scar on the eyebrow. They then proceed to plot the death of their enemies. Orestes goes to meet Aegisthus is close by sacrificing, and presently returns with the corpse, at which Electra hurls back the taunts and jeers he had heaped on her in his lifetime. She had sent to her mother saying she had given birth to a boy and asking her to come immediately.

Orestes quails before the coming murder, but Electra bids him be loyal to his father. Clytemnestra on her arrival querulously defends her past, alleging as her pretext not the death of Iphigeneia but the presence of a rival, Cassandra. Electra after refuting her invites her inside the wretched hut to offer sacrifice for her newly born child, where she is slain by Orestes. At the end of the play the Dioscuri, Castor and Pollux, bid Pylades marry Electra, tell Orestes he will be purified in Athens and prophesy that Menelaus and Helen, just arrived from Egypt, will bury Agisthus real Helen never went to Troy, a wraith of her being sent there with Paris.

The startling realism of this drama is apparent. The poverty of Electra, the more certain identification of Orestes by a scar than by a lock of hair, the mention of Cassandra as the real motive for the murder of Agamemnon all indicate that Euripides was not content with the accepted legend. His Clytemnestra is a feeble creation even by the side of that of Sophocles.

Stesichorus in a famous poem tells how Helen blinded him for maligning her; she never went to Troy; it was a wraith which accompanied Paris. Such is the central idea of a very strange play, the *Helen*. The scene is in Egypt. Teucer, banished by his father, meets the real Helen; to her amazement he tells of her evil reputation and of the great war before Troy, adding that Menelaus is sailing home with another Helen. The latter enters, to learn that he is in Egypt, where the real Helen has lived for the last seventeen years. Warned by a prophetess Theonoe that her husband is not far off, Helen comes to be reunited to him. A messenger from the coast announces that the wraith has faded into nothingness.

Helen then warns Menelaus of her difficult position. She is wooed by Theoclymenus, king of the land, brother of Theonoe. Menelaus in despair thinks of killing himself and Helen to escape the tyrant. Theonoe holds their fate in her hands; Helen pleads with her; "It is shameful that thou shouldest know things divine, and not righteousness." Menelaus declares his intention of living and dying with his wife. The prophetess leaves them to discover some means of escape which Helen devises. Pretending that Menelaus is a messenger bringing news of her husband's death at sea, she persuades the tyrant to provide a ship and rowers that Helen may perform the last rites to the dead on the element where he died. At the right moment the Greek sailors overpowered the rowers and sailed home with the united pair.

Very commonly real drama suffers the fate which has overtaken it in this piece; it declines into melodrama. Here are to be found all the stock melodramatic features—a bold hero, a scheming beauty, a confidante, a dupe, the murder of a ship's crew. Massinger piloted Elizabethan drama to a similar end. Given an uncritical audience melodrama is the surest means of filling the house. Reality matters little in such work; the facts of life are like Helen's wraith, when they become unmanageable they vanish into thin air.

About 412 the *Iphigeneia in Tauris* appeared. South Russia was the seat of a cult of Artemis; the goddess spirited Iphigeneia to the place when her father sacrificed her at Aulis. Orestes, bidden by Apollo to steal an image of the goddess to get his final purification, comes on the stage with Pylades; on seeing the temple they are convinced of the impossibility of burgling it. A shepherd describes to Iphigeneia their capture, for strangers were taken and offered to the goddess without exception. One of the two was seized with a vision of the avenging deities; attacked by a band of peasants both were overpowered after a stubborn resistance. Formerly Iphigeneia had pitied the Greeks who landed there; now, warned of Orestes' death by a dream, she determines to kill without mercy. One of them shall die, the other taking back to Greece a letter. Orestes insists on dying himself, reminding Pylades of his duty to Electra. When the letter is brought Pylades swears to fulfil his word, but asks what is to happen if the ship is wrecked. Iphigeneia reads the letter to him; it is addressed to Orestes and tells of his sister's weary exile. After the recognition is completed, Orestes relates the horrors of his life and begs his sister to help him to steal the all-important image.

Thoas, the King of the land, learns from her that the two Greeks are guilty of kindred murder; their presence has defiled the holy image which needs purification in the sea as well as the criminals. The priestess obtains permission to bind the captives and take the image to be cleansed with private mystic rites. The plot succeeds; Orestes' ship puts in; after a struggle the three board it, carrying the image with them. Thoas is prevented from pursuit by an intervention of Athena.

Goethe used this play for his drama of the same name; he made Thoas the lover of Iphigeneia, whom he represents as the real image whom Orestes is to remove. Her departure is not compassed by a stratagem, but is permitted by the King, a man of singular nobility and self-denial.

The *Phaenissae* has been much admired in all ages. Jocasta tells how after the discovery of his identity Oedipus blinded himself but was shut up by his two sons whom he cursed for their impiety. Eteocles then usurped the rule while Polyneices called an Argive host to attack Thebes. A Choral description of this army is succeeded by an unexpected entry into the city of Polyneices who meets his mother and tells her of his life in exile. She sends for Eteocles in the hope of reconciling her two sons. Polyneices promises to disband his forces if he is restored to his rights, but Eteocles, enamoured of power, refuses to surrender it. Jocasta vainly points out to him the burden of rule, nor can she persuade Polyneices not to attack his own land.

When the champions have taken up their position at the gates, Teiresias tells Creon that Thebes can be saved by the sacrifice of his own son Menoeceus. Creon refuses to comply and urges his son to escape. Pretending to obey Menoeceus threw himself from the city walls. The struggle at the gates is followed by a challenge to Polyneices issued by Eteocles to settle the dispute in single combat. Jocasta and Antigone rush out to intervene, too late. They find the two lying side by side at death's door. Eteocles is past speech, but Polyneices bids farewell to his mother and sister, pitying his brother "who turned friendship into enmity, yet still was dear". In agony, Jocasta slays herself over her sons' bodies.

Led in by Antigone, Oedipus is banished by Creon, who forbids the burial of Polyneices. After touching the dead Jocasta and his two sons, he passes to exile and rest at Colonus.

The harsh story favoured by Sophocles has been greatly humanised by Euripides, who could not accept all the savagery of the received legend. Apart from the unexplained presence of Polyneices in the city, the plot is excellent. The speeches are vigorous and natural, the characters thoroughly human. The criticising and refining influence of Euripides is manifest throughout, together with a simple and noble pathos.

An ancient critic says of the *Orestes*, written in 408, "the drama is popular but of the lowest morality; except Pylades, all are villains". Electra meets Helen, unexpectedly returned from Egypt to Argos with Menelaus, who sends her daughter Hermione with offerings to the tomb of Agamemnon. Electra's opinion of her is vividly expressed.

> "See how she has tricked out her hair, preserving her beauty;
> she is old Helen still. Heaven abhor thee, the bane of me and my
> brother and Greece."

The Chorus accidentally awakens Orestes who is visited by a wild vision of haunting Furies. When he regains sanity he begs the assistance of Menelaus, his last refuge. His uncle, a broken reed, is saved from committing himself by the entry of Tyndareus, father of Clytemnestra and Helen. He righteously rebukes the bloodthirsty Orestes, though he is aware of the evil in his two daughters. Orestes breaks out into an insulting speech which alienates completely his grandfather. Menelaus, when appealed to again, hurries out to try to win him back.

Pylades suggests that he and Orestes should plead their case before the Argive Assembly, which was to try them for murder of Clytemnestra. A very brilliant and exciting account of the debate tells how the case was lost by Orestes himself, who presumed to lecture the audience on the majesty of the law he himself had broken. He and Electra are condemned to be stoned that very day. Determined to ruin Menelaus before they die, they agree to kill Helen, the cause of all their troubles, and to fire the fortified house in which they live. Electra adds that they should also seize Hermione and hold her as a check on Menelaus' fury for the death of Helen. The girl is easily trapped as she rushes into the house hearing her mother's cries for help. Soon after a Trojan menial drops from the first story. He tells how Helen and Hermione have so far escaped death, but the rest is unknown to him. In a ghastly scene Orestes hunts the wretch over the stage, but finally lets him go as he is not a fit victim for a free man's sword. Almost immediately the house is seen to be ablaze; Menelaus rushes up in a frenzy, but is checked by the sight of Orestes with Hermione in his arms. When Menelaus calls for help, Orestes bids Pylades and Electra light more fires to consume them all. A timely appearance of Apollo with Helen deified by his side saves the situation.

It is plain that Euripides has here completely rejected the old legend. He never makes Orestes even think of pleading Apollo's command to him to slay his mother. He is concerned with the defence which a contemporary matricide might make before a modern Athenian assembly and with the fitting doom of self-destruction which would overtake him. Like *Vanity Fair*, the play shows us the life of people who try to do without God.

The *Bacchae* is one of Euripides' best plays. In the absence of Pentheus the King, Cadmus and Teiresias join in the worship of the new god Dionysus at Thebes. Pentheus returns to find that noble women, including Agave, his own mother, have joined the strange cult brought to the place by a mysterious Lydian stranger "whose hair is neatly arranged in curls, his face like wine, his eyes as full of grace as Aphrodite's".

Teiresias advises him to welcome the god, Cadmus to pretend that he is divine, even if he is only a mortal; this new religion is the natural outlet of the desire for innocent revelry born in both sexes. The Lydian is arrested and brought before Pentheus, whom he warns that the god will save him from insult, but Pentheus hurries him away into a dungeon.

The Chorus of Bacchae are alarmed on hearing a tumult. The stranger appears to tell how Pentheus was made mad by Dionysus in the act of imprisoning him. The King in amazement sees his prisoner standing free before him and becomes furiously angry on hearing that his mother has joined a new revel on Mount Cithaeron. The stranger suggests that he should go disguised as a Bacchante to see the new worship. When he appears transformed, the Lydian comments with exquisite and deadly irony on his appearance. His fate is vividly and terribly painted. Placing him in a pine, the stranger suddenly disappeared, while the voice of Dionysus summoned the rout to punish the spy. Rushing to the tree, the woman tore it up by the roots and then rent Pentheus piecemeal, Agave herself leading them on.

She comes in holding what she imagines to be a trophy. Cadmus slowly reveals to her the horror of her deed, the proof of which is her son's head in her grasp. Dionysus himself comes in to point out that this tragedy is the result of the indignity which Thebes put upon him and his mother Semele. Broken with grief, Agave passes out slowly to her banishment. The Bacchae was composed in Macedonia; it contains all the mystery of the supernatural. Dionysus' character is admirably drawn, while the infatuation of Pentheus is a fitting prelude to his ruin. The cult of Dionysus was essentially democratic, intended for those who could claim no share in aristocratic ritual: hence its popularity and prevalence. We may regard the Bacchae as the poet's declaration of faith in the worship which gave Europe the Drama; it is altogether fitting that he who has left us the greatest number of tragedies should have been chosen by destiny to bequeath us the one drama which tells of one of the adventures of its patron deity.

The *Iphigeneia in Aulis* was written in the last year of the poet's life. Agamemnon sends a private letter to his wife countermanding an official dispatch summoning her and Iphigeneia. This letter is intercepted by Menelaus, who upbraids his brother; later, seeing his distress, he advises him to send the women home again. But public opinion forces the leader to obey Artemis and sacrifice his daughter. When he meets his wife and child, he tries to temporise but fails. Achilles meets Clytemnestra and is surprised to hear that he is to marry Iphigeneia, such being the bait which brought Clytemnestra to Aulis. Learning the real truth, she faces her husband, pleading for their daughter's life. Iphigeneia at first shrinks from death; the army demands her sacrifice, while Achilles is ready to defend her. The knot is untied by Iphigeneia herself, who willingly at last consents to die to save her country.

This excellent play shows no falling in dramatic power; it was imitated by Racine and Schiller. The figures are intensely human, the conflict of duties firmly outlined, the pathos sincere and true, there is no divine appearance to straighten out a tangled plot. Thus Euripides' career ends as it began, with a story of a woman's noble self-sacrifice.

The poet's popularity is indicated by the number of his extant dramas and fragments, both of which exceed in bulk the combined work of Aeschylus and Sophocles. All classes of writers quoted him, philosophers, orators, bishops. In his own lifetime Socrates made a point of witnessing his plays; the very violence of Aristophanes' attack proves Euripides' potent influence; his lost drama *Melanippe* turned the heads of the Athenians, the whole town singing its odes. Survivors of the Sicilian disaster won their freedom by singing his songs to their captors, returning to thank their liberator in person; the fragments of Menander discovered in 1906 contain many reminiscences of him, even slaves quoting passages of him to their masters. For it was the very width of his appeal that made him universally loved; women and slaves in his view were every whit as good as free-born men, sometimes they were far nobler. If drama is the voice of a democracy, the Athenians had found a more democratic mouthpiece than they had bargained for.

With the educated men it was different. They suspected a poet who was upsetting their tradition. Besides, they were asked to crown a person who told them in play after play that they were really like Jason, Menelaus, Polymestor, poor creatures if not quite odious. He made them see with painful clearness that the better sex was the one which they despised, yet which was sure one day to find the utterance to which it had a right in virtue of its greater nobility. The feminism of Euripides is evident through his whole career; it is an insult to our powers of reading to imagine that he was a woman-hater. It is then not to be wondered at that he won the prize only five times, and it can hardly be an accident that he gained it once with the Hippolytus, which on a surface view condemns the female sex.

For the officials could not see that Euripides was not a man only, he was a spirit of development. Privilege and narrowness in every form he hated; he demanded unlimited freedom for the intelligence. The narrow circle of legends, the conventional unified drama, state religion, a pseudo-democracy based on slavery he fearlessly criticised. Rationalism, humanism, free speculation were his watchwords; he was always trying new experiments in his art, introducing politics, philosophy, melodrama and trying to get rid of the chorus wherever he could. He was a living and a contemporary Proteus, pleading like an advocate in a lawsuit, discussing political theory, restating unsolved problems in modern form and seasoning his work with his own peculiar and often elevating pathos. Such a man was anathema to conservative Athens.

But to us he is one of ourselves. He exactly hits off our modern taste, with its somewhat sentimental tendency, its scepticism, love of excitement, and its great complexity. We know we have many moods and passions which strangely blend and thwart each other; these we treat in our novels, and Euripides' plays are a sort of novel, but for the divine appearances in the last scenes. He shows us the inevitable end of actions of beings exactly like ourselves, acting from merely human motives, neither higher nor lower than we, though perhaps disguised under heroic names. He is in a word the first modern poet.

TRANSLATIONS:

A. S. Way, Loeb Series. This verse translation is the most successful; it renders the choric odes with skill.

Professor Gilbert Murray has published verse translations of various plays. He is an authority on the text. His volume on Euripides in the Home University Library is admirable.

Euripides the Rationalist and *Four Plays of Euripides* by A. W. Verrall are well known; the latter is particularly stimulating. The views it expounds are original but not traditional.

See Symonds' *Greek Poets* as above.

ARISTOPHANES

At the end of the *Symposium* Plato represents Socrates as convincing both Agathon, a tragedian, and Aristophanes that the writer of tragedy will be able to write comedy also. That the two forms are not wholly divorced is clear from the history of ancient drama itself: Each dramatist competed with four plays, three tragedies and a Satyric drama. What this last is can be plainly seen in the *Cyclops* of Euripides, which relates in comic form the adventures of Odysseus and Silenus in the monster's company. Further, the tendency of tragedy was inevitably towards comedy. The extant work of Aeschylus and Sophocles is not without comic touches; but the trend is clearer in Euripides who was an innovator in this as in many other matters. Laughter and tears are neighbours; a happy ending is not tragic; loosely connected scenes are the essence of Old Comedy, and loosely written tragic dialogue (common in Euripides' later work) closely resembles the language of comedy, which is practically prose in verse form. The debt which later comedy owed to Euripides is great; reminiscences of him abound; he is quoted directly and indirectly; his stage tricks are adopted and his realistic characters are the very population of the Comic stage.

The logically developed plot is the characteristic of serious drama. Old Comedy, its antithesis, is often a succession of scenes in which the connection is loose without being impossible. In it the unexpected is common, for it is an escape from the conventions of ordinary life, a thing of causes and effects. It might be more accurate to say that farce is a better description of the work which is associated with the name of Aristophanes.

This writer was born about 448, was a member of the best Athenian society of the day, quickly took the first place as the writer of comedy and died about 385. He saw the whole of the Peloponnesian war and has given us a most vivid account of the passions it aroused and its effect on Athenian life. He first won the prize in 425, when he produced the *Acharnians* under an assumed name. Pericles had died in 429; the horrors of war were beginning to make themselves felt; the Spartans were invading Attica, cutting down the fruit-trees and compelling the country folk to stream into the city. One of these, Dicaeopolis enters the stage. It is early morning; he is surprised that there is no popular meeting on the appointed day. He loathes the town and longs for his village; he had intended to heckle the speakers if they discussed anything but peace. Ambassadors from foreign nations are announced; seeing them he conceives the daring project of making a separate peace with the Spartan for eight drachmae. His servant returns with three peaces of five, ten and thirty years; he chooses the last.

A chorus of angry Acharnians rush in to catch the traitor; they are charcoal burners ruined by the invasion. Dicaeopolis seizes a charcoal basket, threatening to destroy it if they touch him. Anxious to spare their townsman, the basket, they consent to hear his defence, which he offers to make with his neck on an executioner's block. He is afraid of the noisy patriotism appealed to by mob-orators and of the lust for condemning the accused which is the weakness of older men. Choosing from Euripides' wardrobe the rags in which Telephus was arrayed to rouse the audience to pity, he boldly ventures to plead the cause of the Spartans, though he hates them for destroying his trees. He asserts that "Olympian Pericles who thundered and lightened and confounded Greece" caused the war by putting an embargo on the food of their neighbour Megara, his pretext being a mere private quarrel.

The Chorus are divided; his opponents send for Lamachus, the swashbuckling general; the latter is discomfited and Dicaeopolis immediately opens a market with the Peloponnesians, Megarians and Boeotians, but not with Lamachus. In an important choral ode the poet justifies his existence. By his criticism he puts a stop to the foreign embassies which dupe the Athenians; he checks flattery and folly; he never bribes nor hoodwinks them, but exposes their harsh treatment of their subjects and their love of condemning on groundless charges the older generation which had fought at Marathon.

The play ends with a trading scene; a Boeotian in exchange for Copaic eels takes an Athenian informer, an article unknown in Boeotia. Lamachus returns wounded while Dicaeopolis departs in happy contrast to celebrate a feast of rustic jollity.

Aristophanes' chief butts were Cleon, Socrates and Euripides; the last is treated with good nature in this play. To modern readers the comedy is important for two reasons; first, it attacks the strange belief that a democracy must necessarily love peace; Aristophanes found it as full of the lust for battle as any other form of government; all it needed was a Lamachus to rattle a sword. Again, the unfailing source of war is plainly indicated, trade rivalry. War will continue as long as there are markets to capture and rivals to exclude from them.

In the next year, 424, Aristophanes produced the *Knights*, the most violent political lampoon in literature. The victim was Cleon who had succeeded Pericles as popular leader. He was at the height of his glory, having captured the Spartan contingent at Pylos, prisoners who were of great importance for diplomatic purposes. The comedy is a scathing criticism of democracy; the subject is so controversial that it will be best to give some extracts without comment.

Two servants of Demos (the People) steal the oracles of the Paphlagonian (the babbler, Cleon) while he is asleep. To their joy they find that he will govern Demos' house only until a more abominable than he shall appear, namely a sausage-seller. That person immediately presenting himself is informed of his high calling. At first he is amazed. "I know nothing of refinement except letters, and them, bad as they are, badly." The answer is:

"Your only fault is that you know them badly; mob-leadership has nothing to do with a man refined or of good character, rather with an ignoramus and a vile fellow."

To his objection that he cannot look after a democracy the reply is,

> "it is easy enough; only go on doing what you are doing now. Mix and chop up everything; always bring the mob over by sweetening it with a few cook-shop terms. You have all the other qualifications, a nasty voice, a low origin, familiarity with the street."

The Paphlagonian Cleon runs in bawling that they are conspiring against the democracy. They call loudly for the Knights, who enter as the Chorus to assist them against Cleon, encouraging the sausage-seller to show the brazen effrontery which is the mob-orator's sole protection, and to prove that a decent upbringing is meaningless. Nothing loth, he redoubles Cleon's vulgarity on his head. Cleon rushes out intending to inform the Upper House of their treasons; the sausage-seller hurries after him, his neck being well oiled with his own lard to make Cleon's slanders slip off. A splendid ode is sung in the meantime; it contains a half-comic account of Aristophanes' training in his art and a panegyric on the old spirit which made Athens great. The sausage-seller returns to tell of Cleon's utter defeat; he is quickly followed by Cleon, who appeals to Demos himself, pointing out his own services.

> "At the first, when I was a member of the Council, I got in vast sums for the Treasury, partly by torture, partly by throttling, partly by begging. I never studied any private person's interest if I could only curry favour with you, to make you master of all Greece."

The sausage-seller refutes him.

> "Your object was to steal and take bribes from the cities, to blind Demos to your villainies by the dust of war, and to make him gape after you in need and necessity for war-pensions. If Demos can only get into the country in peace and taste the barley-cakes again, he will soon find out of what blessings you have rid him by your briberies; he will come back as a dour farmer and will hunt up a vote which will condemn you."

Cleon, the new Themistocles, is deposed from his stewardship.

He appeals to some oracles of Bacis, but the sausage-seller has better ones of Bacis' elder brother Glanis. The Chorus rebuke Demos, whom all men fear as absolute, for being easily led, for listening to the newest comer and for a perpetual banishment of his intelligence. In a second contest for Demos' favours Cleon is finally beaten when it appears that he has kept some dainties in his box while the sausage-seller has given his all. An appeal to an oracle prophesying his supplanter—one who can steal, commit perjury and face it out—so clearly applies to the sausage-seller that Cleon retires.

After a brief absence Demos appears with his new friend—but it is a different Demos, rid of his false evidence and jury system, the Demos of fifty years before. He is ashamed of his recent history, of his preferring doles to battleships. He promises a speedy reform, full pay to his sailors, strict revision of the army service rolls, an embargo on Bills of Parliament. To his joy he recovers the Thirty Years' peace which Cleon had hidden away, and realises at last his longing to escape from the city into the country.

This violent attack on Cleon was vigorously met; Aristophanes was prosecuted and seems to have made a compromise. In his next comedy, the *Clouds* (which was presented in 423) he changes his victim. Strepsiades, an old Athenian, married a high-born wife of expensive tastes; their son Pheidippides developed a liking for horses and soon brought his father to the edge of ruin. The latter requests the son to save him by joining the academy conducted by Socrates, where he can learn the worse argument which enables its possessor to win his case. Aided by it he can rid his father of debt. As the son flatly refuses, the old man decides to learn it himself. Entering the school he sees maps and drawings of all kinds and finally descries Socrates himself, far above his head in a basket, high among the clouds, studying the sun. Strepsiades begs him to teach him the Worse Argument at his own price. After initiating him, Socrates summons his deities the Clouds, who enter as the Chorus. These are the guardian deities of modern professors, seers, doctors, lazy long-haired long-nailed fellows, musicians who cultivate trills and tremolos, transcendental quacks who sing their praises. The old gods are dethroned, a vortex governing the universe. The Chorus tells Socrates to take the old man and teach him everything.

The ode which follows contains the poet's claim to be original.

> "I never seek to dupe you by hashing up the same old theme two or three times, but show my cleverness by introducing ever-new ideas, none alike and all smart."

Socrates returns with Strepsiades, whom he can teach nothing. The Chorus suggest he should bring his son to learn from Socrates how to get rid of debts. At first Pheidippides refuses but finally agrees, though he warns his father that he will rue his act. The Just and Unjust arguments come out of the academy to plead before the Chorus. The former draws a picture of the old-fashioned times when a sturdy race of men was reared on discipline, obedience and morality—a broad-chested vigorous type. In utter contempt the latter brands such teaching as prehistoric. Pleasure, self-indulgence, a lax code of morality and easy tolerance of little weaknesses are the ideal. The power of his words is such that the Just Argument deserts to him.

Strepsiades, coached by his son, easily circumvents two money-lenders and retires to his house. He is soon chased out by his son, who when asked to sing the old songs of Simonides and Aeschylus scorned the idea, humming instead an immoral modern tune of Euripides' making. A quarrel inevitably followed; Strepsiades was beaten by his son who easily proved that he had a right to beat his mother also. Stung to the quick the old man burns the academy; when Socrates and his pupils protest, he tells them they have but a just reward for their godlessness.

The Socrates here pilloried is certainly not the Socrates of history; his teaching was not immoral. But Aristophanes is drawing attention to the evil effects produced by the Sophists, who to the ordinary man certainly included Socrates. The importance of this play to us is clear. We are a nation of half-trained intelligences. Our national schools are frankly irreligious, our teachers people of weak credentials. Parental discipline is openly flouted, pleasure is our modern cult. Jazz bands, long-haired novelists and poets, misty philosophers, anti-national instructors are the idols of many a pale-faced and stunted son of Britain. The reverence which made us great is decadent and openly scoffed at. What is the remedy? Aristophanes burnt out the pestilent teachers. We had better not copy him till we are satisfied that the demand for them has ceased. A nation gets the instruction for which it is morally fitted. There is but one hope; we must follow the genuine Socratic method, which consisted of quiet individual instruction. Only thus will we slowly and patiently seize this modern spirit of unrest; our object should be not to suppress it—it is too sturdy, but to direct its energies to a better and a more noble end.

Finding that the *Clouds* had been too wholesome to be popular, Aristophanes in 422 returned to attack Cleon in the *Wasps*. Early in the morning Bdelycleon (Cleon-hater) with his two servants is preventing his father Philocleon from leaving the house to go to the jury-courts. The old man's amusing attempts to evade their vigilance are frustrated, whereupon he calls for assistance. Very slowly a body of old men dressed as wasps, led by boys carrying lanterns, finds its way to the house to act as Chorus. They make many suggestions to the father to escape; just as he is gnawing through the net over him his son rushes in. The wasps threaten him with their formidable stings. After a furious conflict truce is declared. Bdelycleon complains of the inveterate juryman's habit of accusing everybody who opposes them of aiming at establishing a tyranny. Father and son consent to state their case for the Chorus to decide between them.

Philocleon glories in the absolute power he exercises over all classes; his rule is equal to that of a king. To him the greatest men in Athens bow as suppliants, begging acquittal. Some of these appeal to pity, others tell him Aesop's fables, others try to make him laugh. Most of all, he controls foreign policy through his privilege of trying statesmen who fail. In return for his duties he receives his pay, goes home and is petted by his wife and family. Bdelycleon opens thus:

> "it is a hard task, calling for a clever wit and more than comic genius to cure an ancient disease that has been breeding in the city."

After giving a rough estimate of the total revenue of Athens, he subtracts from it the miserable sum of three obols which the jurymen receive as pay. Where does the remainder go? It is evident that the jurymen are the mere catspaw of the big unscrupulous politicians who get all the profit and incur none of the odium. This argument convinces both the Chorus and Philocleon, old heroes of Marathon who created the Empire.

The latter asks what he is to do. His son promises to look after him, allowing him to gratify at home his itch for trying disputes. Two dogs are brought in; by a trick the son makes his father acquit instead of condemn. He then dresses him up decently and instructs him in the etiquette of a dinner-party, whither they proceed. But the old man behaves himself disgracefully, beating everyone in his cups. He appears with a flute-girl and is summoned for assault by a vegetable-woman, whose goods he has spoiled, and by a professional accuser. His insolence to his victims is checked by his son who thrusts him into the house before more accusers can appear.

It is sometimes believed that democracy is a less corrupt form of polity than any other. Aristophanes in this play exposes one of its greatest weaknesses.

Flattered by the sense of power which the possession of the vote brings with it, the enfranchised classes cannot always see that they easily become the tools of the clever rogues who get themselves elected to office by playing on the fears of the electors. The Athenian voter was as easily scared by the word "tyranny" as the modern elector is by "capital". The result is the same. Not only do the so-called lower orders sink into an ignorant slavery; they use their power so brainlessly and so mercilessly that they are a perfect bugbear to the rest.

Literary men's prophecies rarely come true. In 421 the *Peace*, produced in March, was followed almost immediately by a compact between Athens and Sparta for fifty years. An old farmer, Trygaeus, sails up to heaven on the back of a huge beetle, bidding his family farewell for three days. He meets Hermes, who tells him that Zeus in disgust has surrendered men to the war they love. War himself has hidden Peace in a deep pit, and has made a great mortar in which he intends to grind civilisation to powder. He looks for the Athenian pestle, Cleon, but cannot find him—the Spartan pestle Brasidas has also been mislaid; both were lost in Thrace. Before he can find another pestle Trygaeus summons all men to pull Peace out of her prison. Hermes at first objects, but is won over by offers of presents. At length the goddess is discovered with her two handmaids, Harvest and Mayfair.

A change immediately comes over the faces of men. In pure joy they laugh through their bruises. Hermes explains to the farmers who form the Chorus why Peace left the earth. It was the trade rivalry which first drove her away; at Athens the subject cities fomented strife with Sparta, then the country population flocked to the city, where they fell easy victims to the public war-mongers, who found it profitable to continue the struggle. The god then offers to Trygaeus Harvest as a bride to make his vineyards fruitful. In the ode which follows the poet claims that he first made comedy dignified

> "with great thoughts and words and refined jests, not lampooning individuals but attacking the Tanner war-god."

Returning to earth Trygaeus sends Harvest to the Council, while the marriage sacrifice is made ready. A soothsayer endeavours to impose on the rustics with prophecies that the Peace will be a failure. Trygaeus refutes him with a quotation from Homer. "Without kin or law or home is a man who loveth harsh strife between peoples." The makers of agricultural implements quickly sell all their stock, while the makers of helmets, crests and breastplates find their market gone. A glad wedding song forms the epilogue.

Aristophanes believed that the war meant an extinction of civilisation and loathed it because it was useless. What would he have thought of the barbarous and bloodthirsty Great War of our own day? The causes which produced both struggles were identical—trade rivalry and a set of jingoes who found that war paid. But he was mistaken in believing that peace was the normal condition of Greek life. He was born just before the great period began during which Pericles gave Greece a long respite from quarrels, and seems to have been quite nonplussed by what to him was an abnormal upheaval. His bright hopes soon faded and he seems to have given up thinking about peace or war during a period of eight years. In the meanwhile Athens had attacked Sicily; perhaps a change had come over comedy itself owing to legal action. At any rate, the old and virulent type of political abuse was becoming a thing of the past; the next play, the *Birds*, produced in 414, abandons Athens altogether for a new and charming world in which there was a rest from strife.

Two Athenians, Peithetairus (Persuasive) and Euelpides (Sanguine) reach the home of the Hoopoe bird, once a mortal, to find a happier place than their native city. Suddenly, as the bird describes the happy careless life of his kind, Peithetairus conceives the idea of founding a new bird city between earth and heaven. The Hoopoe summons his friends to hear their opinion; as they come in he names them to the wondering Athenians. At first the Birds threaten to attack the mortals, their natural enemies. They listen, however, to Peithetairus' words of wisdom.

> "Nay, wise men learn much from their foes, for good counsel saves everything. We cannot learn from a friend, but an enemy quickly forces the truth upon us. For example, cities learn from their enemies, not their friends, to create high walls and battleships, and such are the salvation of children, home and substance."

A truce is made. Peithetairus tells them the Birds once ruled the world but have been deposed, becoming the prey of those who once worshipped them. They should ring round the air, like Babylon, with mighty baked bricks and send an ultimatum to the gods, demanding their lost kingdom and forbidding a passage to earth; another messenger should descend to men to require from them due sacrifices. The Birds agree; the two companions retire to Hoopoe's house to eat the magic root which will turn them into winged things. After a choral panegyric on the bird species Peithetairus returns to name the new city Cloudcuckootown, whose erection is taken in hand. Impostors make their appearance, a priest to sacrifice, a poet to eulogise, an oracle-dealer to promise success, a mathematician to plan out the buildings, an overseer and a seller of decrees to enact by-laws; all are summarily ejected by Peithetairus.

News comes that the city is already completed. Suddenly Iris darts in, on her way to earth to demand the accustomed sacrifices from men which the new city has interrupted; she is sent back to heaven to warn the gods of their coming overthrow. A herald from earth brings tidings that more than a myriad human beings are on their way to settle in the city. A parent-beater first appears, then a poet, then an informer—all being firmly dealt with. Prometheus slips in under a parasol, to advise Peithetairus to demand from Zeus his sceptre and with it the lady Royalty as his bride. Poseidon, Heracles and an outlandish Triballian god after a long discussion make terms with the new monarch, who goes with them to fetch his bride. A triumphant wedding forms the conclusion.

The purpose of this comedy has been the subject of much discussion. As a piece of literature it is exquisite. It lifts us out of a world of hard unpleasant fact into a region where life is a care-free thing, bores or impostors are banished and the reign of the usurper ends. The play is not of or for any one particular period; it is really timeless, appealing to the ineradicable desire we all have for an existence of joy and light, where dreams always come true and hope ends only in fulfilment. It is therefore one of man's deathless achievements; the power of its appeal is evident from the frequency with which it has been revived—it was staged at Cambridge this very year. Staged it will be as long as men are what they are.

Having learned that men are a naturally combative race, lusting for blood, the poet saw it was hopeless to bring them to terms. Nor could he for ever live in Cloudcuckootowns; he therefore bethought him of another expedient for obtaining peace. In 411 he imagines the women of Athens, Peloponnese and Boeotia combining to force terms on the men by deserting their homes, under the leadership of *Lysistrata*. She calls a council of war, explaining her plot to capture the Acropolis. A Chorus of men rush in to smoke them out, armed with firebrands, but are met by a Chorus of women bearing pitchers to quench the flames. An officer of the Council comes to argue with Lysistrata, who points out that in the first part of the war (down to 421) the women had kept quiet, though aware of men's incompetence; now they have determined to control matters. They are possessed of the Treasury, their experience of household economy gives them a good claim to organise State finance; they grow old in the absence of their husbands; a man can marry a girl however old he is. A woman's prime soon comes; if she misses it, she sits at home looking for omens of a husband; women make the most valuable of all contributions to the State, namely sons. The officer retires to report to the Council.

Lysistrata, seeing a weakness in the women's resolution, encourages them with an oracle which promises victory if they will only persist. A herald speedily arrives from Sparta announcing a similar defection in that city. Ambassadors of both sides are brought to Lysistrata who makes a splendid speech.

> "I am a woman, but wit is in me and I have no small conceit of myself. Having heard many speeches from my father and elder men I am not ill-informed. Now that I have caught you I will administer to you the rebuke you richly deserve. You sprinkle altars from the same lustral-bowl, like relatives, at Olympia, Pylae, Delphi and many other places. Though the barbarian enemy is on you in armed force, you destroy Greek men and cities."

She points out that both sides have been guilty of injustice; both should make surrenders and agree to a peace which is duly ratified. The Chorus of men believe that Athenian ambassadors should go to Sparta in their cups:—

> "As it is, whenever we go there sober, we immediately see what mischief we can make. We never hear what they say; what

they do not say we conjecture and never bring back the same tale about the same facts."

Odes of thanksgiving wind up the piece.

Exactly twenty years earlier Euripides in the *Medea* had written the first protest against women's subjection to an unfair social lot. By a strange irony of fortune his most severe critic Aristophanes was the first man in Europe to give utterance to their claim to a political equality. True, he does so in a comedy, but he was speaking perhaps more seriously than he would have us think. Women do contribute sons to the State; they do believe that they are as capable as men of judging political questions—with justice, in a system where no qualifications but twilight opinions are necessary. On this ground they have won the franchise. Nor has the feminist movement really begun as yet. We may see women in control of our political Acropolis, forcing the world to make peace to save our chances of becoming ultimately civilised.

The *Thesmophoriazousae*, staged in 411, is a lampoon on Euripides. That poet with his kinsman Mnesilochus calls at the house of Agathon, a brother tragedian whose style is amusingly parodied. Euripides informs him that the women intend to hold a meeting to destroy him for libel; they are celebrating the feast of the Thesmophoria. As Agathon refuses an invitation to go disguised and defend Euripides, Mnesilochus undertakes the dangerous duty; his disguise is effected on the stage with comic gusto. At the meeting the case against the poet is first stated; he has not only lampooned women, he has taught their husbands how to counter their knaveries and is an atheist. Mnesilochus defends him; women are capable of far more villainies than even Euripides has exposed. The statement of these raises the suspicions of the ladies who soon unmask the intruder, inquiring of him the secret ritual of the Thesmophoria.

One of them goes to the Town Council to find out what punishment they are to inflict.

Mnesilochus meanwhile snatches a child from the arms of one of them, holding it as a hostage. To his amazement it turns out to be a wine-stoup. He vainly tries some of the dodges practised in Euripides' plays to bring him to the rescue. The Chorus meantime expose the folly of calling women evil.

> "If we are a bane, why do you marry us? Why do you forbid us to walk abroad or to be caught peeping out? Why use such pains to preserve this evil thing? If we do peep out, everybody wants this bane to be seen; if we draw back in modesty, every man is much more anxious to see this pest peep out again. At any rate, no woman comes into the city after stealing public money fifty talents at a time."

A better plan would be

> "to give the mothers of famous sons the right of place in festivals; those whose sons are evil should take a lower place."

In an amusing series of scenes Euripides enters dressed up as some of his own characters to save Mnesilochus. A borough officer enters with a policeman whom he orders to bind the prisoner and guard him. More disguises are adopted by Euripides who succeeds at last in freeing his kinsman by pretending to be an old woman with a marriageable daughter whom the policeman can have at a price. When the latter goes to fetch the money Euripides and his relative disappear.

The poet has in this play very skilfully palmed off on Euripides his own attack on women. We have already seen what Euripides' attitude was to the neglected sex. Feminine deceit has been a stock theme in all ages; it had already been treated in Greek literature and was to be passed through Roman literature to the Middle Ages, in which period it received more than its due share of attention. In itself it is a poor theme, good enough perhaps as a stand-by, for it is sure to be popular. Those who pose as woman-haters might consider the words of the Chorus in this play.

The most violent attack on Euripides was delivered after his death by Aristophanes in the *Frogs*, written in 405. This famous comedy is so well-known that a brief outline will suffice. It falls into two parts. The first describes the adventures of Dionysus who with his servant Xanthias descends to the lower world to bring back Euripides. The god and his servant exchange parts according as the persons they meet are friendly or hostile. In the second part the three great tragedians are brought on the scene. Euripides, who has just died, tries to claim sovereignty in Hades; Sophocles, "gentle on earth and gentle in death" withdraws his claim, leaving Aeschylus to the contest. The two rivals appoint Dionysus, the patron of drama, to act as umpire. In a series of admirable criticisms the weaknesses of both are plainly indicated. Finally Dionysus decides to take back Aeschylus.

This play is as popular as the Birds. It contains one or two touches of low comedy, but these are redeemed by the spirit of inexhaustible jollity which sets the whole thing rocking with life and gaiety. It is an original in Greek literature, being the first piece of definitely literary criticism. A long experience had made the sense of the stage a second nature to Aristophanes who here criticises two rival schools of poetry as a dramatist possessed of inside professional knowledge. So far his work is of the same class as Cicero's *De Oratore* and Reynolds' *Discourses*. His object, however, was not to preserve a balance of impartiality but to condemn Euripides as a traitor to the whole tradition of Attic tragedy. He does so, but not without giving his reasons—and these are good and true. No person is qualified to judge the development of Greek tragedy who has not weighed long and carefully the second portion of the *Frogs*.

In 393 Aristophanes broke entirely new ground in the *Ecclesiazousae* (women in Parliament), a discussion of social and economic problems. Praxagora assembles the women of Athens to gain control of the city. They meet early in the morning, disguise themselves with beards and open the question.

"The decisions of men in Parliament are to reflecting people like the derangements of drunken men. I am disgusted with our policy, we always employ unscrupulous leaders. If one of them is honest for one day, he is a villain for ten. Doling out public money, men have eyes only for what they can make out of the State. Let women govern; they are the best at providing money and are not likely to be deceived in office, for they are well versed in trickery."

They proceed to the Assembly to execute their plot.

On the opening of the discussion one Euaeon proposed a scheme of wholesale spoliation of the property owners to support the poor. Then a white-faced citizen arose and proposed flatly that women should rule, that being the one thing which had never yet been tried. The motion was carried with great enthusiasm, the men declaring that "an old proverb says all our senseless and foolish decisions turn out for good". When Praxagora returns to the stage, she declares she intends to introduce a system of absolute communism. All citizens are to live and dine in common and possess wives in common, existing on the work of slaves. Any person who refuses to declare his wealth is to be punished by losing his rations, "the punishment of a man through his belly being the worst insult he can suffer". A vivid description of the workings of the new system ends the play.

Aristophanes is no doubt criticising Plato's *Republic*, but allowing for altered circumstances we cannot go far wrong if we see here a picture of the suggested remedy for the social distress which is inseparable from a great war. At Athens, beaten and impoverished, there must have been widespread discontent; the foundation upon which society was built must have been criticised, its inequalities being emphasised by idealists and intriguers alike. Our own generation has to face a similar situation. We have seen women in Parliament and we are deluged by a flood of communistic idealism emanating from Russia. Its one commendation is that it has never yet been tried among us and many simple folk will applaud the philosophy which persuades itself that all our mistakes will somehow come right in the end. The problem of finding somebody to do the work was easily solved in ancient Athens where the slaves were three times as numerous as the free. England, possessing no slaves, would under communism be unable to feed herself and would die of starvation.

The *Plutus*, written in 388 is a singular work. An honest old man Chremylus enters with Carion "his most faithful and most thievish servant". They are holding fast a blind old man, in obedience to an oracle of Apollo. After a little questioning the stranger admits that he is Plutus, the god of wealth. Wild with joy they invite him to their house. He does not like houses, for they have never brought him to any good.

> "If I enter a stingy man's abode, he immediately digs me deep in the earth and denies he has ever seen me. If I enter a crazy man's home, given to dicing and fast living, I am soon ejected naked."

Learning that Chremylus is honest and poor he consents to try once again.

The rumour gets abroad that Chremylus has suddenly grown rich; his acquaintance reveal their true characters as they come to question him about his luck. The goddess Poverty enters, to be cross-examined by Chremylus who has suggested that Plutus should recover his sight under the healing care of Asclepius. Before the care is effected, she points out the dangers of his project. He is well-meaning, but foolish; Poverty is not Mendicancy, it means a life of thrift, with nothing left over but with no real want; it is the source of the existence of all the handicrafts, nor can the slaves be counted on to do the work if everybody becomes rich, for nobody will sell slaves if he has money already. Riches on the other hand are the curse of many; wealth rots men, causing gout, dropsy and bloated insolence; the gods themselves are poor, otherwise they would not need human sacrifice.

The cure is successful; Plutus recovers his eyes and can see to whom he gives his blessings; the good and the rascals alike receive their due reward. The change which wealth produces in men's natures is most admirably depicted in the Epilogue.

This is an Allegory dramatised with no little skill. The piece is full of the shrewdest hits at our human failings, aimed, however, with no ill-nature. Aristophanes' power of characterisation here shows no falling-off. Fortune's fickleness is proverbial and has received frequent literary treatment. Men's first prayer is for wealth; poverty, according to Dr. Johnson, is evidently a great evil because it needs such a long defence. Yet it is only the well-meaning but utterly unpractical idealists who desire to make us all prosperous—

"How that may change our nature, that's the question."

Some are not fit for riches, being ignorant of their true function; self-indulgence and moral rottenness follow wealth; because of the abuse of the power which wealth brings, we are taught that it is hard for the rich to enter the kingdom of heaven.

It is difficult to convey an adequate impression of Aristophanes to the English reader. Long excerpts are impossible and undesirable. Comedy is essentially a mirror of contemporary life; it contains all kinds of references to passing political events and transient forms of social life; its turns of language are peculiar to its own age. We who are familiar with Shakespeare know that one of our chief difficulties in reading him is the constant reference to what was obvious to the Elizabethan public but is dark to us. Yet the plays of Aristophanes in an English translation such as that of Frere read far more like modern work than the comedies of Ben Jonson, for the society in which Aristophanes moved was far more akin to ours. It was democratic, was superficially educated, was troubled by socialistic and communistic unrest exactly as we are. Some of our modern thinkers would be surprised to find how many of their dreamings were discussed twenty-three centuries ago by men quite as intelligent and certainly as honest.

Aristophanes' greatest fault is excessive conservatism. He gives us a most vivid description of the evils and abuses of his own time, yet has no remedy except that of putting back the hands of the clock some fifty years. Marathon, Aeschylus, the nascent democracy were his ideal and he was evidently put out by the ending of the period of "Periclean calm." He then has no solution for the problems in front of him. But it might be asked whether a dramatist's business is not rather to leave solutions to the thinker, concerning himself only with mirroring men's natures.

With singular courage and at no small personal risk this man attacked the great ones of his day, scourging their hypocrisies and exposing the real tendencies of their principles. If he has opened our eyes to the objections to popular government and popular poetry and has made us aware of the significance of the feminist movement, let us be thankful; we shall be more on our guard and be less easily persuaded that problems are new or that they are capable of a final solution.

On the other hand, we shall find in him qualities of a most original type. His spirits are inexhaustible, he laughs heartily and often without malice at the follies of the mass of men; Cleon and Euripides were anathema to him, but the rest he treats as Fluellen did Pistol: "You beggarly knave, God bless you". His lyrics must be classed with the best in Greek poetry. Like Rabelais this rollicking jolly spirit disguises his wisdom under the mask of folly, turning aside with some whimsical twist just when he is beginning to be too serious. He will repay the most careful reading, for his best things are constantly turning up when least expected. His political satire ceasing with the death of Cleon, he turned to the land of pure fancy among the winged careless things; he then raised the woman's question, started literary criticism and ended with Allegory. To few has such a noble cycle of work been vouchsafed; we owe him at least a debt of remembrance, for he loved us as our brother.

TRANSLATIONS:

Frere (verse). This spirited version of five plays is justly famous. Various plays have been rendered into verse by Rogers (Bell). The translation is on the whole rather free. The volumes contain excellent introductions and notes.

No prose translation of outstanding merit has appeared.

The Greek tragedians have not received their due from translators and admirers. There is nothing in English drama inspired by Greece to compare with the French imitations of Seneca, Plautus and Terence.

HERODOTUS

Greek historical literature follows the same course of development as Greek poetry; it begins in epic form in Ionia and ends in dramatic type at Athens.

Herodotus, "the father of History", was born at Halicarnassus in Asia Minor about 484 B.C. He travelled widely over the East, Egypt, North Africa and Greece. He was acquainted with the Sophoclean circle, joined the Athenian colony at Thurii in South Italy and died there before the end of the century. His subject was the defeat of the Persian attack on Greece and falls into three main divisions. In the first three books he tells how Persian power was consolidated: in the next three he shows how it flooded Russia, Thrace and Greece, being stemmed at Marathon in 490; the last three contain the story of its final shattering at Salamis and Plataea in 480 and of the Greek recoil on Asia in 479. It is thus a "triple wave of woes" familiar to Greek thought. His dialect is Ionic, which he adopted because it was the language of narrative poetry and prose.

His introduction leads at once into Romance; he intends to preserve the memory of the wonderful deeds of Greeks and Barbarians, the cause of their quarrel being the abductions of women, Io, Europe, Medea, Helen. A more recent aggressor was Croesus, King of Lydia, who attacked the Greek seaboard. The earlier reigns of Lydian kings are recounted in a series of striking narratives. Gyges was the owner of the famous magic ring which made its possessor invisible. His policy of expansion was continued by his son and grandson. But Croesus, his great-grandson, was the wealthiest of all, extending his realm from as far as the Halys, the boundary of Cyrus' Persian Empire. Solon's famous but fictitious warning to him to "wait till the end comes before deciding whether he had been happy" left him unmoved. Soon clouds began to gather. A pathetic misadventure robbed him of his son; the growing power of Persia alarmed him and he applied to Delphi for advice. The oracle informed him that if he crossed the Halys he would ruin a mighty Empire and suggested alliance with the strongest state in Greece. Finding that Athens was still torn by political struggles consequent upon the romantic banishments and restorations of Peisistratus, he joined with Sparta which had just overcome a powerful rival, Tegea in Arcadia.

Croesus crossed the Halys in 554. After fighting an indecisive battle he retired to his capital Sardis. Cyrus unexpectedly pursued him. The Lydian cavalry stampeded, the horses being terrified by the sight and odour of the Persian camel corps. Croesus shut himself up in Sardis which he thought impregnable. An excellent story tells how the Persians scaled the most inaccessible part of the fortress. Croesus was put on a pyre and there remembered the words of Solon. Cyrus, dreading a similar revolution of fortune, tried in vain to save him from the burning faggots; the fire was too fierce for his men to quench, but Apollo heard Croesus' prayer and sent a rainstorm which saved him. Being reproached by the fallen monarch who had poured treasure into his temple, Apollo replied that he had staved off ruin for three full years, but could not prevail against Fate; besides, Croesus should have asked whose Empire he was to destroy; at least Apollo had delivered him from death. The Lydian portion ends with a graphic description of laws, customs and monuments.

The rise of Persia is next described. Assyria, whose capital was Nineveh, was destroyed by Cyaxares of Media, whose capital was Ecbatana. His son Astyages in consequence of a dream married his daughter Mandané to a Persian named Cambyses. A second dream made him resolve to destroy her child Cyrus who, like Oedipus, was saved from exposure by a herdsman. Later, on learning Cyrus' identity, Astyages punished Harpagus whom he had bidden to remove the child. Harpagus sowed mutiny in the Median army, giving the victory to the Persians in 558. Cyrus proceeded to attack the Asiatic Greeks, of whom the Phocaeans left their home to found new states in Corsica and Southern Gaul; the other cities surrendered. Babylon was soon the only city in Asia not subject to Persia. Cyrus diverted the course of the Euphrates and entered the town in 538. In an attack on Tomyris, queen of a Scythian race, Cyrus was defeated and slain in 529.

His son Cambyses determined to invade Egypt, the eternal rival of the Mesopotamian kings. Herodotus devotes his second book to a description of the marvels of Egypt, through which he travelled as far as Elephantiné on the border of Ethiopia. He opens with a plain proof that Egypt is not the most ancient people, for some children were kept apart during their first two years, nobody being allowed to speak with them. They were then heard to say distinctly the word "bekos" which was Phrygian for "bread". This evidence of Phrygian antiquity satisfied even the Egyptians.

In this second book there is hardly a single leading feature of Egyptian civilisation which is not discussed. The Nile is the life of the land; being anxious to solve the riddle of its annual rise, Herodotus dismisses as unreasonable the theory that the water is produced by the melting snow, for the earth becomes hotter as we proceed further south, and there cannot be snow where there is intense heat. The sun is deflected from its course in winter, which derangement causes the river to run shallow in that season. The religious practice of the land are well described, including the process of embalming; oracles, animals, medicine, writing, dress are all treated. He notes that in Egyptian records the sun has twice risen in the west and twice set in the east.

A long list of dynasties is relieved with many an excellent story, notably the very famous account of how Rhampsonitis lost his treasures and failed to find the robber until he offered him a free pardon; having found him he said the Egyptians excelled all the world in wisdom, and the robber all the Egyptians. The Pyramids are described; transmigration is discussed and emphasis is laid upon the growing popularity of Greek mercenaries. The book closes with the brilliant reign of Amasis, who made overtures to the Greek oracles, allied himself with Samos and permitted the foundation of an important Greek colony at Naucratis.

The third book opens with the invasion of Egypt by Cambyses in 525 on account of an insult offered him by Amasis. A Greek mercenary named Phanes gave the Persians information of the one means of attacking through the desert. After a fierce battle at Pelusium Egypt was beaten; for years afterwards skulls of both armies lay around, the Persian heads being easily broken by a pebble, the Egyptian scarcely breakable by stones. In victory Cambyses outraged Psammenitus, the defeated King; a fruitless expedition against Ethiopia and the Ammonians followed. The Egyptians were stirred by the arrival of their calf-god Apis; Cambyses mockingly wounded him and was punished with madness, slaying his own kindred and committing deeds of impiety.

At that time Egypt was leagued with the powerful island of Samos, ruled by Polycrates, a tyrant of marvellous good fortune. Suspecting some coming disaster to balance it, Amasis urged him to sacrifice his dearest possession to avert the evil eye. Polycrates threw his ring into the sea; it was retrieved by a fisherman. On hearing this, Amasis severed his alliance.

In the absence of Cambyses two Magi brothers stirred up revolt in Susa, one pretending to be Smerdis, the murdered brother of Cambyses. That monarch wounded himself in the thigh as he mounted his horse. The wound festered and caused speedy death. Meanwhile the false Smerdis held the sovereignty. He was suspected by Otanes, a noble whose daughter Phaedymé was married to him. At great personal risk she discovered that the King was without ears, a manifest proof that he was a Magian. Otane thens joined with six other conspirators to put the usurper down. Darius, son of Hystaspes, warned them that their numbers were too large for secrecy, advising immediate action. The two pretenders had meanwhile persuaded Prexaspes, a confidant of Cambyses, to assure the Persians that Smerdis really ruled. Prexaspes told the truth and then threw himself to death from the city walls. This news forced the conspirators' hands; rushing into the palace, they were luckily able to slay the usurpers.

The next question was, who should reign? Herodotus turned these Persians into Greeks, making them discuss the comparative merits of monarchy, oligarchy and democracy. They decided that their horses should choose the next king; he whose steed should first neigh should rule. Darius had a cunning groom named Oebares; that evening he took the horse and his mare into the market-place; next morning on reaching the same spot the horse did not fail to seat his master on the throne in 521. A review of the Persian Empire follows, with a description of India and Arabia.

Polycrates did not long survive. He was the first Greek to conceive the idea of a maritime empire. He was foully murdered by the Persian Oroetes, who decoyed him to the mainland by an offer of treasure and then crucified him. In the retinue of Polycrates was a physician, Democedes of Croton, who was captured by Oroetes. His fame spread to Susa at a time when no court doctor could treat Darius' sprained foot. Democedes was sent for and effected the cure; later he healed the Queen Atossa of a boil. Instructed by him she advised Darius to send a commission of fifteen Persians to spy out the Greek mainland under Democedes' guidance. After an exciting series of adventures the physician succeeded in returning to his native city. But the idea of an invasion of Greece had settled on Darius' mind. First, however, he took Samos, giving it to Syloson, Polycrates' brother who years before in Egypt had made him a present of a scarlet cloak while he was a mere guardsman. Darius consolidated his power in Asia by the capture of the revolted province of Babylon through the self-sacrifice of Zopyrus, son of one of the seven conspirators. The vivid story of his devotion is one of the very greatest things in Herodotus.

Persia being thus mistress of all Asia, of Samos and the seaboard, began to dream of subduing Greece itself. But first Darius determined to conquer his non-Greek neighbours. The fourth book describes the attack which Darius himself led against the Scythians in revenge for the twenty-eight years' slavery they inflicted on the Medes. A description of Scythia is relieved by an account of the circumnavigation of Africa by the Phoenicians and the voyage of Scylax down the Indus and along the coast of Africa to Egypt.

The war on the Scyths was dramatic and exciting, both sides acting in the spirit of chivalry. Crossing the Bosporus, Darius advanced through Thrace to the Danube which he spanned with a bridge. The Scyths adopted the favourite Russian plan of retreating into the interior, destroying the crops and hovering round the foe; they further led the Persians into the territories of their own enemies. This process at last wearied Darius; he sent a herald to challenge them to a straight contest or to become his vassals. The reply came that if Darius wished a conflict he had better outrage their ancestral tombs; as for slavery, they acknowledged only Zeus as their master. But the threat of slavery did its work. A detachment was sent to the Danube to induce the Ionian Greeks to strike for freedom by breaking down the bridge they were guarding, thus cutting off Darius' retreat. To the King himself a Scythian herald brought a present of a bird, a mouse, a frog and five arrows, implying that unless his army became one of the creatures it would perish by the arrows. The Scyths adopted guerilla tactics, leaving the Persians no rest by night and offering no battle by day. At last Darius began his retreat. One division of the Scythian horsemen reached the bridge before their foes, again asking the Ionians to destroy it. The Greeks pretended to consent, breaking down the Scythian end of it. Darius at last came to the place; to his dismay he found the bridge demolished. He bade an Egyptian Stentor summon Histiaeus, the Greek commandant, who brought up the fleet and saved the Persian host which retired into Asia.

In 509 a second expedition was dispatched against Barca, a colony of Cyrene. The history of the latter is graphically described, the first king being Battus, the Stammerer, who founded it in obedience to the directions of Apollo. Cyrene was brought under Cambyses' sway by Arcesilaus who had been banished. He misinterpreted an oracle and cruelly killed his enemies in Barca. When he was assassinated in that town his mother Pheretima fled from the metropolis Cyrene to Aryandes, the Persian governor in Egypt. Backed by armed force she besieged Barca which resisted bravely for nine months; at the end of that term an agreement was made that Barca should pay tribute and remain unassailed as long as the ground remained firm on which the treaty was made. But the Persians had undermined the spot, covering planks of wood with a loose layer of earth. Breaking down the planks they rushed in and took the town, Pheretima exacting a horrible vengeance. Yet she herself died soon after, eaten of worms. "Thus," remarks the historian, "do men, by too severe vengeances, draw upon their own heads the divine wrath."

The fifth book begins the concentration on purely Greek history. Darius had left Megabazus in command in Europe, retiring himself to Sardis. In that city he was much struck by the appearance of a Paeonian woman and ordered Megabazus to invade the country. He subdued it and Macedonia in 506-4, but in the process some of his commanders were punished for an insult to Macedonian women, revenge being taken by Alexander, son of King Amyntas; a bride shut the lips of a party sent to discover their fate. In Thrace, Megabazus began to suspect Histiaeus, the Ionian who had saved Darius and in return had been given a strong town, Myrcinus on the River Strymon. The King by a trick drew Histiaeus to Sardis and took him to the Capital, leaving his brother Artaphernes as governor in Sardis. But Histiaeus had been succeeded in Miletus by his nephew Aristagoras; to him in 502 came certain nobles from Naxos, one of the Cyclades isles, begging restoration from banishment. He decided to apply to Artaphernes for Persian help; this the viceroy willingly gave as it would further the Persian progress to the objective, the Greek mainland, across the Aegean in a direct line. The Persian admiral Megabates soon quarrelled with Aristagoras about the command and informed the Naxians of the coming attack. The expedition thus failed. Aristagoras, afraid to face Artaphemes whose treasure he had wasted, decided on raising a revolt of the whole of Ionia; at that very moment a slave came to him from his uncle in Susa with a message tattooed on his head, bidding him rebel.

Aristagoras first applied to Sparta for aid. When arguments failed, he tried to bribe the king Cleomenes. In the room was the King's little daughter Gorgo. Hearing Aristagoras gradually raise his offer from ten to fifty talents, the child said, "Father, depart, or the stranger will corrupt thee". Aristagoras received a better welcome at Athens. That city in 510 had expelled Hippias, the tyrant son of Peisistratus, who appealed to Artaphernes for aid. Hearing this, the Athenians sent an embassy asking the satrap not to assist the exile, but the answer was that if they wished to survive, they must receive their ruler back. Aristagoras therefore found the Athenians in a fit frame of mind to listen. They lent him a fleet of twenty sail and marched with him to Sardis which they captured and burned in 501. The revolt speedily spread over all the Asiatic sea-coast. On hearing of the Athenians for the first time, Darius directed a slave to say to him thrice a day, "Sire, remember the Athenians". He summoned Histiaeus and accused him of complicity in the revolt, but Histiaeus assured him of his loyalty and obtained permission to go to the coast. Meanwhile the Persians took strong action against the rebels, subduing many towns and districts. The book ends with the flight of Aristagoras to Myrcinus and his death in battle against the Thracians in 496.

The next book opens with the famous accusation of Histiaeus by Artaphernes: "Thou hast stitched this boot and Aristagoras hath put it on." Histiaeus in fear fled to his own city Miletus; being disowned there, he for a time maintained a life of privateering, but was eventually captured and crucified by Artaphernes. The Ionian revolt had been narrowed down to Miletus and one or two less important towns. The Greeks assembled a fleet, but a spirit of insubordination manifesting itself they were defeated at sea in the battle of Lade in 495. Next year Miletus fell but was treated with mercy. At Athens the news caused the greatest consternation; a dramatic poet named Phrynichus ventured to stage the disaster; the people wept and fined him a thousand talents, forbidding any similar presentation in future. Stamping out the last embers of revolt in Asia the Persians coasted along Thrace; before their advance the great Athenian Miltiades was compelled to fly from the Dardanelles to his native city. In 492 Mardonius was appointed viceroy of Asia Minor. He reorganised the provincial system and then attempted to double the perilous promontory of Athos, but only a remnant of his forces returned to Asia.

Next year Darius sent to all the Greek cities demanding earth and water, the tokens of submission. The islanders obeyed including Aegina, the deadly foe of Athens. A protest made by the latter led to a war between the two states in which Athens was worsted. Sparta itself had just been torn by an internal dissension between two claimants of the throne, one of whom named Demaratus had been ejected and later fled to the Persian court. The great expedition of 490 sailed straight across the Aegean, commanded by Datis and Artaphernes. Their primary objective was Eretria in Euboea, a city which had assisted the Ionians in their revolt. The town was speedily betrayed, the inhabitants being carried aboard the Persian fleet. Guided by Hippias the armament landed at the bay of Marathon, twenty-five miles from Athens. A vain appeal was sent to Sparta for succours; Athens, supported by the little Boeotian city of Plataea, was left to cope with the might of Persia.

It was fortunate that the Athenians could command the services of Miltiades who had already had some experience of the Persian methods of attack. The details of the great battle that followed depend upon the sole authority of Herodotus among the Greek writers. Many difficulties are caused by his narrative, but it seems certain that Miltiades was in command on the day on which the battle was actually fought. He apparently clung to the hills overlooking the plain and bay of Marathon until the Persian cavalry were unable to act. Seizing the opportunity, he led his men down swiftly to the combat; his centre which had been purposely weakened was thrust back but the two wings speedily proved victorious, then converged to assist the centre, finally driving the foe to the sea where a desperate conflict took place. The Persians succeeded in embarking and promptly sailed round the coast to Athens, but seeing the victors in arms before the town they sailed back to Asia. The Spartan reinforcements which arrived too late for the battle viewed the Persian dead and returned after praising the Athenians.

A slight digression tells the amusing story how the Athenian Hippocleides in his cups lost the hand of the princess of Sicyon because he danced on his head and waved his legs about, shouting that he didn't care. The great victor Miltiades did not long survive his glory. His attempt to reduce the island of Paros, which had sided with Persia, completely failed. Returning to Athens he was condemned and fined, shortly after dying of a mortified thigh.

In the third portion Herodotus gradually rises to his greatest height of descriptive power. Darius resolved on a larger expedition to reduce Greece. He made preparations for three years, then a revolt in Egypt delayed his plans and his career was cut short by death in 485. His successor Xerxes was disinclined to invade Europe, but was overborne by Mardonius his cousin. A canal was dug across the peninsula of Athos, a bridge was built over the Hellespont, and provisions were collected. A detailed account of the component forces is given, special mention being made of Artemisia, Queen of Herodotus' own city, who was to win great glory in the campaign. The army marched over the Hellespont and along the coast, the fleet supporting it; advancing through Thessaly, it reached the pass of Thermopylae, opposite Euboea, in 480.

On the Greek side was division; the Spartans imagined that their duty was to save the Peloponnese only; they were eager to build a wall across the isthmus of Corinth, leaving the rest of Greece to its fate. But Athens had produced another genius named Themistocles. Shortly before the invasion the silver mines at Laureium in Attica had yielded a surplus; he persuaded the city to use it for building a fleet of two hundred sail to be directed against Aegina. When the Athenians got an oracle from Delphi which stated that they would lose their land but be saved by their wooden walls, he interpreted the oracle as referring to the fleet. Under his management the city built more ships. The Council of Greece held at the Isthmus of Corinth decided that an army should defend Thermopylae while the fleet supported it close by at Artemisium. The Persian fleet had been badly battered in a storm as it sailed along the coast of Magnesia, nearly four hundred sail foundering; the remainder reached safe anchorage in the Malian gulf, further progress being impossible till the Greek navy was beaten or retired.

At Thermopylae the advance-guard was composed of Spartans led by Leonidas who determined to defend the narrow pass. A Persian spy brought the news to Xerxes that this small body of warriors were combing their hair. The King sent for Demaratus, the ex-Spartan monarch, who assured him that this was proof that the Spartans intended to fight to the death. After a delay of four days the fight began. The Spartans routed all their opponents including the famous Immortals, the Persian bodyguard. At length a traitor Ephialtes told Xerxes of a path across the mountains by which Leonidas could be taken in the rear. Learning from deserters and fugitives that he had been betrayed, Leonidas dismissed the main body, himself advancing into the open. After winning immortal glory he and his men were destroyed and the way to Greece lay open to the invader.

In three naval engagements off Artemisium the Greek fleet showed its superiority; a detachment of two hundred sail had been sent round the island of Euboea to block up the exit of the channel through which the Greek navy had to retreat, but a storm totally destroyed this force. When the army retreated from Thermopylae the Greek ships were obliged to retire to the Isthmus; in spite of much opposition the Athenians compelled Eurybiades the Spartan admiral to take up his station at Salamis, whither the Persian navy followed. Their army had advanced through Boeotia, attacking Delphi on the way. The story was told how Apollo himself defended his shrine, hurling down rocks on the invaders and sending supernatural figures to discomfit them. Entering Attica the barbarian host captured a deserted

Athens, Xerxes sending the glad news to his subjects in the Persian capital.

The Greeks were with difficulty persuaded not to abandon the sea altogether. Themistocles was bitterly opposed in his naval policy by Adeimantus, the Corinthian; it was only by threatening to leave Greece with their fleet that the Athenians were able to bring the allies to reason. By a stroke of cunning Themistocles forced their hands; a messenger went to Xerxes with news of the Greek intention to retreat; on hearing this the Persians during the night blocked up the passages round Salamis and landed some of their best troops on a little island called Psyttaleia. The news of this encircling movement was brought to the allies by Aristides, a celebrated Athenian who was in exile, and was confirmed by a Tenian ship which deserted from the Persians. Next morning the Greeks sailed down the strait to escape the blockade and soon the famous battle began. Among the brave deeds singled out for special mention none was bolder than that of Artemisia who sank a friend to escape capture. The remainder of the Persian captains had no chance of resisting, being huddled up in a narrow channel. Seeing Artemisia's courage Xerxes remarked that his men had become women, his women men. The rout of the invaders was quickly completed, the chief glory being won by Aegina and Athens; the victory was consummated by the slaughter of the troops on Psyttaleia. The Persian monarch sent tidings of this defeat to his capital and in terror of a revolt in Ionia decided to retreat, leaving Mardonius in command of picked troops. He hurriedly passed along the way he had come, almost disappearing from Herodotus' story.

Mardonius accompanied him to Thessaly and Macedonia; he sent Alexander, King of the latter country, as an envoy to Athens, offering to rebuild the temples and restore all property in exchange for an alliance. Hearing the news the Spartans in fear for themselves sent a counter-embassy. The Athenian reply is one of the great things in historical literature. "It was a base surmise in men like the Spartans who know our mettle. Not all the gold in the world would tempt us to enslave our own countrymen. We have a common brotherhood with all Greeks, a common language, common altars and sacrifices, common nationality; it would be unseemly to betray these. We thank you for your offer to support our ruined families, but we will bear our calamities as we may and will not burden you. Lead out your troops; face the enemy in Boeotia and there give him battle."

The last book relates the consequences of the Athenian reply to Alexander. Mardonius advanced rapidly to Athens, which he captured a second time. The Spartans were busy keeping the feast of Hyacinthia; only an Athenian threat to come to terms with the foe prevailed on them to move. Mardonius soon evacuated Attica, the ground being too stony for cavalry, and encamped near Plataea. The Greeks followed, taking the high ground on Mount Cithaeron. A brave exploit of the Athenian infantry in defeating cavalry heartened the whole army. After eleven days' inaction, Mardonius determined to attack, news of his plan being brought secretly at night to the Athenians by Alexander. The Spartans, afraid of facing the Persians, exchanged places with the Athenians; when this movement was discovered by Mardonius, he sent a challenge to the Spartans to decide the battle by a single conflict between them and his Persian division. Receiving no reply, he let his cavalry loose on the Greeks who began to retire to a place called the Island, where horse could not operate. This action took place during the night. When morning broke the battle began. The Persian wicker shields could not resist their enemies' weapons; the host fled and after Mardonius fell was slaughtered in heaps. The Greek took vengeance on the Thebans who had acted with the Persians, of whom a mere remnant reached Asia under the command of Artabazus.

The victorious Greek fleet had advanced as far as Delos, commanded by Leotychides, a Spartan of royal blood. To them came an embassy from Samos, urging an attack on the Persians encamped on Mycale. It is said that the battle was fought on the same day as that of Plataea and that a divine rumour ran through the Greek army that their brothers had gained the day. In the action at Mycale the Athenians took the palm of valour, bursting the enemy's line and storming his entrenchments. This victory freed Ionia; it remained only to open the Dardanelles. The Spartans returned home, but the Athenians crossed from Abydos in Asia to Sestos, the strongest fortress in the district. The place was starved into surrender; with its capture ends the story of Persia's attempt to destroy European civilisation.

In this great Epic nothing is more obvious than the terror the Greeks felt when they first faced the Persians. The numbers arrayed against them were overwhelming, their despondency was justifiable. It required no little courage from a historian to tell the awkward truth—that Herodotus did tell it is no small testimony to his veracity. Yet only a little experience was needed to convince the Greeks that they were superior on both land and sea. Once the lesson was learned, they never forgot it. Mycale is the proof that they remembered it well. This same consciousness of superiority animated two other Greek armies, one deserted in the middle of Asia Minor, yet led unmolested by Xenophon through a hostile country to the shores of the Black Sea—the other commanded by Alexander the Great who planted Greek civilisation over every part of his conquests, from the coast to the very gates of Persia itself.

Modern history seems to have lost all powers of interesting its readers. It is as dull as political economy; it suspects a stylist, questions the accuracy of its authorities, tends to minimise personal influence on events, specialises on a narrow period, emphasises constitutional development, insists on the "economic interpretation" of an age and at times seems quite unable to manage with skill the vast stores of knowledge on which it draws. To it Herodotus is often a butt for ridicule; his credulity, inability to distinguish true causes, belief in divine influences, love of anecdote and chronological vagueness are serious blemishes. But to us Herodotus is literature; we believe that he himself laughs slyly at some of the anecdotes he has rendered more piquant by a pretended credulity; this quick-witted Greek would find it paid him to assume innocence in order to get his informers (like his critics) to go on talking. Like Froissart, Joinville, de Comines and perhaps even like Macaulay he wishes to write what will charm as well as what will instruct.

Yet as a historian Herodotus is great; he sifts evidence, some of which he mentions only to reject it; the substantial accuracy of his statements has been borne out by inscriptions; in fact, his value to-day is greater than it was last century. If a man's literary bulk is measured by the greatness of his subject, Herodotus cannot be a mean writer. His theme is nothing less than the history of civilisation itself as far as he could record it; his broad sweep of narrative may be taken to represent the wide speculation of a philosophic historian as opposed to the narrower and more intense examination of a short period which is characteristic of the scientific historian. He tells us of the first actual armed conflict between East and West, the never-ending eternally romantic story. As Persia fought Greece, so Rome subdued Carthage, Crusader attacked Saladin, Turkey submerged half Europe, Russia contended with Japan. The atmosphere of Herodotus is the unchanging East of the Bible, inscrutable Egypt, prehistoric Russia, barbarous Thrace, as well as civilised Greece, Africa, India; had he never written, much information would have been irretrievably lost, for example, the account of one of the "Fifteen decisive battles" in history. Let him be judged not as a candidate for some Chair of Ancient History in some modern University, but as the greatest writer of the greatest prose-epic in the greatest literature of antiquity.

Of his inimitable short stories it is difficult to speak with measured praise; it is dangerous to quote them, they are so perfect that a word added or omitted might spoil them. His so-called digressions have always some cogent reason in them; they are his means of including in the panorama a scene essential to its completeness. The narrow type of history writing has been tried for some centuries; all that it seems able to accomplish is to go on narrowing itself until it cannot enjoy for recording or remembering. It is a refreshing experience to move in the broad open regions of history in which Herodotus trod. If it is impossible to combine accurate research with the ecstasy of pure literature, be it so. Herodotus will be read with joy and laughter and sometimes with tears when some of our modern historians have been superseded by persons even duller than themselves.

TRANSLATIONS:

Rawlinson's edition with a version contains essays of the greatest value. It has been the standard for two generations and is not likely to be superseded.

The Loeb Series contains a version by A. D. Godley.

The great annotated edition of the text by R. W. Macan (Oxford) is the result of a lifetime's work. It contains everything necessary to confirm the claims of the historian.

The Great Persian War, by Grundy (London), is valuable.

See Bury, *Ancient Greek Historians* (Macmillan).

THUCYDIDES

History, like an individual's life, is a succession of well-defined periods. Herodotus took as his subject a long cycle of events; the shorter period was first treated by Thucydides who introduced methods which entitle him to be regarded as the first modern historian. Born in Attica in 471 he was a victim of the great plague, was exiled for his failure to check Brasidas at Eion in 424 and spent the rest of his life in collecting materials for his great work. His death took place about 402.

His preface is remarkable as outlining his creed. First he states his subject, the Peloponnesian war of 431-404; he then tests by an appeal to reason the statements in old legends and in Homer, arguing from analogy or from historical survivals in his own time to prove that various important movements were caused or checked by economic influence. He uses his imagination to prove that the importance of an event cannot be decided from the extant remains of its place of origin, for if only the ruins of both Sparta and Athens were left, Sparta would be thought to be insignificant and Athens would appear twice as powerful as she really is. Poetical exaggeration is easy and misleading, and ancient history is difficult to determine by absolute proofs.

"Men accept statements about their own national past from one another without testing them."

"To most men the search for truth implies no effort; they prefer to turn to the first accounts available."

"It was difficult for me to write an exact narrative of the speeches actually made; I have therefore given the words that might have been expected of each speaker, adhering to the broad meaning of what was really uttered. The facts I have not taken from any chance person, nor have I given my own impressions, but have as accurately as possible written a detailed account of what I witnessed myself or heard from others. The discovery of these facts was laborious owing to conflicting statements and confused memories and party favour. Perhaps the unromantic nature of my record will make it uninteresting; but if any person will judge it useful because he desires to consider a clear account of actual facts and of what is likely to recur at some future time, I shall be content. As a compilation it is rather an eternal possession than a prize-essay for a moment."

The essentially modern idea of history writing is here perfectly evident.

Having pointed out the significance of the war, not only to Greece but to the whole of the world, he gives its causes. To him the real root of the trouble was Sparta's fear of Athenian power: the alleged pretexts were different. The rise of Athens is rapidly described, her building of the walls broken down by the Persians, her control of the island-states in a Delian league which eventually became the nucleus of her Empire, her alliance with Megara, a buffer-state between herself and Corinth. This last saved her from fears of a land invasion; when she built for Megara long walls to the sea she incurred the intense anger of Corinth which smouldered for years and at last caused the Peloponnesian conflagration. The reduction of Aegina in 451 compensated for the loss of Boeotia and Egypt. Eventually the Thirty Years' Peace was concluded in 445; Athens gave up Megara, but retained Euboea; her definite policy for the future was concentration on a maritime empire; she controlled nearly all the islands of the Aegean and was mistress of the Saronic gulf, Aegina, "the eyesore of the Peiraeus", having fallen.

But if she was to confine her energies to the sea, it was essential that she should be mistress of all the trade-routes which in ancient history usually ran along the coast. On both east and west she found Corinth in possession; a couple of quarrels with this city ruptured the peace. In the west, Corinth had founded Corcyra (Corfu); this daughter colony quarrelled with her mother and prevailed. In itself Corcyra was of little importance in purely Greek politics, but it happened to possess a large navy and commanded the trade-route to Sicily, whence came the corn supply. When threatened with vengeance by Corinth, she appealed to Athens, where ambassadors from Corinth also appeared. Their arguments are stated in the speeches which are so characteristic of Thucydides. The Athenians after careful consideration decided to conclude a defensive alliance with Corcyra, for they dreaded the acquisition of her navy by Corinth. But circumstances turned this into an offensive alliance, for Corinth attacked and would have won a complete victory at sea but for timely Athenian succour. In the east Athens was even more vitally concerned in trade with the Hellespont, through which her own corn passed. On this route was the powerful Corinthian city Potidaea, situate on the western prong of Chalcidice. It had joined the Athenian confederacy but had secured independence by building strong walls. When the Athenians demanded their destruction and hostages as a guarantee, the town revolted and appealed to the mother-city Corinth. A long and costly siege drained Athens of much revenue and distracted her attention; but worst of all was the final estrangement of the great trade rival whom she had thwarted in Greece itself by occupying Megara, in the west by joining Corcyra, and in the east by attacking Potidsea.

The final and open pretext for war was the exclusion of Megara from all Athenian markets; this step meant the extinction of the town as a trading-centre and was a definite set-back to the economic development of the Peloponnese, of which Corinth and Megara were the natural avenues to northern Greece. The cup was full; Athenian ambition had run its course. The aggrieved states of the Peloponnese were invited to put their case at Sparta; Corinth drew a famous picture of the Athenian character, its restlessness, energy, adaptability and inventiveness. "In the face of such a rival," they added,

> "Sparta hesitates; in comparison Spartan methods are antiquated, but modern principles cannot help prevailing; in a stagnant state conservative institutions are the best, but when men are faced with various difficulties great ingenuity is essential; for that reason Athens through her wide experience has made more innovations."

An Athenian reply failed to convince the allies of her innocence; one of the Spartan Ephors forced the congress to declare that Athens had violated the peace. A second assembly was summoned, at which the Corinthians in an estimate of the Athenian power gave reasons for believing it would eventually be reduced. They further appealed to what has never yet failed to decide in favour of war—race antagonism; the Athenians and her subjects were Ionians, whereas the Peloponnesians were mainly Dorians. The necessary vote for opening hostilities was secured; but first an ultimatum was presented. If Athens desired peace she must rescind the exclusion acts aimed at Megara. At the debate in the Athenian assembly Pericles, the virtual ruler, gave his reason for believing Athens would win; he urged a demand for the withdrawal of Spartan Alien Acts aimed at Athens and her allies and offered arbitration on the alleged grievances.

It is well to repeat the causes of this war: trade rivalry, naval competition, race animosity and desire for predominance. Till these are removed it is useless to expect permanent peace in spite of Leagues or Tribunals or Arbitration Courts. Further, it should be noted that Thucydides takes the utmost care to point out the excellent reasons the most enlightened statesmen had for arriving at contradictory conclusions; the event proved them all wrong without exception. The future had in store at least two events which no human foresight could discover, and these proved the deciding factors in the conflict.

The war began in 431 by a Theban attack on Plataea, the little town just over the Attic frontier which had been allied with Athens for nearly a century and protected her against invasion from the north. This city had long been hated by Thebes as a deserter from her own league; it alone of Boeotian towns had not joined the Persians. Burning with the desire to capture it, a body of Thebans entered the place by night, seizing the chief positions. But in the morning their scanty numbers were apparent; recovering from panic the Plataeans overwhelmed the invaders and massacred them. This open violation of the treaty kindled the war-spirit. Both sides armed, Sparta being more popular as pretending to free Greece from a tyrant. Their last ambassador on leaving Athenian territory said: "This day will be the beginning of mighty woes for Greece".

The Spartans invaded Attica, cutting down the fruit trees and forcing the country folk into the city; the Athenians replied by ravaging parts of Peloponnese and Megara. The funeral of the first Athenian victims of the war was the occasion of a remarkable speech. Pericles in delivering it expounds the Athenian ideal of life.

> "We do not compete with other constitutions, we are rather a pattern for the rest. In our democracy all are equal before the law; each man is promoted to public office not by favour but by merit,

according as he can do the State some service. We love beauty in its simplicity, we love knowledge without losing manliness. Our citizens can administer affairs both private and public; our working classes have an adequate knowledge of politics. To us the most fatal error is the lack of theoretical instruction before we attempt any duty. In a word, I say that Athens is an education for all Greece; individually we can prove ourselves competent to face the most varied forms of human activity with the maximum of grace and adaptability.... We have forced the whole sea and every land to open to our enterprise. Look daily at the material power of the city and love her passionately. Her glory was won by men who did their duty and sacrificed themselves for her. The whole world is the sepulchre of famous men; their memory is not only inscribed on pillars in their own country, it lives unwritten in the hearts of men in alien lands."

At the beginning of the next year a calamity which no statesman could have foreseen overtook Athens. A mysterious plague of the greatest malignity scourged the city, the mortality being multiplied among the crowds of refugees. The city's strength was seriously impaired, public and private morality were undermined, inasmuch as none knew how long he had to live. Discouraged by it and by the invasions the Athenians sent a fruitless embassy to Sparta and tinned in fury on Pericles. He made a splendid defence of his policy and gave them heart to continue the struggle; he pointed out that it was better to lose their property and save the State than save their property and lose the State; their fleet opened to them the world of waters over which they could range as absolute masters. Soon afterwards he died, surviving the opening of the war only two years and a half; his character and abilities received due acknowledgment from Thucydides.

At this point Sparta decided to destroy Plataea, the Athenian outpost in Boeotia. A very brilliant description of the siege and counter-operations reveals very clearly the Spartan inability to attack walled towns and explains their objection to fortified friends. Leaving the town guarded they retired for a time, to complete the work later. The war began to spread beyond the Peloponnese to the north of the Corinthian gulf, the control of which was important to both sides. The Acarnanians were attacked by Sparta and appealed to the Athenian admiral Phormio. Two naval actions in the gulf revealed the astonishing superiority of the Athenian navy on the high seas. Threatened in her corn supply in the west, Sparta began to intrigue with the outlying kingdoms on the north-east, the "Thraceward parts" on the trade-route being the objective.

A spirit of revolt against Athenian rule appeared in Lesbos, which seceded in 428. The chief town in this non-Ionic island was Mytilene, which sent ambassadors to Sparta. Their speech clearly explains how the Athenians were able to keep their hold on their policy; her policy (like that of Rome) was to divide the allies by carefully grading their privileges, playing off the weak against the stronger. The Spartans proved unable to help and the Athenians easily blockaded the city, capturing it early in 427. In their anger they at first decided to slay all the inhabitants, but a better feeling led to a reconsideration next day. In the Assembly two great speeches were delivered. Pericles had been succeeded by Cleon, to whom Thucydides seems to have been a little unjust. He opened his speech with the famous remark that a democracy cannot govern an Empire; it is liable to sudden fits of passion which make a consistent policy impossible. He himself never changed his plans, but his audience were different.

> "You are all eyes for speeches, all ears for deeds; you judge of the possibility of a project from good speeches; accomplished facts you believe not because you see them but because you hear them from smart critics. You are easily duped by some novel plan, but you refuse to adhere to what has been proved sound. You are slaves to every new oddity and have nothing but contempt for what is familiar. Every one of you would like to be a good speaker, failing that, to rival your orators in cleverness. You are as quick to guess what is coming in a speech as you are slow at foreseeing its consequences. In a word, you live in some non-real world."

He pleaded for the rigorous application of the extreme penalty already voted.

He was opposed by Diodotus, who appealed to the same principle as Cleon did expediency.

> "No penalty will deter men, not even the death penalty. Men have run through the whole catalogue of deterrents in the hope of securing themselves against outrage, yet offences still are common. Human nature is driven by some uncontrollable master passion which tempts it to danger. Hope and Desire are everywhere and are most mischievous, for they are invisible. Fortune too is as powerful a means of exciting men. At tunes she stands unexpectedly at their side and leads them to take risks with too slender resources. Most of all she tempts cities, for they are contending for the greatest prizes, liberty or domination. It is absolutely childish then to imagine that when human nature is bent on performing a thing it will be deterred by law or any other force. If revolting cities are quite sure that no mercy will be shown, they will fight to the last, bequeathing the victors only smoking ruins. It would be more expedient to be merciful and thus save the expenses of a long siege."

This saner view prevailed. The doctrine of a "ruling passion" is a remarkable contribution to Greek political thought, the abstract personifications reading like the work of a poet or philosopher. An exciting race against time is most graphically described. After great exertions the ship bearing the reprieve arrived just in time to save Mytilene. This act of mercy stands in sinister contrast with the treatment the unhappy Plataeans received from the liberators of Greece. The citizens were captured, Athens having strangely abandoned them in spite of her promise to help. They were allowed to commemorate their services to Greece, appealing in a most moving speech to the sacred ground of their city, the scene of the immortal battle. All was in vain. The Thebans accused them of flat treachery to Boeotia, securing their condemnation. Corcyra similarly proved unprofitable; it was afflicted by fratricidal dissensions which coloured one of Thucydides' darkest pictures. As the war went on it became clearer that it was a struggle between two rival political creeds, democracy and oligarchy. To the partisans all other ties were of little value, whether of blood or race or religion; only frenzied boldness and unquestioning obedience to a party organisation were of any consequence. This wretched spirit of feud was destined in the long run to spell the doom of the Greek cities. In 427 the first mention was made of the will-of-the-wisp which in time led Athens to her ruin. In her anxiety to intercept the Peloponnesian corn she supported Leontini against Syracuse, the leading Sicilian state. In Acarnania the capable general Demosthenes after a series of movements not quite fruitless succeeded in bringing peace to the jarring mountain tribes.

In 425 a most important event took place. As an Athenian squadron was proceeding to Sicily it was forced to put in at Pylos, where many centuries later Greece won a famous victory over the Turks. Demosthenes, though he had no official command, persuaded his comrades to fortify the place as a base from which to harry Spartan territory. It was situated in the country which had once belonged to the Messenians who for generations had been held down by the Spartan oligarchs. Deserters soon began to stream in; the gravity of the situation was recognised by the Spartan government who landed more than four hundred of their best troops on the island of Sphacteria at the entrance to the bay. These were speedily isolated by the Athenian navy; and news of the event filled all Greece with excitement. A heated discussion took place at Athens, where Cleon accused Nicias, the commander-in-chief, of slackness in not capturing the blockaded force. Spartan overtures for a peace on condition of the return of the isolated men proved vain; after a lively altercation with Nicias Cleon made a promise to capture the Spartans within thirty days, a feat which he accomplished with the aid of Demosthenes. Nearly three hundred were found to prefer surrender to death; these were conveyed to Athens and were an invaluable asset for bargaining a future peace.

A further success was the capture of Nisaea, the port of Megara, in 424, but an attempt to propagate democracy in Boeotia ended in a severe defeat at Delium; the fate of Plataea was a bad advertisement in an oligarchically governed district. Worse was to follow. Brasidas, a Spartan who had greatly distinguished himself at Pylos, passed through Thessaly with a volunteer force, reaching Thrace and capturing some important towns; the loss of one of these, Eion, caused the exile of the historian, who was too late to save it. In 423 a truce for one year was arranged between the combatants, but Brasidas ignored it, sowing disaffection among the Athenian allies. His personal charm gave them a good impression of the Spartan character and his offer of liberty was too attractive to be resisted. His success was partly due to a deliberate misrepresentation of the Athenian power which proved greater than it seemed to be. The two real obstacles to peace were Brasidas and Cleon; at Amphipolis they met in battle; a rash movement gave the Spartan an opportunity for an attack. He fell in action, but the town was saved. Cleon was killed in the same battle and the path to peace was clear. The truce for one year developed into a regular settlement in 421, Nicias being responsible for its negotiation in Athens. The chief clause provided that Athens should recover Amphipolis in exchange for the Spartan captives.

The members of the Peloponnesian league considered themselves betrayed by this treaty, for their hated rival Athens had not been humbled. Corinth was the ringleader in raising disaffection. She determined to create a new league, including Argos, the inveterate foe of Sparta. This state had stood aloof from the war, nursing her strength and biding her time for revenge. When Sparta failed to restore Amphipolis, the war party at Athens, led by Alcibiades, formed an alliance with Argos to reduce Sparta; but this policy alienated Corinth, who refused to act with her trade rival. An Argive attack on Arcadia ended in the fierce battle of Mantinea in 418, in which Sparta won a complete victory. Argos was forced to come to terms, the new league was dissolved and Athens was once more confronted by her combined enemies, her diplomacy a failure and her trump-card, the Sphacterian prisoners, lost.

Next year she was guilty of an act of sheer outrage. Her fleet descended on the island of Melos, which had remained neutral, though its inhabitants were colonists from the Spartan mainland close by. Nowhere does the dramatic nature of Thucydides' work stand more clearly revealed than in his account of this incident. He represents the Athenian and Melian leaders as arguing the merits of the case in a regular dialogue, essentially a dramatic device. The Athenian doctrine of Might and Expediency is unblushingly preached and acted upon, in spite of Melian protests; the island was captured, its population being slain or enslaved. Such an act is a fitting prelude to the great disaster which forms the next act of Thucydides' drama.

In 416 Athens proceeded to develop her design of subjugating Sicily. Segesta was at feud with Selinus; as the latter city applied to Syracuse for aid, the former bethought her of her ancient alliance with Athens. Next year the Sicilian ambassadors arrived with tales of unlimited wealth to finance an expedition. Nicias, the leader of the peace party, vainly counselled the Assembly to refrain; he was overborne by Alcibiades, whose ambition it was to reduce not only Sicily but Carthage also. When the expedition was about to sail most of the statues of Hermes in the city were desecrated in one night. Alcibiades, appointed to the command with Nicias and Lamachus, was suspected of the outrage, but was allowed to sail. The fleet left the city with all the pomp and ceremony of prayer and ritual, after which it showed its high spirits in racing as far as Aegina.

In Sicily itself Hermocrates, the great Syracusan patriot, repeatedly warned his countrymen of the coming storm, advising them to sink all feuds in resistance to the common enemy. He was opposed by Athenagoras, a democrat who, true to his principles, suspected the story as part of a militarist plot to overthrow the constitution. His speech is the most violent in Thucydides, but contains a passage of much value.

> "The name of the whole is People, that of a part is Oligarchy; the rich are the best guardians of wealth, the educated class

can make the wisest decisions, the majority are the best judges of speeches. All these classes in a democracy have equal power both individually and collectively. But oligarchy shares the dangers with the many, while it does not merely usurp the material benefits, rather it appropriates and keeps them all."

The Athenians received a cold welcome wherever they went. At Catana they found their state vessel waiting to convey Alcibiades home to stand his trial; he effected his escape on the homeward voyage, crossing to the Peloponnese. The great armament instead of thrusting at Syracuse wasted its time and efficiency on side-issues, mainly owing to the cold leadership of Nicias. This valuable respite was used to the full by Hermocrates, who at a congress held at Camarina was insistent on the racial character of the struggle between themselves who were Dorians and the Ionians from Athens. This national antipathy contributed greatly to the final decision of the conflict.

Passing to Sparta, Alcibiades deliberately betrayed his country. His speech is of the utmost importance.

His view of democracy is contemptuous. "Nothing new can be said of what is an admitted folly." He then outlined the Athenian ambition; it was to subdue Carthage and Sicily, bring over hosts of warlike barbarians, surround and reduce the Peloponnese and then rule the whole Greek-speaking world. He advised his hearers to aid Sicilian incapacity by sending a Spartan commander; above all, he counselled the occupation of Deceleia, a town in Attica just short of the border, through which the corn supply was conveyed to the capital; this would lead to the capture of the silver-mines at Laureium and to the decrease of the Athenian revenues. He concluded with an attempt to justify his own treachery, remarking that when a man was exiled, he must use all means to secure a return.

The Spartans had for some time been anxious to open hostilities; an act of Athenian aggression gave them an opportunity. Meanwhile in Sicily Lamachus had perished in attacking a Syracusan cross-wall. Left in sole command, Nicias remained inactive, while Gylippus, despatched from Sparta, arrived in Syracuse just in time to prevent it from capitulating. The seventh book is the record of continued Athenian disasters. Little by little Gylippus developed the Syracusan resources. First he made it impossible for the Athenians to circumvallate the city; then he captured the naval stores of the enemy, forcing them to encamp in unhealthy ground. Nicias had begged the home government to relieve him of command owing to illness. Believing in the lucky star of the man who had taken Nissea they retained him, sending out a second great fleet under Demosthenes. The latter at once saw the key to the whole situation. The Syracusan cross-wall which Nicias had failed to render impassable must be captured at all costs. A night attack nearly succeeded, but ended in total defeat. Demosthenes immediately advised retreat; but Nicias obstinately refused to leave. In the meantime the Syracusans closed the mouth of their harbour with a strong boom, penning up the Athenian fleet. The famous story of the attempt to destroy it calls out all the author's powers of description. He draws attention to the narrow space in which the action was fought. As long as the Athenians could operate in open water they were invincible; but the Syracusans not only forced them to fight in a confined harbour, they strengthened the prows of their vessels, enabling them to smash the thinner Athenian craft in a direct charge. The whole Athenian army went down to the edge of the water to watch the engagement which was to settle their fate. Their excitement was pitiable, for they swayed to and fro in mental agony, calling to their friends to break the boom and save them. After a brave struggle, the invaders were routed and driven to the land by the victorious Syracusans.

Retreat by land was the only escape. A strategem planned by Hermocrates and Nicias' superstitious terrors delayed the departure long enough to enable the Syracusans to secure the passes in the interior. When the army moved away the scene was one of shame and agony; the sick vainly pleaded with their comrades to save them; the whole force contrasted the proud hopes of their coming with their humiliating end and refused to be comforted by Nicias, whose courage shone brightest in this hour of defeat. Demosthenes' force was isolated and was quickly captured; Nicias' men with great difficulty reached the River Assinarus, parched with thirst. Forgetting all about their foes, they rushed to the water and fought among themselves for it though it ran red with their own blood. At last the army capitulated and was carried back to Syracuse. Thrown into the public quarries, the poor wretches remained there for ten weeks, scorched by day, frost-bitten by night. The survivors were sold into slavery.

> "This was the greatest achievement in the war and, I think, in Greek history the most creditable to the victors, the most lamentable to the vanquished. In every way they were utterly defeated; their sufferings were mighty; they were destroyed hopelessly; ships, men, everything perished, few only returning from the great host."

So ends the most heartrending story in Greek history, told with absolute fidelity by a son of Athens and a former general of her army.

The last book is remarkable for the absence of speeches; it is a record of the continued intrigues which followed the Sicilian disaster. Upheavals in Asia Minor brought into the swirl of plots Tissaphernes, the Persian satrap, anxious to recover control of Ionia hitherto saved by Athenian power. In 412 the Athenian subjects began to revolt, seventeen defections being recorded in all. At Samos a most important movement began; the democrats rose against their nobles, being guaranteed independence by Athens. Soon they made overtures to Alcibiades who was acting with the Spartan fleet; he promised to detach Tissaphernes from Sparta if Samos eschewed democracy, a creed odious to the Persian monarchy. The Samians sent a delegation to Athens headed by Pisander, who boldly proposed Alcibiades' return, the dissolution of the democracy in Samos and alliance with Tissaphernes. These proposals were rejected, but the democracy at Athens was not destined to last much longer, power being usurped by the famous Four Hundred in 411. The Samian democracy eventually appointed Alcibiades general, while in Athens the extremists were anxious to come to terms with Sparta. This movement split the Four Hundred, the constitution being changed to that of the Five Thousand, a blend of democracy and oligarchy which won Thucydides' admiration; the history concludes with the victory of the Athenians in the naval action at Cynossema in 410.

The defects of Thucydides are evident; his style is harsh, obscure and crabbed; it is sometimes said that he seems wiser than he really is mainly because his language is difficult; that if his thoughts were translated into easier prose our impressions of his greatness would be much modified. Yet it is to be remembered that he, like Lucretius, had to create his own vocabulary. It is a remarkable fact that prose has been far more difficult to invent than poetry, for precision is essential to it as the language of reasoning rather than of feeling. Instead of finding fault with a medium which was necessarily imperfect because it was an innovation we should be thankful for what it has actually accomplished. It is not always obscure; at times, when "the lion laughed" as an old commentator says, he is almost unmatched in pure narrative, notably in his rapid summary of the Athenian rise to power in the first book and in the immortal Syracusan tragedy of the seventh.

His merits are many and great; his conciseness, repression of personal feeling, love of accuracy, careful research, unwillingness to praise overmuch and his total absence of preconceived opinion testify to an honesty of outlook rare in classical historians. Because he feels certain of his detachment of view, he quite confidently undertakes what few would have faced, the writing of contemporary history. Nowadays historians do not trust themselves; we may expect a faithful account of our Great War some fifty years hence, if ever. Not so Thucydides; he claims that his work will be a treasure for all time; had any other written these words we should have dismissed them as an idle boast.

For he is the first man to respect history. It was not a plaything; it was worthy of being elevated to the rank of a science. As such, its events must have some deep causes behind them, worth discovering not only in themselves as keys to one particular period, but as possible explanations of similar events in distant ages. Accordingly, he deemed it necessary to study first of all our human nature, its varied motives, mostly of questionable morality, next he studied international ethics, based frankly on expediency. The results of these researches he has embodied (with one or two exceptions) in his famous speeches. He surveyed the ground on which battles were fought; he examined inscriptions, copying them with scrupulous care; he criticised ancient history and contemporary versions of famous events, many of which he found to be untrue. Further, his anxiety to discover the real sources of certain policies made it necessary for him to write an account of seemingly purposeless action in wilder or even barbarous regions such as Arcadia, Ambracia, Macedonia; in consequence his work embraces the whole of the Greek world, as he said it would in his famous preface.

As an artist, he is not without his merits. The dramatic nature of his plan has been frequently pointed out; to him the main plot is the destruction not of Athens, but of the Periclean democracy, the overthrow thereof being due to a conflict with another like it; hence the marked change in the last book, in which the main dramatic interest has waned. This dramatic form has, however, defeated its own objects sometimes, for all the Thucydidean fishes talk like Thucydidean whales.

To us he is indispensable. We are a maritime power, ruling a maritime empire, our potential enemies being military nations. He has warned us that democracy cannot govern an empire. Perhaps our type of this creed is not so full of the lust for domination and aggrandisement as was that of Athens; it may be suspected that we are virtuous mainly because we have all we need and are not likely to be tempted overmuch. But there is the other and more subtle danger. The enemies within the state betrayed Deceleia which safeguarded the food-supply. We have many Deceleias, situate along the great trade-routes and needing protection. Once these are betrayed we shall not hold out as Athens did for nearly ten years; ten weeks at the outside ought to see our people starving and beaten, fit for nothing but the payment of indemnities to the power which relieves us of our inheritance.

TRANSLATIONS:—

The earliest is by Hobbes, the best is by Jowett, Oxford. Though somewhat free, it renders with vigour the ideas of the original text.

The Loeb Series has a version by Smith.

Thucydides Mythistoricus, Cornford (Arnold), is an adverse criticism of the historian; it points out the inaccuracies which may be detected in his work.

Clio Enthroned by W. R. M. Lamb, Cambridge, should be read in conjunction with the above. The author adopts the traditional estimate of Thucydides.

See also Bury, *Ancient Greek Historians,* as above.

PLATO

Shortly after the outbreak of the Peloponnesian war Plato was born, probably in 427. During the eighty years of his life he travelled to Sicily at least twice, founded the Academy at Athens and saw the beginning of the end of the Greek freedom. He represents the reflective spirit in a nation which seems to appear when its development is well advanced. After the madness of a long war the Athenians, stripped of their Empire for a time, sought a new outlet for their restless energies and started to conquer a more permanent kingdom, that of scientific speculation about the highest faculties of the human mind.

The death of Socrates in 399 disgusted Plato; democracy apparently was as intolerant as any other form of political creed. His writings are in a sense a vindication of the honesty of his master, although the picture he draws of him is not so true to life as that of Xenophon. The dialogues fall into two well-marked classes; in the earlier the method and inspiration is definitely Socratic, but in the later Socrates is a mere peg on which Plato hung his own system. In itself the dialogue form was no new thing; Plato adopted it and made it a thing of life and dramatic power, his style being the most finished example of exalted prose in Greek literature. The order in which the dialogues were written is a thorny problem; there is good reason for believing that Plato constantly revised some of them, removing the inconsistencies which were inevitable while he was feeling his way to the final form which his speculations assumed. It is perhaps best to give an outline of a series which exhibits some regular order of thought.

It is sometimes thought that Philosophy has no direct bearing on practical questions. A review of the *Crito* may dispel this illusion. In it Socrates refuses to be tempted by his young friend Crito who offers to secure his escape from prison and provide him a home among his own friends. The question is whether one ought to follow the opinions of the majority on matters of justice or injustice, or those of the one man who has expert knowledge, and of Truth. The laws of Athens have put Socrates in prison; they would say;

> "by this act you intend to perpetrate your purpose to destroy us and the city as far as one man can do so. Can any city survive and not be overturned in which legal decisions have no force, but are rendered null by private persons and destroyed?"

Socrates had by his long residence of seventy years declared his satisfaction with the Athenian legal system. The laws had enabled him to live in security; more, he could have taken advantage of legal protection in his trial, and if he had been dissatisfied could have gone away to some other city. What sort of a figure would he make if he escaped? Wherever he went he would be considered a destroyer of law; his practice would belie his creed; finally, the Laws say,

> "if you wish to live in disgrace, after going back on your contract and agreement with us, we will be angry with you while you are alive and in death our Brother Laws will give you a cold welcome; they will know that you have done your best to destroy our authority."

Sound and concrete teaching like this is always necessary, but is hardly likely to be popular. The doctrine of disobedience is everywhere preached in a democracy; violation of contracts is a normal practice and law-breakers have been known to be publicly feasted by the very members of our legislative body.

A different lesson is found in the *Euthyphro*. After wishing Socrates success in his coming trial, Euthyphro informs him that he is going to prosecute his father for manslaughter, assuring him that it would be piety to do so. Socrates asks for a definition of piety. Euthyphro attempts five—"to act as Zeus did to his father"; "what the gods love"; "what all the gods love"; "a part of righteousness, relating to the care of the gods"; "the saying and doing of what the gods approve in prayer and sacrifice". Each of these proves inadequate; Euthyphro complains of the disconcerting Socratic method as follows:

> "Well, I do not know how to express my thoughts. Every one of our suggestions always seem to have legs, refusing to stand still where we may fix it down. Nor have I put into them this spirit of moving and shifting, but you, a second Daedalus."

It is noticeable that no definite result comes from this dialogue; Plato was within his rights in refusing to answer the main question. Philosophy does not pretend to settle every inquiry; her business is to see that a question is raised. Even when an answer is available, she cannot always give it, for she demands an utter abandonment of all prepossessions in those to whom she talks—otherwise there will be no free passage for her teaching. Though refuted, Euthyphro still retained his first opinions, for his first and last definitions are similar in idea. To such a person argument is mere waste of time.

An admirable illustration of Plato's lightness of touch is found in the *Laches*. The dialogue begins with a discussion about the education of the young sons of Lysimachus and Melesias. Soon the question is raised "What is courage?" Nicias warns Laches about Socrates; the latter has a trick of making men review their lives; his practice is good, for it teaches men their faults in time; old age does not always bring wisdom automatically. Laches first defines courage as the faculty which makes men keep the ranks in war; when this proves inadequate, he defines it as a stoutness of spirit. Nicias is called in; he defines it as "knowledge of terrors and confidence in war"; he is soon compelled to add "and knowledge of all good and evil in every form"—in a word, courage is all virtue combined. The dialogue concludes that it is not young boys but grown men of all ages who need a careful education. This spirited little piece is full of dramatic vigour—the remarks of Laches and Nicias about each other as they are repeatedly confuted are most human and diverting.

Literary criticism is the subject of the *Ion*. Coming from Ephesus, Ion claimed to be the best professional reciter of Homer in all Greece. Acknowledging that Homer made him all fire, while other poets left him cold, he is made to admit that his knowledge of poetry is not scientific; otherwise he would have been able to discuss all poetry, for it is one. Socrates then makes the famous comparison between a poet and a magnet; both attract an endless chain, and both contain some divine power which masters them. Ecstasy, enthusiasm, madness are the best descriptions of poetic power. Even as a professional reciter Ion admits the necessity of the power of working on men.

> "When I am on the platform I look on my audience weeping and looking warlike and dazed at my words. I must pay attention to them; if I let them sit down weeping, I myself shall laugh when I receive my fee, but if they laugh I myself shall weep when I get nothing."

Homer is the subject of the *Hippias Minor*. At Olympia Hippias once said that every single thing that he was wearing was his own handiwork. He was a most inventive person—one of his triumphs being an art of memory. In this dialogue he prefers the Iliad to the Odyssey because Achilles was called "excellent" and Odysseus "versatile". Socrates soon proves to him that Achilles was false too, as he did not always keep his word. He reminds Hippias that he never wastes time over the brainless, though he listens carefully to every man. In fact, his cross-examination is a compliment. He never thinks the knowledge he gains is his own discovery, but is grateful to any who can teach him. He believes that unwitting deceivers are more culpable than deliberate tricksters. Hippias finds it impossible to agree with him, whereupon Socrates says that things are for ever baffling him by their changeability; it is pardonable that unlearned men like himself should err; when really wise people like Hippias wander in thought, it is monstrous that they are unable to settle the doubts of all who appeal to them.

Channides, the young boy after whom the dialogue was named, was the cousin and ward of Critias, the infamous leader of the Thirty Tyrants. On being introduced to him Socrates starts the discussion "What is self-control?" The lad makes three attempts to answer; seeing his confusion, Critias steps in, "angry with the boy, like a poet angry with an actor who has murdered his poems". But he is not more successful; his three definitions are proved wanting.

> "Like men who, seeing others yawn, themselves yawn, he too was in perplexity. But because he had a great reputation, he was put to shame before the audience and refused to admit his inability to define the word."

The dialogue gives no definite answer to the discussion. It is a vivid piece of writing; the contrast between the young lad and the elder cousin whose pet phrases he copies is very striking.

In the *Lysis* the characters and the conclusion are similar. Lysis is a young lad admired by Hippothales. The first portion of the dialogue consists of a conversation between Lysis and Socrates; the latter recommends the admirer to avoid foolish converse. On the entry of Lysis' friend Menexenus, Socrates starts the question "What is friendship?" It appears that friendship cannot exist between two good or two evil persons, but only between a good man and one who is neither good nor bad, exactly as the philosopher is neither wise nor ignorant, yet he loves knowledge. Still this is not satisfactory; up conclusion being reached, Socrates winds up with a characteristic remark; they think they are friends, yet cannot say what friendship is. This dialogue was carefully read by Aristotle before he gave his famous description in the Ethics: "A friend is a second self". Perhaps Socrates avoided a definite answer because he did not wish to be too serious with these sunny children.

The *Euthydemus* is an amusing study of the danger which follows upon the use of keen instruments by the unscrupulous. Euthydemus and his brother Dionysodorus are two sophists by trade to whom words mean nothing at all; truth and falsehood are identical, contradiction being an impossibility. As language is meaningless, Socrates himself is quickly reduced to impotence, recovering with difficulty. Plato was no doubt satirising the misuse of the new philosophy which was becoming so popular with young men. When nothing means anything, laughter is the only human language left. The *Cratylus* is a similarly conceived diversion. Most of it is occupied with fanciful derivations and linguistic discussions of all kinds. It is difficult to say how far Plato is serious. Perhaps the feats of Euthydemus in stripping words of all meaning urged him to some constructive work — for Plato's system is essentially destructive first, then constructive. At any rate, he does insist on the necessity for determining a word's meaning by its derivation, and points out that a language is the possession of a whole people.

In the *Protagoras* Socrates while a young man is represented as meeting a friend Hippocrates, who was on his way to Protagoras, a sophist from Abdera who had just arrived at Athens. Socrates shows first that his friend has no idea of the seriousness of his action in applying for instruction to a sophist whose definition he is unable to give.

> "If your body had been in a critical condition you would have asked the advice of your friends and deliberated many days before choosing your doctor. But about your mind, on which depends your weal or woe according as it is evil or good, you never asked the advice of father or friend whether you ought to apply to this newly-arrived stranger. Hearing last night that he was here, you go to him to-day, ready to spend your own and your friends' money, convinced that you ought to become a disciple of a man you neither know nor have talked with."

They proceed to the house of Callias, where they find Protagoras surrounded by strangers from every city who listened spell-bound to his voice.

Protagoras readily promises that Hippocrates would be taught his system which offers "good counsel about his private affairs and power to transact and discuss political matters". Socrates' belief that politics cannot be taught provokes one of the long speeches to which Plato strongly objected because a fundamental fallacy could not be refuted at the outset, vitiating the whole of the subsequent argument. Protagoras recounted a myth, proving that shame and justice were given to every man; these are the basis of politics. Further, cities punish criminals, implying that men can learn politics, while virtue is taught by parents and tutors and the State. Socrates asks whether virtue is one or many. Protagoras replies that there are five main virtues, knowledge, justice, courage, temperance and piety, all distinct. A long rambling speech causes Socrates to protest; his method is the short one of question and answer. By using some very questionable reasoning he proves that all these five virtues are identical. Accordingly, if virtue is one it can be taught, not however, by a sophist or the State, but by a philosopher, for virtue is knowledge.

This conclusion is thoroughly in harmony with Socrates' system. Yet it is probably false. Virtue is not mere knowledge, nor vice ignorance. If they were, they would be intellectual qualities. They are rather moral attributes; experience soon proves that many enlightened persons are vicious and many ignorant people virtuous. The value of this dialogue is its insistence upon the unity of virtue. A good man is not a bundle of separate excellences; he is a whole. Possessing one virtue he potentially has them all.

The *Gorgias* is a refutation of three distinct and popular notions. Gorgias of Leontini used to invite young men to ask him questions, none of whom ever put to him a query absolutely new. It soon appears that he is quite unable to define Rhetoric, the art by which he lived. Socrates said it was a minister of persuasion, that it in the long run concerned itself with mere Opinion, which might be true or false, and could not claim scientific Knowledge. Further, it implied some morality in its devotees, for it dealt with what was just or unjust. Polus, a young and ardent sophist, was compelled to assent to two very famous doctrines, first that it is worse to do evil than to experience it, second, that to avoid punishment was the worst thing for an offender. But a more formidable adversary remained, one Callicles, the most shameless and unscrupulous figure perhaps in Plato's work. His creed is a flat denial of all authority, moral or intellectual. It teaches that Law is not natural, but conventional; that only a slave puts up with a wrong, and only weak men seek legal protection. Philosophy is fit only for youths, for philosophers are not men of the world. Natural life is unlimited self-indulgence and public opinion is the creation of those who are too poor to give rein to their appetites; the good is pleasure and infinite self-satisfaction is the ideal. Socrates in reply points out the difference between the kinds of pleasures, insists on the importance of Scientific knowledge of everything, and proves that order is requisite everywhere—its visible effects in the soul being Justice and Wisdom, not Riot. To prevent injustice some art is needed to make the subject as like as possible to the ruler; the type of life a man leads is far more important than length of days. The demagogue who like Callicles has no credentials makes the people morally worse, especially as they are unable to distinguish quacks from wise men. Nor need philosophers trouble much about men's opinions, for a mob always blames the physician who wishes to save it. A delightful piece of irony follows, in which Socrates twits Callicles for accusing his pupils of acting with injustice, the very quality he instils into them. Callicles, though refuted, advises Socrates to fawn on the city, for he is certain to be condemned sooner or later; the latter, however, does not fear death after living righteously.

Most men have held doctrines similar to those refuted here. There is an idea abroad that what is "natural" must be intrinsically good, if not godlike. But it is quite clear that "Nature" is a vague term meaning little or nothing—it is higher or lower and natural in both forms. Those who wish to know the lengths of impudence to which belief in the sacredness of "Nature" can bring human beings might do worse than read the *Gorgias*.

Plato's dramatic power and fertility of invention are displayed fully in the *Symposium*. Agathon had won the tragic prize and invited many friends to a wine-party. After a slight introduction a proposition was carried that all should speak in praise of Love. First a youth Phaedrus describes the antiquity of love and gives instances of the attachments between the sexes. Pausanias draws the famous distinction between the Heavenly and the Vulgar Aphrodite; the true test of love is its permanence. A doctor, Eryximachus, raises the tone of the discussion still further. To him Love is the foundation of Medicine, Music, Astronomy and Augury. Aristophanes tells a fable of the sexes in true comic style, making each of them run about seeking its other half. Agathon colours his account with a touch of tragic diction. At last it is Socrates' turn. He tells what he heard from a priestess called Diotima. Love is the son of Fulness and Want; he is the intermediary between gods and men, is active, not passive; he is desire for continuous possession of excellent things and for beautiful creation which means immortality, for all men desire perpetual fame which can come only through the science of the Beautiful. In contemplation and mystical union with the Divine the soul finds its true destiny, satisfying itself in perfect love.

At this moment Alcibiades arrives from another feast in a state of high intoxication. He gives a most marvellous account of Socrates' influence over him and likens him in a famous passage to an ugly little statue which when opened is all gold within. At the end of the dialogue one of the company tells how Socrates compelled Aristophanes and Agathon to admit that it was one and the same man's business to understand and write both tragedy and comedy—a doctrine which has been practised only in modern drama.

In this dialogue we first seem to catch the voice of Plato himself as distinct from that of Socrates. The latter was undoubtedly most keenly interested in the more human process of questioning and refuting, his object being the workmanlike creation of exact definitions. But Plato was of a different mould; his was the soaring spirit which felt its true home to be the supra-sensible world of Divine Beauty, Immortality, Absolute Truth and Existence. Starting with the fleshly conception of Love natural to a young man, he leads us step by step towards the great conclusion that Love is nothing less than an identification of the self with the thing loved. No man can do his work if he is not interested in it; he will hate it as his taskmaster. But when an object of pursuit enthrals him it will intoxicate him, will not leave him at peace till he joins his very soul with it in union indissoluble. This direct communication of Mind with the object of worship is Mysticism. It is the very core of the highest form of religious life; it purifies, ennobles, and above all it inspires. To the mystic the great prophet is the Athenian Plato, whose doctrine is that of the Christian "God is love" converted into "Love is God". It is not entirely fanciful to suggest that Plato, in saying farewell to the definitely Socratic type of philosophy, gave his master as his parting gift the greatest of all tributes, a dialogue which is really the "praise of Socrates".

The intoxication of Plato's thought is evident in the *Phaedrus*. This splendid dialogue marks even more clearly the character of the new wine which was to be poured into the Socratic bottles. Phaedrus and Socrates recline in a spot of romantic beauty along the bank of the Ilissus. Phaedrus reads a paradoxical speech supposed to be written by Lysias, the famous orator, on Love; Socrates replies in a speech quite as unreal, praising as Lysias did him who does not love. But soon he recants—his real creed being the opposite. Frenzy is his subject—the ecstasy of prophecy, mysticism, poetry and the soul. This last is like a charioteer driving a pair of horses, one white, the other black. It soars upwards to the region of pure beauty, wisdom and goodness; but sometimes the white horse, the spirited quality of human nature, is pulled down by the black, which is sensual desire, so that the charioteer, Reason, cannot get a full vision of the ideal world beyond all heavens. Those souls which have partially seen the truth but have been dragged down by the black steed become, according to the amount of Beauty they have seen, philosophers, kings, economists, gymnasts, mystics, poets, journeymen, sophists or tyrants. The vision once seen is never quite forgotten, for it can be recovered by reminiscence, so that by exercise each man can recall some of its glories.

The dialogue then passes to a discussion of good and bad writing and speaking. The truth is the sole criterion of value, and this can be obtained only by definition; next there must be orderly arrangement, a beginning, a middle and an end. In rhetoric it is absolutely essential for a man to study human nature first; he cannot hope to persuade an audience if he is unaware of the laws of its psychology; not all speeches suit all audiences. Further, writing is inferior to speaking, for the written word is lifeless, the spoken is living and its author can be interrogated. It follows then that orators are of all men the most important because of the power they wield; they will be potent for destruction unless they love the truth and understand human nature; in short, they must be philosophers.

The like of this had nowhere been said before. It opened a new world to human speculation. First, the teaching about oratory is of the highest value. Plato's quarrel with the sophists was based on their total ignorance of the enormous power they exercised for evil, because they knew not what they were doing. They professed to teach men how to speak well, but had no conception of the science upon which the art of oratory rests. In short, they were sheer impostors. Even Aristotle had nothing to add to this doctrine in his treatise on *Rhetoric*, which contains a study of the effects which certain oratorical devices could be prophesied to produce, and provides the requisite scientific foundation. Again, the indifference to or the ridicule of truth shown by some sophists made them odious to Plato. He would have none of their doctrines of relativity or flux. Nothing short of the Absolute would satisfy his soaring spirit. He was sick of the change in phenomena, the tangible and material objects of sense. He found permanence in a world of eternal ideas. These ideas are the essence of Platonism. They are his term for universal concepts, classes; there are single tangible trees innumerable, but one Ideal Tree only in the Ideal world beyond the heavens. Nothing can possibly satisfy the soul but these unchanging and permanent concepts; it is among them that it finds its true home. Lastly, the tripartite division of the nature of the soul here first indicated is a permanent contribution to philosophy. Thus Plato's system is definitely launched in the *Phaedrus*. His subsequent dialogues show how he fitted out the hulk to sail on his voyages of discovery.

The *Meno* is a rediscussion on Platonic principles of the problem of the *Protagoras*: can virtue be taught? Meno, a general in the army of the famous Ten Thousand, attempts a definition of virtue itself, the principle that underlies specific kinds of virtues such as justice. After a cross-examination he confesses his helplessness in a famous simile: Socrates is like the torpedo-fish which benumbs all who touch it. Then the real business begins. How do we learn anything at all? Socrates says by Reminiscence, for the soul lived once in the presence of the ideal world; when it enters the flesh it loses its knowledge, but gradually regains it. This theory he dramatically illustrates by calling in a slave whom he proves by means of a diagram to know something of geometry, though he never learned it. Thus the great lesson of life is to practise the search for knowledge—and if virtue is knowledge it will be teachable.

But the puzzle is, who are the teachers? Not the sophists, a discredited class, nor the statesmen, who cannot teach their sons to follow them. Virtue then, not being teachable, is probably not the result of knowledge, but is imparted to men by a Divine Dispensation, just as poetry is. But the origin of virtue will always be mysterious till its nature is discovered beyond doubt. So Plato once more declares his dissatisfaction with a Socratic tenet which identified virtue with knowledge.

The *Phaedo* describes Socrates' discussion of the immortality of the soul on his last day on earth. Reminiscence of Ideas proves pre-existence, as in the *Meno*; the Ideas are similarly used to prove a continued existence after death, for the soul has in it an immortal principle which is the exact contrary of mortality; the Idea of Death cannot exist in a thing whose central Idea is life. Such in brief is Socrates' proof. To us it is singularly unconvincing, as it looks like a begging of the whole question. Yet Plato argues in his technical language as most men do concerning this all-important and difficult question. That which contains within itself the notion of immortality would seem to be too noble to have been created merely to die. The very presence of a desire to realise eternal truth is a strong presumption that there must be something to correspond with it. The most interesting portion of this well-known dialogue is that which teaches that life is really an exercise for death. All the base and low desires which haunt us should be gradually eliminated and replaced by a longing for better things. The true philosopher at any rate so trains himself that when his hour comes he greets death with a smile, the life on earth having lost its attractions.

Such is the connection between the *Meno* and the *Phaedo*; the life that was before and the life that shall be hereafter depend upon the Ideal world. That salvation is in this life and in the practical sphere of human government is possible only through a knowledge of these Ideas is the doctrine of the immortal *Republic*. This great work in ten books is well known, but its unique value is not always recognised. It starts with a discussion of Justice. Thrasymachus, a brazen fellow like Callicles in the *Gorgias*, argues that Justice is the interest of the stronger and that law and morality are mere conventions. The implications of this doctrine are of supreme importance. If Justice is frank despotism, then the Eastern type of civilisation is the best, wherein custom has once for all fixed the right of the despot to grind down the population, while the sole duty of the latter is to pay taxes. The moral reformation of law becomes impossible; no adjustment of an unchanging decree to the changing and advancing standard of public morality can be contemplated; constitutional development, legal reformation and the great process by which Western peoples have tried gradually to make positive law correspond with Ethical ideals are mere dreams.

But the verbal refutation of Thrasymachus does not satisfy Glaucus and Adeimantus who are among Socrates' audience. In order to explain the real nature of Justice, Socrates is compelled to trace from the very beginning the process by which states have come into existence. Economic and military needs are thoroughly discussed. The State cannot continue unless there is created in it a class whose sole business it is to govern. This class is to be produced by communistic methods; the best men and women are to be tested and chosen as parents, their children being taken and carefully trained apart for their high office. This training will be administered to the three component parts of the soul, the rational, the spirited and the appetitive, while the educational curriculum will be divided into two sections, Gymnastic for the body and Artistic for the mind—the latter including all scientific, mathematical and literary subjects. After a careful search, in this ideal state Justice, the principle of harmony which keeps all classes of the community coherent, will show itself in "doing one's own business".

Yet even this method of describing Justice is not satisfactory to Plato, who was not content unless he started from the universal concepts of the Ideal world. The second portion of the dialogue describes how knowledge is gained. The mind discards the sensible and material world, advancing to the Ideas themselves. Yet even these are insufficient, for they all are interconnected and united to one great and architectonic Idea, that of the Good; to this the soul must advance before its knowledge can be called perfect. This is the scheme of education for the Guardians; the philosophic contemplation of Ideas, however, should be deferred till they are of mature age, for philosophy is dangerous in young men. Having performed their warlike functions of defending the State, the Guardians are to be sifted, those most capable of philosophic speculation being employed as instructors of the others. Seen from the height of the Ideal world, Justice again turns out to be the performance of one's own particular duties.

This ideal society Plato admits to be a difficult aim for our weak human nature; he stoutly maintains, however, that "a pattern of it is laid up in heaven", man's true home. He mournfully grants that a declension from excellence is often possible and describes how this rule of philosophers, if established, would be expected to pass through oligarchy to democracy, the worst form of all government, peopled by the democratic man whose soul is at war with itself because it claims to do as it likes. The whole dialogue ends in an admirable vision in which he teaches that man chose his lot on earth in a preexisting state.

Such is a fragmentary description of this masterpiece. What is it all about? First it is necessary to point out a serious misconception. Plato is not here advocating universal communism; his state postulates a money-making class and a labouring class also. Apart from the fact that he explicitly mentions these and allows them private property, it would be difficult to imagine that they are not rendered necessary by his very description of Justice. Not all men are fit for government—and therefore those who are governed must "do their particular business" for which they are fitted; in some cases it is the rather mean business of piling up fortunes. Communism is advocated as the only means of creating first and then propagating the small Guardian caste. Nor again is the caste rigid, for some of the children born of communistic intercourse will be unfit for their position and will be degraded into the money-making or property owning section. Communism to Plato is a high creed, too high for everybody, fit only for the select and enlightened or teachable few.

Nor is the *Republic* an instance of Utopian theorising. It is a criticism of contemporary Greek civilisation, intended to remove the greatest practical difficulty in life. Man has tried all kinds of governments and found none satisfactory. All have proved selfish and faithless, governing for their own interests only. Kings, oligarchs, democrats and mob-leaders have without exception regarded power as the object to be attained because of the spoils of office. Political leadership is thus a direct means of self-advancement, a temptation too strong for weak human nature. As a well-known Labour leader hinted, five thousand a year does not often come in men's way. There is only one way of securing honest government and that is Plato's. A definite class must be created who will exercise political power only, economic inclinations of any sort disqualifying any of its members from taking office. The ruling class should rule only, the money-making class make money only. In this way no single section will tax the rest to fill its own pockets. The one requisite is that these Guardians should be recognised as the fittest to rule and receive the willing obedience of the rest. If any other sane plan is available for preserving the governed from the incessant and rapacious demands of tax-collectors, no record of it exists in literature. Practical statesmanship of a high and original order is manifest in the *Republic*; in England, where the official qualifications for governing are believed to be equally existent in everybody whether trained or untrained in the art of ruling, the *Republic*, if read at all, may be admired but is sure to be misunderstood.

It seems that Plato's teaching at the Academy raised formidable criticism. The next group of dialogues is marked by metaphysical teaching. The *Parmenides* is a searching examination of the Ideas. If these are in a world apart, they cannot easily be brought into connection with our world; a big thing on earth and the Idea of Big will need another Idea to comprehend both. Besides, Ideas in an independent existence will be beyond our ken and their study will be impossible. Socrates' system betrays lack of metaphysical practice; at most the Ideas should have been regarded as part of a theory whose value should have been tested by results. This process is exemplified by a discussion of the fundamental opposition between the One and the infinite Many which are instances of it.

This criticism shows the advantage Plato enjoyed in making Socrates the mouthpiece of his own speculations; he could criticise himself as it were from without. He has put his finger on his own weak spot, the question whether the Ideas are immanent or transcendent. The results of this examination were adopted by the Aristotelian school, who suggested another theory of Knowledge.

The *Philebus* discusses the question whether Pleasure or Knowledge is the chief good. A metaphysical argument which follows that of the *Parmenides* ends in the characteristic Greek distinction between the Finite and the Infinite. Pleasure is infinite, because it can exist in greater or less degree; there is a mixed life compounded of finite and infinite and there is a creative faculty to which mind belongs. Pleasure is of two kinds; it is sometimes mixed with pain, sometimes it is pure; the latter type alone is worth cultivating and includes the pleasures of knowledge. Yet pleasure is not an end, but only a means to it. It cannot therefore be the Good, which is an end. Knowledge is at its best when it is dealing with the eternal and immutable, but even then it is not self-sufficient—it exists for the sake of something else, the good. This latter is characterised by symmetry, proportion and truth. Knowledge resembles it far more than even pure pleasure.

The *Theaetetus* discusses more fully the theory of knowledge. It opens with a comparison of the Socratic method to midwifery; it delivers the mind of the thoughts with which it is in travail. The first tentative definition of knowledge is that it is sensation. This is in agreement with the Protagorean doctrine that man is the measure of all things. Yet sensation implies change, whereas we cannot help thinking that objects retain their identity; if knowledge is sensation a pig has as good a claim to be called the measure of all things as a man. Again, Protagoras has no right to teach others if each man's sensations are a law unto him. Nor is the Heracleitean doctrine much better which taught that all things are in a state of flux. If nothing retains the same quality for two consecutive moments it is impossible to have predication, and knowledge must be hopeless. In fact, sensation is not man's function as a reasoning being, but rather comparison. Neither is knowledge true opinion, for this at once demands the demarcation of false opinion or error; the latter is negative, and will be understood only when positive knowledge is determined. Perhaps knowledge is true opinion plus reason; but it is difficult to decide what is gained by adding "with reason", words which may mean either true opinion or knowledge itself, thus involving either tautology or a begging of the question. The dialogue at least has shown what knowledge is not.

Locke, Berkeley and Hume, the eighteenth century sensation philosophers, were similarly refuted by Kant. The mind by its mere ability to compare two things proves that it can have two concepts at least before it at the same time, and can retain them for a longer period than a mere passing sensation implies. Yet the problem of knowledge still remains as difficult as Plato knew it to be.

"Is the Sophist the same as the Statesman and the Philosopher?" Such is the question raised in the *Sophist*. Six definitions are suggested, all unsatisfactory. The fixed characteristic of the Sophist is his seeming to know everything without doing so; this definition leads straight to the concept of false opinion, a thing whose object both is and is not. "That which is not" provokes an inquiry into what is, Being. Dualism, Monism, Materialism and Idealism are all discussed, the conclusion being that the Sophist is a counterfeit of the Philosopher, a wilful impostor who makes people contradict themselves by quibbling.

The *Politicus* carries on the discussion. In this dialogue we may see the dying glories of Plato's genius. In his search for the true pastor or king he separates the divine from the human leader; the true king alone has scientific knowledge superior to law and written enactments which men use when they fail to discover the real monarch. This scientific knowledge of fixed and definite principles can come only from Education. A most remarkable myth follows, which is practically the Greek version of the Fall. The state of innocence is described as preceding a decline into barbarism; a restoration can be effected only by a divine interposition and by the growth of a study of art or by the influence of society. The arts themselves are the children of a supernatural revelation.

The *Timaeus* and the long treatise the *Laws* criticise the theories of the Republic. The former is full of world-speculations of a most difficult kind, the latter admits the weakness of the Ideal State, making concessions to inevitable human failings.

Though written in an early period, the *Apology* may form a fitting end to these dialogues. Socrates was condemned on the charge of corrupting the Athenian youth and for impiety. To most Athenians he must have been not only not different from the Sophists he was never weary of exposing, but the greatest Sophist of them all. He was unfortunate in his friends, among whom were Critias the infamous tyrant and Alcibiades who sold the great secret. The older men must have regarded with suspicion his influence over the youth in a city which seemed to be losing all its national virtues; many of them were personally aggrieved by his annoying habit of exposing their ignorance. He was given a chance of escape by acknowledging his fault and consenting to pay a small fine. Instead, he proposed for himself the greatest honour his city could give any of her benefactors, public maintenance in the town-hall.

His defence contains many superb passages and is a masterpiece of gentle irony and subtle exposure of error. Its conclusion is masterly.

> "At point of death men often prophesy. My prophecy to you, my slayers, is that when I am gone you will have to face a far more serious penalty than mine. You have killed me because you wish to avoid giving an account of your lives. After me will come more accusers of you and more severe. You cannot stop criticism except by reforming yourselves. If death is a sleep, then to me it is gain; if in the next world a man is delivered from unjust judges and there meets with true judges, the journey is worth while. There will be found all the heroes of old, slain by wicked sentences; them I shall

meet and compare my agonies with theirs. Best of all, I shall be able to carry out my search into true and false knowledge and shall find out the wise and the unwise. No evil can happen to a virtuous man in life or in death. If my sons when they grow up care about riches more than virtue, rebuke them for thinking they are something when they are naught. My time has come; we must separate. I go to death, you to life; which of the two is better only God knows."

Two lessons of supreme importance are to be learned from Plato. In the first place he insists on credentials from the accepted teachers of a nation. On examination most of them, like Gorgias, would be found incapable of defining the subjects for the teaching of which they receive money. The sole hope of a country is Education, for it alone can deliver from ignorance, a slavery worse than death; the uneducated person is the dupe of his own passions or prejudices and is the plaything of the horde of impostors who beg for his vote at elections or stampede him into strikes.

Again, the possibility of knowledge depends upon accurate definition and the scientific comparisons of instances. These involve long and fatiguing thought and very often the reward is scanty enough; no conclusion is possible sometimes except that it is clear what a thing cannot be. The human intelligence has learned a most valuable lesson when it has recognised its own impotence at the outset of an inquiry and its own limitations at the end thereof. Knowledge, Good, Justice, Immortality are conceptions so mighty that our tiny minds have no compasses to set upon them. Better far a distrust in ourselves than the somewhat impudent and undoubtedly insistent claim to certitude advanced by the materialistic apostles of modern non-humanitarianism. When questioned about the ultimates all human knowledge must admit that it hangs upon the slender thread of a theory or postulate. The student of philosophy is more honest than others; he has the candour to confess the assumptions he makes before he tries to think at all.

At times it must be admitted that Plato sounds very unreal. His faults are clear enough. The dialogue form makes it very easy for him to invent questions of such a nature that the answer he wants is the only one possible. Again, his conclusions are often arrived at by methods or arguments which are frankly inadmissible; in the earlier dialogues are some very glaring instances of sheer logical worthlessness. Frequently the whole theme of discussion is such that no modern philosopher could be expected to approve of it. A supposed explanation of a difficulty is sometimes afforded by a myth, splendid and poetical but not logically valid. Inconsistencies can easily be pointed out in the vast compass of his speculations. It remained for Aristotle to invent a genuine method of sorting out a licit from an illicit type of argument.

These faults are serious. Against them must be placed some positive excellences. Plato was one of the first to point out that there is a problem; a question should be asked and an answer found if possible, for we have no right to take things for granted. More than this, he was everywhere searching for knowledge, ridding himself of prejudice, doing in perfect honesty the most difficult of all things, the duty of thinking clearly. These thoughts he has expressed in the greatest of all types of Greek prose, a blend of poetic beauty with the precision of prose.

But Plato's praise is not that he is a philosopher so much as Philosophy itself in poetic form. His great visions of the Eternal whence we spring, his awe for the real King, the real Virtue, the real State "laid up in Heaven" fill him with an inspired exaltation which lifts his readers to the Heaven whence Platonism has descended. There are two main types of men. One is content with the things of sense; using his powers of observation and performing experiments he will become a Scientist; using his powers of speculation he will become an Aristotelian philosopher; putting his thoughts into simple and logical order, he will write good prose. The other soars to the eternal principles behind this world, the deathless forms or the general concepts which give concrete things their existence. These perfect forms are the main study of the Artist, Poet, Sculptor, whose work it is to give us comfort and pleasure unspeakable. So long as man lives, he must have the perfection of beauty to gladden him, especially if Science is going to test everything by the ruler or balance or crucible. This love of Beauty is exactly Platonism. It has never died yet. From Athens it spread to Alexandria, there to start up into fresh life in the School of which Plotinus is the chief; its doctrines are described for the English reader in Kingsley's *Hypatia*. It planted its seed of mysticism in Christianity, with which it has most strange affinities. At the Renaissance this mystic element caught the imagination of northern Europe, notably Germany. Passing to England, it created at Cambridge a School of Platonists, the issue of whose thought is evident in the poetry of Coleridge and Wordsworth. Its last outburst has been the Transcendental teaching of the nineteenth century, so curiously Greek and non-Greek in its essence.

For there is in our nature that undying longing for communion with the Divine which the mere thought of God stirs within us. Our true home is in the great world where Truth is everything, that Truth which one day we, like Plato, shall see face to face without any quailing.

TRANSLATIONS:

The version in 4 volumes by Jowett (Oxford) is the standard. It contains good introductions.

The *Republic* has been translated by Davies and Vaughan.

Two volumes in the Loeb Series have appeared.

A new method of translation of Plato is needed. The text should be clearly divided into sections; the steps of the argument should be indicated in a skeleton outline. Until this is done study of Plato is likely to cause much bewilderment.

Plato and Platonism, by Pater, is still the best interpretation of the whole system.

DEMOSTHENES

One of the most disquieting facts that history teaches is the inability of the most enlightened and patriotic men to "discern the signs of the times". To us the collapse of the Greek city-states seems natural and inevitable. Their constant bickerings and petty jealousies justly drew down upon them the armed might of the ambitious and capable power which destroyed them. Their fate may fill us with pity and our admiration for those who fought in a losing cause may prejudice us against their enslavers. But just as the Norman Conquest in the long run brought more blessing than misery, so the downfall of the Greek commonwealths was the first step to the conquering progress of the Greek type of civilisation through the whole world. Our Harold, fighting manfully yet vainly against an irresistible tendency, has his counterpart in the last defender of the ancient liberties of Greece.

Demosthenes was born in 384 of a well-to-do business man who died eight years later. The guardians whom he appointed appropriated the estate, leaving Demosthenes and his sister in straitened circumstances. On coming of age the young man brought a suit against his trustees in 363, of whom Aphobus was the most fraudulent. Though he won the case, much of his property was irretrievably lost. Nor were his first efforts at public speaking prophetic of future greatness. His voice was thin, his demeanour awkward, his speech indistinct; his style was laboured, being an obvious blend of Thucydides with Isaeus, an old and practised pleader. Yet he was ambitious and determined; he longed to copy the career of Pericles, the noblest of Athenian statesmen. The stories of his self-imposed exercises and their happy issue are well known; his days he spent in declaiming on the sea-shore with pebbles in his mouth, his nights in copying and recopying Thucydides; the speeches which have come down to us show clearly the gradual evolution of the great style well worthy of the greatest of all themes, national salvation.

It will be necessary to explain a convention of the Athenian law courts. A litigant was obliged to plead his own case; if he was unable to compose his own speech, he applied to some professional retailer of orations who would write it for him. The art of these speech-writers was of varying excellence. A first-class practitioner would not only discover the real or the supposed facts of the dispute, he would divine the real character of his client, and write the particular type of speech which would seem most natural on such a person's lips. Considerable knowledge of human nature was required in such an exciting and delicate profession, although the author did not always succeed in concealing his identity. Demosthenes had his share of this experience; he wrote for various customers speeches on various subjects; one concerns a dowry dispute, another a claim for compensation for damage caused by a water-course, another deals with an adoption, another was written for a wealthy banker. Assault and battery, ship-scuttling, undue influence of attractive females on the weaker sex, maritime trickery of all kinds, citizen rights, are all treated in the so-called private speeches, of which some are of considerable value as illustrating legal or mercantile or social etiquette.

Public suits were of the same nature; the speeches were composed by one person and delivered by another. Such are the speech against *Androtion* for illegal practices, against *Timocrates* for embezzlement and the important speech against *Aristocrates*, in which for the first time Demosthenes seems to have become aware of the real designs of Macedonia. The speech against the law of *Leptines*, delivered in 354 by Demosthenes himself, is of value as displaying the gradual development of his characteristic style; in it we have the voice and the words of the same man, who is talking with a sense of responsibility about a constitutional anomaly.

But for us the real Demosthenes is he who spoke on questions of State policy. This subject alone can call out the best qualities in an orator as distinct from a rhetorician; the tricks and bad arguments which are so often employed to secure condemnation or acquittal in a law court are inapplicable or undignified in a matter of vital national import. But before the great enemy arose to threaten Greek liberty, it happened that Fortune was kind enough to afford Demosthenes excellent practice in a parliamentary discussion of two if not three questions of importance.

In 354 there was much talk of a possible war with Persia. Demosthenes first addresses the sword-rattlers. "To the braggarts and jingoes I say that it is not difficult—not even when we need sound advice—to win a reputation for courage and to appear a clever speaker when danger is very near. The really difficult duty is to show courage in danger and in the council-chamber to give sounder advice than anybody else." His belief was that war was not a certainty, but it would be better to revise the whole naval system. A detailed scheme to assure the requisite number of ships in fighting-trim follows, so sensible that it commands immediate respect. The speaker estimates the wealth of Attica, maps it out into divisions, each able to bear the expense of the warships assigned to it. To a possible objection that it would be better to raise the money by increased taxation he answers with the grim irony natural to him (he seems to be utterly devoid of humour).

> "What you could raise at present is more ridiculous than if you raised nothing at all. A hundred and twenty talents? What are they to the twelve hundred camels which they say carry Persia's revenues?"

He refuses to believe that a Greek mercenary army would fight against its country, while the Thebans, who notoriously sided with Persia in 480, would give much for an opportunity of redeeming this old sin against Greece.

> "The rest of the Greeks, as long as they considered the Persian their common enemy, had numerous blessings; but when they began to regard him as their friend they experienced such woes as no man could have invented for them even in his curses. Whom then Providence and Destiny have shown useless as a friend and most advantageous as a foe, shall we fear? Rather let us commit

no injustice for our own sakes and save the rest from commotion and strife."

Such is the outline of the speech on the *Navy-boards*. Two years later he displayed qualities of no mean order. Sparta and Thebes were quarrelling for the leadership. Arcadia had revolted from Sparta, the centre of the disaffection being *Megalopolis*; ambassadors from the latter city and from Sparta begged Athenian aid. In the heat of the excitement men's judgments were not to be trusted. "The difficulty of giving sound advice is well known," says the orator.

> "If a man tries to take a middle course and you have not the patience to hear, he will win the approval of neither party but will be maligned by both. If such a fate awaits me, I would rather appear to be talking nonsense than allow any party to deceive you into what I know is not your wisest policy."

The question was, should Athens join Thebes or Sparta, both ancient foes?

> "I would like to ask those who say they hate either, whether they hate the one for the sake of the other or for your sake. If for the sake of the other party, then you can trust neither, for both are mad; if for your sake, why do they try to strengthen one of these two cities unduly? You can with perfect ease keep Thebes weak without making Sparta strong, as I will prove. You will find that the main cause of woe and ruin is unwillingness to act with simple honesty."

After a rapid calculation of possibilities he suggests the following plan.

> "War between Thebes and Sparta is certain. If Thebes is beaten to the ground, as she deserves to be, Sparta will not be unduly powerful, for these Arcadian neighbours will restore the balance; if Thebes recovers and saves herself, she will still be weak if you ally yourselves with Arcadia and protect her. It is expedient then in every way neither to sacrifice Arcadia nor let that country imagine that it survives through its own power or through any other power than yours."

The calm voice of the cool-headed statesman is everywhere audible in this admirable little speech.

The power of discounting personal resentment and thinking soberly is apparent in the speech for the *Freedom of Rhodes*, delivered about this time. Rhodes had offended Athens by revolting in the Social war of 357-5 with the help of the well-known Carian king Mausolus. For a time that monarch had treated Rhodes well; later he overthrew the democracy and placed the power in the hands of the oligarchs. When Queen Artemisia succeeded to the throne of Caria the democrats begged Athens to aid them in recovering their liberty. Deprecating passion of any kind, Demosthenes points out the real question at issue. The record of the oligarchs is a bad one; to overthrow the democracy they had won over some of the leading citizens whom they banished when they had attained their object. Their faithless conduct promised no hope of a firm alliance with Athens. The Rhodian question was to be the acid test of her political creed.

> "Look at this fact, gentlemen. You have fought many a war against both democracies and oligarchies, as you well know. But the real object of these wars perhaps none of you considers. Against democracies you fight for private grievances which cannot be settled in public, or for territory or boundaries or for domination. Against oligarchies you fight for none of these things, but for your constitution and freedom. I would not hesitate to say that I consider it more to your advantage should become democratic and fight you than turn oligarchic and be your friends. I am certain that it would not be difficult for you to make peace with free-constitutions; with oligarchies your friendship would not even be secure, for it is impossible that they in their lust for power could cherish kindness for a State whose policy is based on freedom of speech."

> "Even if we were to say that Rhodes richly deserves her sufferings, this is the wrong time to gloat. Prosperous cities ought always to show that they desire every good for the unfortunate, for the future is dark to us all."

His conclusion is this.

> "Any person who abandons the post assigned to him by his commander you disfranchise and exclude from public life. Even so all who desert the political tradition bequeathed you by your ancestors and turn oligarchs you ought to banish from your Council. As it is you trust politicians who you know for certain side with your country's enemies."

These three speeches indicate plainly enough the kind of man who was soon to make himself heard in a more important question. Instead of a frothy and excitable harangue that might have been looked for in a warm-blooded Southern orator we find a dignified and apparently cool-headed type of speech based on sound sense, full of practical proposals, fearless, manly and above all noble because it relies on righteousness. An intelligence of no mean order has in each case discarded personal feeling and has pointed out the one bed-rock fact which ought to be the foundation of a sound policy. More than this; for the first time an Attic orator has deliberately set to work to create a new type of prose, based on a cadence and rhythm. This new language at times runs away with its inventor; experience was to show him that in this matter as in all others the consummate artist hides the art whereof he is master.

By 352 Greece had become aware that her liberties were to be threatened not from the East, but from Macedonia. Trained in the Greek practice of arms and diplomacy, her king Philip within seven years had created a powerful military system. His first object was to obtain control of a seaboard. In carrying out this policy he had to reduce Amphipolis on the Strymon in Thrace, Olynthus in Chalcidice, and Athenian power centralised in Potidaea, a little south of Olynthus, and on the other side of the Gulf of Therma in Pydna and Methone. Pydna he secured in 357 by trickery; Amphipolis had passed under his control through inexcusable Athenian slackness earlier in the same year. Potidaea fell in 356 and Methone, the last Athenian stronghold, in 353. Pagasae succumbed in 352; with it Philip obtained absolute command of the sea-coast.

In the same year a Macedonian attempt to pass Thermopylae was met by vigorous Athenian action; a strong force held the defile, preventing a further advance southward. In the next year the Athenian pacifist party was desirous of dropping further resistance. This policy caused the delivery of the *First Philippic*. It is a stirring appeal to the country to shake off its lethargy. Nothing but personal service would enable her to recover the lost strongholds. "In my opinion," it says, "the greatest compelling power that can move men is the disgrace of their condition. Do you desire to stroll about asking one another for news? What newer news do you want than that a Macedonian is warring down Athens? Philip sick or Philip dead makes no difference to you. If he died you would soon raise up for yourselves another Philip if you continue your present policy."

With statesmanlike care Demosthenes makes concrete proposals for the creation of a standing force of citizens ready to serve in the ranks; at present their generals and captains are puppets for the pretty march-past in the public square. He estimates the cost of upkeep and shows that it is possible to maintain a force in perfect efficiency; he lays particular stress on creating a base of operations in Macedonia itself, otherwise fleets sailing north might be checked by trade winds. "Too late" is the curse of Athenian action; a vacillating policy ruins every expedition.

> "Such a system was possible earlier, but now we are on the razor's edge. In my opinion some god in utter shame at our history has inspired Philip with his restlessness. If he had been content with his conquests and annexations, some of you would be quite satisfied with a position which would have branded our name with infamy and cowardice; as it is, perhaps his unceasing aggressions and lust for extension might spur you—unless you are utterly past redemption."

He grimly refutes all those well-informed persons who "happen to know" Philip's object—we had scores of them in our own late war.

> "Why, of course he is intoxicated at the magnitude of his successes and builds castles in the air; but I am quite sure that he will never choose a policy such that the most hopeless fools here are likely to know what it is, for gossipers are hopeless fools."

It should be remembered that these are the words of a young man of thirty-four, unconnected with any party, yet capable of forming a sane policy. That they are great words will be obvious to anyone who replaces the name of Philip by that of his country's enemy; the result is startling indeed.

The last and most formidable problem Philip had yet to solve, the destruction of Olynthus, the centre of a great confederation of thirty-two towns. Military work against it was begun in 349 and led at once to an appeal to Athens for assistance. The pacifists and traitors were busy intriguing for Philip; Demosthenes delivered three speeches for Olynthus. The *First Olynthiac* sounds the right note.

> "The present crisis all but cries aloud saying that you must tackle the problem your own selves if you have any concern for salvation. The great privilege of a military autocrat, that he is his own Cabinet, Commander-in-Chief, and Chancellor of the Exchequer, that he is everywhere personally in service with his army, gives him an enormous advantage for the speedy and timely performance of military duties, but it makes him incapable of obtaining from Olynthus the truce he longs for. Olynthus now knows she is fighting not for glory or territory but to avoid ejection and slavery. She has before her eyes his treatment of Amphipolis and Pydna. In a word, despotism is a thing no free country can trust, especially if it is its neighbour."

He warns his hearers that once Olynthus falls, there is nothing to hinder Philip from marching straight on Athens.

A definite policy is then suggested.

> "Carping criticism is easy; any person can indulge in it; but only a statesman can show what is to be done to meet a pressing difficulty. I know well enough that if anything goes wrong you lose your tempers not with the guilty persons, but with the last speaker. Yet for all that, no thought of private safety will make me conceal what I believe to be our soundest course of action."

By a perfectly scandalous abuse, the surplus funds of the State Treasury had been doled out to the poor to enable them to witness plays in the theatre, on the understanding that the doles should cease if war expenses had to be met. In time the lower orders came to consider the dole as their right, backed by the demagogues refused to surrender it. This theatre-fund Demosthenes did not yet venture to attack, for it was dangerous to do so. He had no alternative but to propose additional taxes on the rich. He concludes with an admirable peroration.

> "You must all take a comprehensive view of these questions and bear a hand in staving off the war into Macedonia. The rich must spend a little of their possessions to enjoy the residue without fear; the men of military age must gain their experience of war in Philip's country and make themselves formidable defenders of their own soil; the speakers must facilitate an enquiry into their own conduct, that the citizen body may criticise their policy according to the political situation at the moment. May the result be good on every ground."

The *Second Olynthiac* strikes a higher note, that of indignant protest against the perfidy of Macedonian diplomacy.

> "When a State is built on unanimity, when allies in a war find their interests identical, men gladly labour together, bearing their troubles and sticking to their task. But when a power like Philip's is strong through greed and villainy, on the first pretext or the slightest set-back the whole system is upset and dismembered. Injustice and perjury and lies cannot win a solid power; they survive for a brief and fleeting period and show many a blossom of promise perhaps, but time finds them out; their leaves soon wither away. Houses or ships need foundations of great strength; policies require truth and righteousness as their origin and first principles. Such are not to be found in Philip's career."

A history of Macedonian progress shows the weak places in the system.

> "Success throws a veil over these at present, for prosperity shrouds many a scandal. If he makes one false step, all his vices will come into the clearest relief; this will soon become obvious under Heaven's guidance, if you will only show some energy. As long as a man is in health, he is unaware of his weaknesses, but when sickness overtakes him, his whole constitution is upset. Cities and despots are the same; while they are invading their neighbours their secret evils are invisible, but when they are in the grip of an internal war these weaknesses all become quite evident."

An exhortation to personal service is succeeded by a protest against a parochial view of politics which causes petty jealousies and paralyses joint action. The whole State should take its turn at doing some war duty.

In the *Third Olynthiac* Demosthenes takes the bull by the horns. The insane theatre-doles were sapping the revenues badly needed for financing the fight for existence. Olynthus at last was aware of her danger; she could be aided not by passing decrees, but by annulling some.

> "I will tell you quite plainly I mean the laws about the theatre-fund. When you have done that and when you make it safe for your speakers to give you the best advice, then you may expect somebody to propose what you all know is to your interest. The men to repeal these laws are those who proposed them. It is unfair that they who passed them should be popular for damaging the State while a statesman who proposes a measure which would benefit us all should be rewarded with public hatred. Before you have set this matter right you cannot expect to find among you a superman who will violate these laws with impunity or a fool who will run his head into a manifest noose."

With the same superb courage he tackles the demagogues who are the cause of all the mischief.

> "Ever since the present type of orator has appeared who asks anxiously, 'What do you want? What can I propose? What can I give you?' the city's prestige has melted in compliment; the net

result is that these men have made their fortunes while the city is disgraced."

A bitter contrast shows how the earlier popular leaders made Athens wealthy, dominant and respected; the modern sort had lost territory, spent a mint of money on nothing, alienated good allies and raised up a trained enemy. But there is one thing to their credit, they had whitewashed the city walls, had repaired roads and fountains. And the trade of public speaking is profitable. Some of the demagogues' houses are more splendid than the public buildings; as individuals they have prospered in exact proportion as the State is reduced to impotence. In fact, they have secured control of the constitution; their system of bribery and spoon-feeding has tamed the democracy and made it obedient to the hand. "I should not be surprised," he continues,

"if my words bring me into greater trouble than the men who have started these abuses. Freedom of speech on every subject before you is not possible—I am surprised that you have not already howled me down."

The doles he compares to the snacks prescribed by doctors; they cannot help keep a patient properly alive and will not allow him to die. Personal service and an end of gratuities is insisted upon.

"Without adding or taking away, only slightly altering our present chaos, I have suggested a uniform scheme whereby each man can do the duties fitted to his years and his opportunities. I have nowhere proposed that you should divide the earnings of the workers among the unemployable, nor that you should slack and amuse yourselves and be reduced to beggary while somebody else is fighting for you—for that is what is happening now."

What a speech is here! Doles, interruptions of men who tell the truth, organised democratic corruption, waste of public money on whitewash are familiar to the unhappy British tax-payer. Where is our Demosthenes who dare appeal to the electorate to sweep the system and its prospering advocates back into the darkness?

Having captured Olynthus in 348 and razed it to the ground, Philip attacked Euboea. A further advance was checked by a disgraceful peace engineered by Philocrates and Aeschines in 346. The embassy which obtained it was dodged by Philip until he had made the maximum of conquest; he had excluded the Phocians from its scope, a people of primary importance because they controlled Thermopylae, but a week after signing the peace he had destroyed Phocian unity and usurped their place on the great Council which met at Delphi. This evident attack on the liberty of southern Greece raised a fever of excitement at Athens. The war-party clamoured for instant action; strangely enough Demosthenes advised his city to observe the peace. In contrast with his fiery audience he speaks with perfect coolness and calm. He reviews the immediate past, explains the shameful part played by an actor Neoptolemus who persuaded Athens to make the peace, then realised all his property and went to live in Macedon; he describes the good advice he gave them which they did not follow, and bases his claim to speak not on any cleverness but on his incorruptibility.

> "Our true interest reveals itself to me in its real outlines as I judge the existing situation. But whenever a man throws a bribe into the opposite scale it drags the reason after it; the corrupt person will never afterwards have any true or sane judgment about anything."

In the present case the real point at issue is clear enough. It is a question of fighting not Philip but the whole body of states who were represented at the Delphic Council, for they would fly to arms at once if Athens renounced *the Peace*; against such a combination she could not survive, just as the Phocians could not cope with the combined attack of Macedonia, Thessaly and Thebes, natural enemies united for a brief moment to achieve a common end. After all, a seat on the Delphic Council was a small matter; only fools would go to war for an unsubstantial shadow.

Firmly planted in Greece itself, Philip started intriguing in Peloponnesus, supporting Argos, Megalopolis and Messene against Sparta. An embassy to these three cities headed by Demosthenes warned them of the treacherous friendship. Returning to Athens in 344 he delivered his *Second Philippi*, which contains an account of the speeches of the recent tour. Philip acted while Athens talked.

> "The result is inevitable and perhaps reasonable; each of you excels in that wherein you are most diligent—he in deeds, you in words."

Hence comes the intrigue against Sparta. He can dupe stupid people like the Thebans, or the Peloponnesians; warning therefore is necessary. To the latter he said:—

> "You now stare at Philip offering and promising things; if you have any sense, pray you may never see him practising his tricks and evasions. Cities have invented all kinds of protections and safeguards such as stockades, walls, trenches—all of which are made by hand and expensive. But men of sense have inherited from Nature one defence, good and salutary—especially democrats against despots—namely, mistrust. If you hold fast to this, you will never come to serious harm. You hanker after liberty, I suppose. Cannot you see that Philip's very title is the exact negation of it? Every king or despot is a foe to freedom and an adversary of law. Beware lest while seeking to be quit of a war you find a master."

He then mentions the silly promises of advantages to come which induced Athens to make the infamous Peace, and quotes the famous remark whereby the traitor gang raised a laugh while in the act of selling their country. "Demosthenes is naturally a sour and peevish fellow, for he drinks water." Drawing their attention to this origin of all their trouble, he asks them to remember their names—at the same time remarking that even if a man deserved to die, punishment should be suspended if it meant loss and ruin to the State.

The next three years saw various Macedonian aggressions, especially in Thrace. That country on its eastern extremity formed the northern coast of the Dardanelles, named the Chersonese, important as safeguarding the corn supplies which passed through the Straits. It had been in the possession of Miltiades, was lost in the Peloponnesian war and was partly recovered by Timotheus in 863. Diopeithes had been sent there with a body of colonists in 346. Establishing himself in possession, he took toll of passing traders to safeguard them against pirates and had collided with the Macedonian troops as they slowly advanced to the Narrows. Philip sent a protest to Athens; in a lively debate *on the Chersonese* early in 341 Demosthenes delivered a great speech.

First of all he shows that Diopeithes is really the one guarantee that Philip will not attack Attica itself. In Thrace is a force which can do great damage to Macedonian territory.

> "But if it is once disbanded, what shall we do if Philip attacks the Chersonese? Arraign Diopeithes, of course—but that will not improve matters. Well then, send reinforcements from here—if the winds allow us. Well, Philip will not attack—but there is nobody to guarantee that."

He suggests that Diopeithes should not be cast off but supported. Such a plan will cost money, but it will be well spent for the sake of future benefits.

> "If some god were to guarantee that if Athens observes strict neutrality, abandoning all her possessions, Philip would not attack her, it would be a scandal, unworthy of you and your city's power and past history to sacrifice the rest of Greece. I would rather die than suggest such action."

He then turns to the pacifists, pointing out that it is useless to expect a peace if the enemy is bent on a war of extermination. None but fools would wait till a foe admits he is actually fighting if his actions are clearly hostile. The traitors who sell the city should be beaten to death, for no State can overcome the foe outside till it has chastised the enemy within. The record of Macedonian duplicity follows; the hectoring insolence of Philip is easily explained; Athens is the only place in the world in which freedom of speech exists; so prevalent is it that even slaves and aliens possess it. Accordingly Philip has to stop the mouths of other cities by giving them territory for a brief period, but Athens he can rob of her colonies and be sure of getting praise from the anti-national bribe-takers. He concludes with a striking and elevated passage describing the genuine statesman.

> "Any man who to secure your real interests opposes your wishes and never speaks to get applause but deliberately chooses politics as his profession (a business in which chance exercises greater influence than human reason), being perfectly ready to answer for the caprices is a really brave and useful citizen. I have never had recourse to the popular arts of winning favour; I have never used low abuse or stooped to humour you or made rich

men's money public; I continue to tell you what is bound to make me unpopular among you and yet advance your strength if only you will listen-so unenviable is the counsellor's lot."

A deep and splendid courage in hopelessness is here manifest.

A little later in the same year was delivered the last and greatest of all the patriotic speeches, the *Third Philippic*. Early in the speech the whole object of the Macedonian threat is made apparent—the jugular veins of Athens, her trade-routes.

> "Any man who plots and intrigues to secure the means of my capture is at war with me, even if he has not fired a shot. In the last event, what are the danger-spots of Athens? The Hellespont, Megara and Euboea, the Peloponnese. Am I to say then that a man who has fired this train against Athens is at peace with her?"

Then the plot against all Greek liberty is explained.

> "We all recognise the common danger, but we never send embassies to one another. We are in such a sorry plight, so great a gulf has been fixed between cities by intrigue that we are incapable of doing what is our duty and our interest; we cannot combine; we can make no confederation of mutual friendship and assistance; we stare at the man as he grows greater; each of us is determined to take advantage of the time during which another is being ruined, never considering or planning the salvation of Greece. Every one knows that Philip is like a recurring plague or a fit of some malevolent disease which attacks even those who seem to be out of his reach. Remember this; all the indignities put on Greece by Sparta or ourselves were at least the work of genuine sons of the land; they may be likened to the wild oats of some heir to a great estate—if they were the excesses of some slave or changeling we all would have considered them monstrous and scandalous. But that is not our attitude to Philip and his diplomacy, though he is not a Greek or a relation; rather he is not born even of decent barbarian parents—he is a cursed wretch from Macedonia which till recently could not supply even a respectable servant."

The bitterness of this is intense in a man who generally refrains from anything undignified in a public speech.

The cause of this disunion is bribery. In former times

> "it was impossible to buy from orators or generals knowledge of the critical moment which fortune often gives to the careless against the industrious. But now all our national virtues have been sold out of the market; we have imported in their place the goods which have tainted Greek life to the very death. These are—envy for every bribe-taker, ridicule for any who confesses his guilt, hatred for every one who exposes him. We have far more warships and soldiers and revenue to-day, but they are all useless, unavail-

ing and unprofitable owing to treason."

To punish these seems quite hopeless.

> "You have sunk to the very depth of folly or craziness or I know not what. Often I cannot help dreading that some evil angel is persecuting us. For some ribaldry or petty spite or silly jest—in fact, for any reason whatsoever you invite hirelings to address you, and laugh at their scurrilities."

He points to the fate of all the cities whom Philip flattered.

> "In all of them the patriots advised increased taxation—the traitors said it was not necessary. They advised war and distrust—the traitors preached peace, till they were caught in the trap. The traitors made speeches to get votes, the others spoke for national existence. In many cases the masses listened to the pro-Macedonians not through ignorance, but because their hearts failed them when they thought they were beaten to their knees."

The doom of these cities it was not worth while to describe overmuch.

> "As long as the ship is safe, that is the time for every sailor and their captain to be keen on his duties and to take precautions against wilful or thoughtless upsetting of the craft. But once the sea is over the decks, all zeal is vain. We then who are Athenians, while we are safe with our great city, our enormous resources, our splendid reputation—what shall we do?"

The universal appeal of this white-hot speech is its most noteworthy feature. The next year the disgraceful peace was ended, the free theatre-tickets withdrawn. All was vain. In 338 Athens and Thebes were defeated at Chaeroneia; the Cassandra prophecies of the great patriot came true. In 330 one more triumph was allowed him. He was attacked by the traitor Aeschines and answered him so effectively in his speech *on the Crown* that his adversary was banished. A cloud settled over the orator's later life; he outlived Alexander by little more than a year, but when Antipater hopelessly defeated the allies at Crannon in 322 he poisoned himself rather than live in slavery.

Of all the orators of the ancient world none is more suitable for modern use than Demosthenes. It is true that he is guilty of gross bad taste in some of his speeches—but rarely in a parliamentary oration. Cicero is too verbose and often insincere. Demosthenes is as a rule short, terse and forcible. It is the undoubted justice of his cause which gives him his lofty and noble style. He lacks the gentler touch of humour—but a man cannot jest when he sees servitude before the country he loves. With a few necessary alterations a speech of Demosthenes could easily be delivered to-day, and it would be successful. Even Philip is said to have admitted that he would have voted for him after hearing him, and Aeschines after winning applause for declaiming part of Demosthenes' speech told his audience that they ought to have heard the beast.

Yet all this splendid eloquence seems to have been wasted. The orator could see much that was dark to his contemporaries, and spoke prophecies true though vain. But the greatest thing of all was concealed from his view. The inevitable day had dawned for the genuinely Greek type of city. It was brilliant but it was a source of eternal divisions in a world which had to be unified to be of any service. Its absurd factions and petty leagues were really a hindrance to political stability. Further, the essential vices of democracy cried aloud for a stern master, and found him. Treason, bribery, appeals to an unqualified voting class, theft of rich men's property under legal forms, free seats in the theatre, belittlement of a great empire, pacifism, love of every state but the right one—these are the open sores of popular control. For such a society only one choice is possible; it needs discipline either of national service or national extinction. Its crazy cranks will not disappear otherwise. Modern political life is democratic; those who imagine that the voice of the majority is the voice of Heaven should produce reasons for their belief. They will find it difficult to hold such a view if they will patiently consider the hard facts of history and the unceasing warnings of Demosthenes.

No account of Greek literature would be complete without a mention of the influence which has revolutionised human thought. It is a strange coincidence that Aristotle was born and died in the same years as Demosthenes. His native town was Stagira; he trained Alexander the Great, presided over the very famous Peripatetic School at Athens for thirteen years and found time to investigate practically every subject of which an ancient Greek could be expected to have any knowledge.

His method was the slow and very patient observation of individual facts. He is the complement of Plato, who tended to neglect the fact for the "idea" or general law or type behind it and logically prior to it. Deductive reasoning was Plato's method—that of the poet or great artist, who worships not what he sees but the unseen perfect form behind; inductive reasoning was Aristotle's method—that of the ordinary man, who respects what he sees that he may by patience find out what is the unseen class to which it belongs. This latter has been the foundation-stone of all modern science; in the main the resemblance between Aristotle's system of procedure and that of the greatest liberators of the human mind, Bacon and Descartes, are more valuable than the differences.

It would be difficult to mention any really great subject on which Aristotle has not left some work which is not to be lightly disregarded. His works are in the form of disjointed notes, taken down at his lectures by his disciples. As a rule they are dry and precise, though here and there rays of glory appear which prove that the master was capable of poetic expression even in prose. A rather fine hymn has been ascribed to him. As we might expect, he is weakest in scientific research, mainly because he could not command the use of instruments familiar to us. That a human being who possessed no microscope should have left such a detailed account of the most minute marks on the bodies of fish and animals is an absolute marvel; so perfect is his description that it cannot be bettered to-day. Cuvier and Linnaeus are great names in Botany; Darwin said that they were mere schoolboys compared with Aristotle—in other words, botanical research had progressed the-wrong way.

Many works have appeared on Ethics and Philosophy; few of them are likely to survive as long as Aristotle's *Ethics* and *Metaphysics* Sometimes our modern philosophers seem to forget their obligation to resemble human beings in their writings. We hear so much of mist and transcendentalism, problems, theories, essays, critiques that a book of Aristotle's dry but exact definition seems like the words of soberness after some nightmare. The man is not assaulting the air; his feet are on firm ground. This is how he proceeds. "Virtue is a mean between excess and defect." In fact, his object appears to have been to teach something, not to mystify everybody and to cover the honourable name of philosophy with ridicule.

It is the same story everywhere. Do we want the best book on *Rhetoric* or *Politics*? Aristotle may supply it, mainly because he took the trouble to classify his instances and show the reason why things not only are of such a kind, but must inevitably be so. A course of Aristotelian study might profitably be prescribed to every person who thinks of talking in public; he would at least learn how to respect himself and his audience, however ignorant and powerful it may be; he would tend to use words in an exact sense instead of indulging in the wild vagueness of speech which is so common and so dangerous. This dry-as-dust philosopher who cut up animals and plants and wrote about public speeches and constitutions found time to give the world a book on Poetry. Modern scientists sometimes deny their belief in the existence of such a thing as poetry, or scoff at its value; no poetic treatise has yet appeared from them, for it seems difficult for modern science to keep alive in its devotees the weakest glimmerings of a sense of beauty. Herein their great founder and father shows himself to be more humane than his so-called progressive children. His *Poetics* was the foundation of literary criticism and shows no sign of being superseded.

Turning his eyes upwards, he gave the world a series of notes on what he saw there. Not possessing a telescope, he could but do his best with the methods available. Let us not jeer at his results; rather let us remember that this same astronomer found time to observe the heavens in addition to revolutionising thought in the brief compass of sixty-two years.

For the miracle of miracles is this man's universality of outlook. It makes us ashamed of our own pretentiousness and swollen-headed pride when we reflect what this great architectonic genius has performed. Just as our bodies have decreased in size with the progress of history, so our intelligences seem to have narrowed themselves since Aristotle's day. Great as our modern scientists are, there is not one of them who would be capable of writing an acknowledged masterpiece on Ethics, Politics, Rhetoric, Poetry, Metaphysics as well as on his own subject.

Nor have we yet mentioned this stupendous thinker's full claim to absolute predominance in intellectual effort. His works on Medicine were known to and appreciated by the Arabs, who translated them and brought them to Spain and Sicily when they conquered those countries. Averroes commented on them and added notes of his own which contributed not a little to the development of the healing art. More than this, and greatest of all, during the later Middle Ages Aristotle's system alone was recognised as possessing universal value; it was taken as the foundation on which the most famous and important Schoolmen erected their philosophies—Chaucer mentions a clerk who possessed twenty books, a treasure indeed in those days; it provided a European Church with a Theology and the cosmopolitan European Universities with a curriculum. Greater honour than this no man ever had or ever can have. Thus, although the Greek city-state seemed to perish in mockery with Demosthenes, yet the Greek spirit of free discussion which died in the great orator was set free in another form in that same year; leaving Aristotle's body, it ranged through the world conquering and civilising. If in our ignorance and bigotry we try to kill Greek literature, we shall find that, like the hero of the *Bacchae*, we are turning our blows against our own selves, to the delight of all who relish exhibitions of perfect folly.

TRANSLATIONS:

Kennedy's edition is the best. It is vigorous and reads almost like an English work.

Butcher's *Demosthenes* is the standard introduction to the speeches.

Many reminiscences of Demosthenes are to be found in the speeches of Lord Brougham.

ARISTOTLE

Politics. Jowett (Oxford). Welldon (Macmillan).

Poetics. Butcher (Macmillan). Bywater (Oxford).

Both contain excellent commentaries and notes.

Ethics. Welldon.

Rhetoric. Welldon. (Contains valuable analysis and notes.)

The article on Greek Science in the *Legacy of Greece* (Oxford) should not be omitted.

Lector House believes that a society develops through a two-fold approach of continuous learning and adaptation, which is derived from the study of classic literary works spread across the historic timeline of literature records. Therefore, we aim at reviving, repairing and redeveloping all those inaccessible or damaged but historically as well as culturally important literature across subjects so that the future generations may have an opportunity to study and learn from past works to embark upon a journey of creating a better future.

This book is a result of an effort made by Lector House towards making a contribution to the preservation and repair of original ancient works which might hold historical significance to the approach of continuous learning across subjects.

HAPPY READING & LEARNING!

LECTOR HOUSE LLP
E-MAIL: lectorpublishing@gmail.com

Lightning Source UK Ltd.
Milton Keynes UK
UKHW010647090820
367908UK00002B/408